Palgrave Studies of Marketing in Emerging Economies

Series Editors
Robert E. Hinson, Department of Marketing and Entrepreneurship, University of Ghana Business School, Legon, Accra, Ghana
Ogechi Adeola, Lagos Business School, Ajah, Lagos, Nigeria

This book series focuses on contemporary themes in marketing and marketing management research in emerging markets and developing economies. Books in the series cover the BRICS (Brazil, Russia, India, China and South Africa), MINT (Mexico, Indonesia, Nigeria and Turkey), CIVETS (Colombia, Indonesia, Vietnam, Egypt, Turkey, and South Africa); EAGLE economies (those which are expected to lead growth in the next ten years, such as Brazil, China, India, Indonesia, South Korea, Mexico, Russia, Taiwan, and Turkey) and all other African countries (classified under developing countries), taking into consideration the demographic, socio-cultural and macro-economic factors influencing consumer choices in these markets. The series synthesizes key subject areas in marketing, discuss marketing issues, processes, procedures and strategies across communities, regions and continents, and also the way digital innovation is changing the business landscape in emerging economies.

Palgrave Studies of Marketing in Emerging Economies presents a unique opportunity to examine and discuss marketing strategy and its implications in emerging economies, thereby filling a gap in current marketing literature.

All chapter submissions to the series will undergo a double blind peer review and all book proposals will undergo a single blind peer review.

More information about this series at
https://link.springer.com/bookseries/16591

Thomas Anning-Dorson · Robert E. Hinson ·
Stanley Coffie · Genevieve Bosah ·
Ibn Kailan Abdul-Hamid
Editors

Marketing Communications in Emerging Economies, Volume II

Conceptual Issues and Empirical Evidence

palgrave
macmillan

Editors
Thomas Anning-Dorson
School of Business Sciences
University of the Witwatersrand
Johannesburg, South Africa

Stanley Coffie
Ghana Institute of Management and Public
Accra, Ghana

Ibn Kailan Abdul-Hamid
University of Ghana Business School
University of Ghana
Accra, Ghana

Robert E. Hinson
Department of Marketing and Entrepreneurship
University of Ghana Business School
Accra, Ghana

Genevieve Bosah
University of Hertfordshire
Hatfield, UK

ISSN 2730-5554 ISSN 2730-5562 (electronic)
Palgrave Studies of Marketing in Emerging Economies
ISBN 978-3-030-81336-9   ISBN 978-3-030-81337-6 (eBook)
https://doi.org/10.1007/978-3-030-81337-6

© The Editor(s) (if applicable) and The Author(s), under exclusive license to Springer Nature Switzerland AG 2022

This work is subject to copyright. All rights are solely and exclusively licensed by the Publisher, whether the whole or part of the material is concerned, specifically the rights of translation, reprinting, reuse of illustrations, recitation, broadcasting, reproduction on microfilms or in any other physical way, and transmission or information storage and retrieval, electronic adaptation, computer software, or by similar or dissimilar methodology now known or hereafter developed.

The use of general descriptive names, registered names, trademarks, service marks, etc. in this publication does not imply, even in the absence of a specific statement, that such names are exempt from the relevant protective laws and regulations and therefore free for general use.

The publisher, the authors and the editors are safe to assume that the advice and information in this book are believed to be true and accurate at the date of publication. Neither the publisher nor the authors or the editors give a warranty, expressed or implied, with respect to the material contained herein or for any errors or omissions that may have been made. The publisher remains neutral with regard to jurisdictional claims in published maps and institutional affiliations.

This Palgrave Macmillan imprint is published by the registered company Springer Nature Switzerland AG
The registered company address is: Gewerbestrasse 11, 6330 Cham, Switzerland

Preface

Marketing communication is fundamental to business success. The effective management of communication with the different stakeholder audiences determines the extent to which brands and corporations gain legitimacy within their context and market of operation. It is a crucial management function that brings the necessary corporate and brand cohesion both within and without. Communication drives the business and value creation processes to ensure that entities function at their optimum to achieve both short and long objectives. In a turbulent environment such as the one created due to the global health pandemic, communication becomes a critical function for the reconstruction of the global economy, individual country level economies, markets, and individual brands. In a turbulent environment, communication becomes the reflective management function that supports strategic alignment and positioning of brands and corporations. Brands and entities wanting to do well within a competitive business environment should refocus their communications.

Emerging and developing countries are the hardest hit of the global pandemic, therefore, having their businesses suffer the most. This book is the first of its kind to highlight some key conceptual issues and provide some critical empirical evidence on marketing communications in and from emerging economies (EEs). The book is principally crafted for entities operating in EEs in order to manage their marketing communications better and more effectively. The book draws on the expertise of multi-disciplinary scholars from emerging economies to share fascinating perspectives on marketing communications. Corporate executives, educators, students, policymakers, and businesses would find this book a useful tool for marketing communication as it lays bare some important strategic and operational insights specific to emerging markets.

This book shares great insight for practice and theory and offers practitioners, students, and research scholars' practical sets of tools for successful marketing communication in EEs. The diversity of the contributors and the opinions and insights shared are such that everyone benefits from the book. The insights come from different functional areas of business and society, and they are captured in ways that enhance learning and equip the practitioner. As EEs continue to drive growth in global trade, such a book becomes timely and appropriate. It offers a suitable contextual understanding of how brands can be successful in such contexts through effective management of marketing communications.

In the thought-provoking chapters, this book tells the story of how marketing communication is evolving and integrating the tools of the current industrial revolution and internet technologies. It dedicates a chapter to the evolving power of public relations and how emerging market firms can deploy such a marketing communication element more effectively. This book discusses critical lessons on marketing communication planning for small businesses with little or no marketing communication budget. The book contains valuable lessons on creating a marketing communication strategy for corporate social responsibility (CSR) in order to enjoy the full benefits of such social investments. The book espouses how a crafted CSR communication strategy is directly and positively linked to brand performance.

The book discusses how to manage customer perception about marketing communication and manage advertising as an element to drive firm performance. Great insight is shared on how firms can use point-of-purchase advertising to nudge consumer behavior positively. This book demonstrates how to appeal to customer emotions by communicating hope in times of despondency. It comes from the premise that brands, through their value propositions, share aspirations that must be fulfilled. Through hope communication, the book offers lessons on ways in which brands can drive growth when they are unable to deliver on the core offering due to uncertainty. The lessons from the book admonish practitioners to focus attention on managing customer emotions through their value communications and paying attention to customer interactions and not just transactions.

The practice and theory-focused nature of this book makes it a valuable tool for practitioners, students, and research scholars. We trust that the insights shared will be imbibed and applied, and we would be grateful to receive feedback from you. We want to thank the contributors for their diligent work in helping to complete this book.

Johannesburg, South Africa	Thomas Anning-Dorson
Accra, Ghana	Robert E. Hinson
Accra, Ghana	Stanley Coffie
Hatfield, UK	Genevieve Bosah
Accra, Ghana	Ibn Kailan Abdul-Hamid

Contents

1 **Introduction to Marketing Communications in Emerging Economies: Conceptual Issues and Empirical Evidence** 1
Thomas Anning-Dorson, Robert E. Hinson, Stanley Coffie, Genevieve Bosah, and Ibn Kailan Abdul-Hamid

2 **Traditional and Contemporary Notions of Marketing Communications** 11
Genevieve Bosah

3 **Power Shift: Analyzing the Changing Role of Public Relations in the Marketing Mix** 37
Ligia A. Trejo

4 **Marketing Communication Planning for SMEs in Emerging Markets** 65
Bright Senanu and Thomas Anning-Dorson

5 **Communicating Corporate Social Responsibility Initiatives: A Focus on COVID-19** 93
Kojo Kakra Twum and Richard Kwame Nimako

Contents

6	**Ithemba Lila Nyuka (Hope is Rising): Responding to Customer Emotions During Uncertainties** *Kelebogile Makhafola and Thomas Anning-Dorson*	125
7	**Perception of Marketing Communication Practice: Evidence from Rural and Community Banks** *Isaac Tandoh, Nicholas Oppong Mensah, and Albert Anani-Bossman*	141
8	**Exploring Drivers of Performance in Advertising Firms in Ghana: A Perspective of Attribution Theory** *Henry Boateng, Ibn Kailan Abdul-Hamid, John Paul B. Kosiba, and Robert E. Hinson*	175
9	**Using Social Media Communication to Enact Brand Purpose During a Global Health Pandemic** *Charmaine du Plessis*	199
10	**Aesthetics Response to Point-of-Purchase Advertising and Purchase Intentions of Groceries** *Kojo Kakra Twum, Andrews Agya Yalley, Kwamena Minta Nyarku, Masud Ibrahim, and Godwyn Manful*	223
11	**Analyzing the Use of Social Media Communication Strategies in Indonesia and Malaysia: Insights and Implications** *Fandy Tjiptono, Ghazala Khan, and Ewe Soo Yeong*	247
12	**Marketing Communications in Emerging Economies: Conclusions and Recommendations** *Stanley Coffie, Thomas Anning-Dorson, Robert E. Hinson, Genevieve Bosah, and Albert Anani-Bossman*	277
Index		297

Notes on Contributors

Ibn Kailan Abdul-Hamid (Ph.D.) is a Lecturer at the University of Professional Studies, Accra, Ghana. He is a Programme Coordinator for the M.A. in Brands and Communications Management at the University of Professional Studies, Accra, Ghana, and also serves as the Track Chair at the Academy of International Business (AIB) Africa Chapter. He has published in reputable journals and is interested in linking theory to practice in emerging markets.

Albert Anani-Bossman (Ph.D.) lectures in Public Relations in the Faculty of Public Relations, Advertising, and Marketing at the Ghana Institute of Journalism, Ghana. He holds a Ph.D. in Communication Science from the University of South Africa (UNISA). His research area of interest includes: PR Research and Evaluation, Public Relations and Communication Management, Organizational Communication, and Crisis Communication.

Thomas Anning-Dorson (Ph.D.) is an Associate Professor, School of Business Sciences, University of the Witwatersrand, Johannesburg, South Africa. He also serves a Researcher with The Fairwork Foundation,

Oxford Internet Institute, University of Oxford; and a fellow at McGill University, Canada on the QES Program. His research interest spans the digital economy, innovation, marketing, strategy, and emerging markets.

Henry Boateng (Ph.D.) is the Director of Institutional Research at D'Youville College. He holds a Ph.D. in Knowledge Management. He researches Information and Knowledge management, social responsibility communications, Social Media, Branding, Corporate and Marketing Communications, Tourism, and Hospitality marketing. He is an Active Research Consultant with special skills in Qualitative, Quantitative, and Mixed Methods Approaches. He has worked on several research projects across the globe. Henry has consulted with several organizations, including the University of Technology Sydney (UTS), Australia, the Multicultural Health Communication Service (MHCS), NSW Australia, and Health Education and Training Institute, NSW Health.

Genevieve Bosah (Ph.D.) is a Researcher and Lecturer at the Department of Media and Communications, University of Hertfordshire, UK. She has worked with media institutions, governments and NGOs and is proficient in qualitative research, capacity development, strategy development and implementation, as well as programme management, journalism, and strategic communications. Before moving to academia, Genevieve held positions in several different capacities and has consulted for international development projects sponsored by USAID and DFID, amongst others. She worked in management and communications consulting, successfully delivering solutions to complex communications needs for individuals, small businesses, and multinational companies.

Stanley Coffie (Ph.D.) is an Associate Professor of Marketing at the Ghana Institute of Management and Public Administration (GIMPA). Coffie previously lectured at Birkbeck College, University of London, UK, where he also obtained his Ph.D. His research interests are in marketing strategy in emerging/developing economies, strategic positioning, and branding in bottom of the pyramid markets, and services marketing. His recent publications are in academic journals and other outlets including: *Journal of Strategic Marketing*, *Thunderbird International Business Review*, *Journal of Product and Brand Management*, *Journal of African Business*, *International Journal of Bank Marketing*, *The Routledge Companion to Contemporary Brand Management and Branding* and *Positioning in Base of the Pyramid Markets in Africa*.

Bright Senanu is a lecturer at the Ghana Institute of Journalism (GIJ). He possesses considerable practical and managerial experience. His research interest covers digital marketing, financial services marketing, consumer culture, customer experience management as well as business-to-business marketing.

Charmaine du Plessis is a professor in the Department of Communication Science, University of South Africa and specializes in brand communication with a focus on social media. She holds a Ph.D. in Communication (Unisa), a Postgraduate Diploma in Marketing (Unisa), and a Certificate in Brand Management (University of Cape Town). She is a rated researcher at the National Research Foundation (NRF) as an acknowledgment for the impact of her research in the field of marketing communication. Prof. du Plessis has published and presented widely, both locally and internationally. She has more than 36 publications in accredited journals, book chapters, and peer-reviewed conference proceedings. She has also recently edited a book on social media research.

Robert E. Hinson (Ph.D.) is a Professor and Head of Department of Marketing and Entrepreneurship at the University of Ghana Business School. He is also the Acting Director of Institutional Advancement at the same institution, Research Associate at the University of the Free State Business School, and an Extraordinary Professor at the North West University School of Business and Governance in South Africa. Robert has authored/edited several books and has over a hundred scientific publications to his credit. He has also served as the Rector of the Perez University College in Ghana. Professor Hinson has for the last twenty-two years, consulted for, and trained several public and private sector institutions globally in the general areas of Marketing, Sales, and Service Excellence; and served as well on the boards of local and international institutions.

Masud Ibrahim is a marketing lecturer at the Department of Management Studies, AAM-University of Skills Training and Entrepreneurial Development. His research interests are in the areas of service innovation, relationship marketing, service recovery, and corporate social responsibility.

Dr. Ghazala Khan (Ph.D.) has over 23 years of tertiary education in Malaysia. A passionate academic Dr. Ghazala has won numerous teaching awards including the Best Lecturer Award for School of Business under the Monash University Student Association in 2005, a feat repeated the following year when she was awarded the same accolade from the Monash University Student Association. Dr. Ghazala is also a quadruple recipient of the PVC's Award for Excellence Teaching between 2008 and 2011. Her research interests lie primarily in consumer behavior, particularly in the areas of consumer socialization and Islamic marketing. She has presented her work at numerous conferences and published in international refereed journals. Ghazala holds a Doctorate from Monash University Australia, Master of Arts in Marketing from University of Northumbria UK, and a Bachelors of Arts from The University of Punjab (Pakistan).

John Paul Basewe Kosiba is a Faculty Member in marketing at the University of Professional Studies, Accra (Ghana). His research focuses on branding, consumer behaviour, internet communication, and business ethics in sub-Saharan Africa. In the field of academia, he has taught management and research-based courses.

Kelebogile Makhafola is a brand strategist and the founder of Maruapula Brand, an integrated brand strategy consultancy that builds brand experiences with socio-economic benefits. As an award-winning businesswoman, WITS Business School M.B.A. candidate, and a 2019 Mandela Washington Fellow, her work seeks to evoke the value merged between business and art—a way to put up a mirror to society by curating impactful brand engagements that turn brand strategies into meaningful human-centric experiences. Her current research studies investigate employer brand activities that may be introduced as effective responses to gig economies within the South African landscape.

Godwyn Manful is the Head of Marketing and Sales of Blueskies Ghana Limited. He has a number of years of experience in working with multinationals in managing marketing and sales. His research interest is marketing communications, international marketing, and sales management.

Nicholas Oppong Mensah (Ph.D.) is an astute scholar and a researcher. He holds a Ph.D. in Agric Business from Kwame Nkrumah University of Science and Technology and is a lecturer at the University of Energy and Natural Resources. He is an experienced researcher and has several publications to his name. His research areas are in Agribusiness, Marketing, Insurance, Communications, and Strategic Management.

Richard Kwame Nimako has an M.B.A. and a Master in Education. He is a lecturer at the Department of Business Administration, Presbyterian University College, Ghana and a marketing consultant. His research areas include integrated marketing communications, customer service, and strategic marketing.

Kwamena Minta Nyarku (Ph.D.) is a senior lecturer at the Department of Marketing and Supply Chain Management, University of Cape Coast, Ghana. He holds a Ph.D. in Marketing from the University of Ghana Business School. His research interests are in the areas of corporate social responsibility, marketing communications, and relationship marketing.

Isaac Tandoh (Ph.D.) is a consummate corporate anthropologist and scholar with 18 years of dutifully earned experience in Corporate Communications, Integrated Marketing Communications, Brand Communications, Journalism, Publishing, and Strategic Management. He has almost two decades of professional engagement serving as a brand strategist and lead spokesperson for both local and international brands. Professional engagements span across multiple industries including Academia, Media, Banking, Publishing, Development Work (INGO), and Consultancy. He holds a Ph.D. in Integrated Marketing Communications from UCN and lectures at the Ghana Institute of Journalism.

Fandy Tjiptono (Ph.D.) is currently a senior lecturer at the School of Marketing and International Business, Victoria University of Wellington (VUW). Prior to joining VUW, he was an academic staff at Monash University Malaysia. He has more than 25 years of teaching experience in Malaysia, Indonesia, Australia, and New Zealand. His main research interest is consumer behavior and marketing practices in Southeast Asia. His research has been published in several reputable journals such as *Journal of Business Ethics*, *European Journal of Marketing*, *Journal of Retailing and Consumer Services*, *Marketing Planning and Intelligence*, *International Journal of Consumer Studies*, *Internet Research*, *Behaviour and Information Technology*, *Journal of Cleaner Production*, *Asia Pacific Journal of Marketing and Logistics*, and *Journal of Travel and Tourism Marketing*. His more than 12 years of consulting experience covers a wide range of industries, such as FMCG, publishing, telecommunication, and banking.

Ligia A. Trejo (M.B.A., ABD) is a native of Honduras, relocated to Miami, FL in 1995 and pursued a Bachelor of Science in Mass Communications at Florida International University. Throughout 20 years of professional experience in media communications, held various positions in cable and broadcast networks primarily targeted toward Hispanics in the United States, most recently as Sr. Director of Sports Programming for the largest Hispanic television network in the United States. In this role, created programming strategies to create audience growth and retention for network sports programming that included strategies for major world sports events such as FIFA World Cup 2014 and UEFA Champions League 2018–2019. Graduate studies included M.B.A. attained from Nova Southeastern University in Davie, FL and currently a third-year DBA student at Florida International University researching the influence of effective communication and trust on employee engagement mediated through employee involvement.

Kojo Kakra Twum is a lecturer at the Department of Business administration at the Presbyterian University College, Ghana. He is a Ph.D. student at the Department of Marketing and Supply Chain Management, University of Cape Coast. He is an upcoming researcher whose research interests include corporate social responsibility, service marketing, and information management systems. He has published in the *Journal of Marketing for Higher Education*, *Journal of Nonprofit and Public Sector Marketing*.

Andrews Agya Yalley (Ph.D.) is a lecturer at the Department of Marketing and Supply Chain Management at the University of Cape Coast, Ghana. His research interests are in the area of marketing communications, service marketing, and political marketing. He has published in reputable journals such as *The Service industries Journal*, *Journal of Political Marketing*, *International Journal of Productivity* and *Performance Management*.

Ewe Soo Yeong (Ph.D.) is currently a lecturer at Monash University Malaysia. Her specialties lie in consumer psychology and experimental research methods. Her current research interest is in consumer decision-making, specifically irrational behavior in decision-making. Other areas of research interest include information processing and message framing. Her multidisciplinary training in Economics, Finance and Marketing is particularly useful when solving research problems. Her work has been published in respected journals such as *Marketing Intelligence and Planning* and *Journal of Behavioral Finance*.

List of Figures

Fig. 2.1	Modernist Paradigm	12
Fig. 2.2	Marketing communication tetrahedron	13
Fig. 2.3	Parallel communication and marketing process	14
Fig. 4.1	The small business communication process (*Source* Longenecker et al. [2003])	70
Fig. 4.2	Stages in the product life cycle (Adapted from Polli and Cook [1969])	75
Fig. 4.3	A model for IMC (*Source* Authors' conceptualization)	76
Fig. 5.1	Strategic CSR communication framework (*Source* Adapted from Du et al. [2010])	102
Fig. 10.1	Research model	233
Fig. 10.2	Cerelac point-of-purchase display	234
Fig. 11.1	A typology of social media marketing strategy	257

List of Tables

Table 2.1	Comparison between traditional and online media	22
Table 2.2	Comparison of traditional marketing and digital marketing	24
Table 4.1	Relevant literature on SME IMC channel options and media planning	80
Table 5.1	Two approaches to CSR communication: Functionalistic and constitutive approach	96
Table 5.2	Three CSR communication strategies on Twitter	99
Table 5.3	COVID-19 CSR reportage in emerging economies	100
Table 5.4	Stages of information processing	103
Table 5.5	CSR communication tools typology	113
Table 7.1	Regional sample size for RCBs	155
Table 7.2	Socio-economic characteristics of clients of RCBs in Ghana	156
Table 7.3	Perceived performance rating of RCBs by clients per communication received by them	157
Table 7.4	Relationship between years of business with RCB and perceived performance rating	158
Table 7.5	Perception of RCBs on marketing communications activities	161

List of Tables

Table 7.6	Marketing mix strategy currently used by RCBs in Ghana by staff perspective	162
Table 7.7	Perception of clients on marketing communication mix adopted by RCBs	166
Table 8.1	Respondent characteristics	185
Table 9.1	The process followed for the general inductive data analysis strategy	210
Table 9.2	Different codes, their underlying meaning and most representative quotes are evident in Theme 1	212
Table 9.3	Different codes, their underlying meaning, and most representative quotes are evident in Theme 2	213
Table 9.4	Different codes, their underlying meaning, and most representative quotes evident in Theme 3	216
Table 10.1	Demographic profile	235
Table 10.2	Descriptive statistics of variables	236
Table 10.3	Reliability and validity	238
Table 10.4	Correlation and Fornell–Lacker criterion analysis	239
Table 10.5	T-statistics of path coefficients	239
Table 11.1	Brief profiles and social media usage of Indonesia and Malaysia	251
Table 11.2	Comparison of usage of top five social media between Indonesia and Malaysia before and during the COVID-19 pandemic	252

1

Introduction to Marketing Communications in Emerging Economies: Conceptual Issues and Empirical Evidence

Thomas Anning-Dorson, Robert E. Hinson, Stanley Coffie, Genevieve Bosah, and Ibn Kailan Abdul-Hamid

1.1 Introduction

The importance of marketing communications to any business and its operational efficiency cannot be overemphasized. Ensuring that all communications within an organization are integrated is the first step to communication success. Entities fail at this struggle with building

---

T. Anning-Dorson (✉)
School of Business Sciences, University of the Witwatersrand, Johannesburg, South Africa

R. E. Hinson
University of Ghana Business School, Accra, Ghana
e-mail: rhinson@ug.edu.gh

S. Coffie
Ghana Institute of Management and Public Administration, Accra, Ghana
e-mail: scoffie@gimpa.edu.gh

© The Author(s), under exclusive license to Springer Nature Switzerland AG 2022
T. Anning-Dorson et al. (eds.), *Marketing Communications in Emerging Economies, Volume II*, Palgrave Studies of Marketing in Emerging Economies, https://doi.org/10.1007/978-3-030-81337-6_1

strong and lasting brands. Failing to integrate marketing communications also create an inconsistent image in the minds of your target audience. The integration helps create a robust communication, which customer-centered and facilitate the customer journey through the buying and consumption process. This book offers pathways that assist firms in emerging economies (EE) create a positive brand image, develop a communication channel between the brand and nurture customer relationships.

As discussed in volume 1 of marketing communication in emerging economies, marketing communication is fundamental to business success. The effective management of communication with the different stakeholder audiences determines the extent to which brands and corporations gain legitimacy within their context and market of operation. It is a crucial management function that brings the necessary corporate and brand cohesion both within and without. Communication drives the business and value creation processes to ensure that entities function at their optimum to achieve both short and long objectives. In a turbulent environment such as the one created as a result of the global health pandemic, communication becomes a critical function for the reconstruction of the global economy, individual country level economies, markets and individual brands.

Emerging and developing countries are the hardest hit of the global pandemic and, therefore, having their businesses suffering the most. In the turbulent environment, communication becomes the reflective management function that supports the strategic alignment and positioning of brands and corporations (Van Ruler & Verčič, 2005). Brands and entities wanting to do well within a competitive business environment should refocus their communications. This book is of the first of its kind to highlight key foundational and contemporary issues of marketing

---

G. Bosah
University of Hertfordshire, Hatfield, UK
e-mail: g.bosah@herts.ac.uk

I. K. Abdul-Hamid
University of Professional Studies, Accra, Ghana

communication specifically crafted for entities operating in Emerging Economies (EEs). The book draws on the expertise of multi-disciplinary scholars from emerging economies to share fascinating perspectives on marketing communications. Corporate executives, educators, students, policymakers and businesses would find this book as a useful tool on marketing communication as it lays bare some important strategic and operational insights specific to emerging markets.

1.2 Marketing Communications, A Critical Business Function

Every business entity aims to have customer success, where the customer responds positively to the firm's marketing efforts. Achieving customer success begins with developing an effective communication channel that seamlessly links the customer and the firm. Such a channel is able to solicit critical customer information before the value production and meet the communication needs of the target market successfully. This requires an intentional approach to communicating with a single voice that reflects and reinforces the brand's value proposition. Such an intentional approach deals with the possible confusion, frustration and arousal of anxiety that may arise within the target customers. Creating an orderly, focused and single-purpose messaging is the main objective of integrated marketing communications (IMC).

Integrated marketing communications offer numerous benefits to a brand. Firms can enjoy these benefits when everyone is on the same page as regards communications, both overt and covert. Implementing IMC within an organization means a total rejection of "a silo mentality" where different parts of the same entity or brand communicate differently. Belch and Belch (2004) assert that IMC is an approach where there is a creation of a unified and seamless opportunity and experience for audiences to interact with the brand. This requires the coming together of all the communication mix elements such as advertising, direct marketing, sponsorship, promotion, public relations and social media communications to achieve a unified communication objective.

Firms and brands that can do the above build a strong brand, which becomes the basis for competitive advantage. IMC brings about improved customer relations, saves resource wastage by eliminating duplication and improves return on communication investments. Managing communications through the IMC approach does not only meet customer needs but that of potential employees and investors. A coordinated marketing communication ensures consistency of brand promise and delivery and an eventual increase in brand equity that helps attract top talent and retain exceptional employees. It also attracts investors and paves the way for better communication integration and legitimization.

1.3 Structure and Contributions of the Book

The initial chapter highlights the evolution within the marketing communication discipline. With all the digital options available to consumers, the traditional methods remain effective. The chapter examines both traditional and contemporary marketing communications and how both can be used effectively in contemporary times. The chapter evaluates the contemporary marketing methods in detail and offers some expedient insight into practice and theory. The chapter discusses the opportunities and challenges brought by digital technologies for marketing communication practice and shows how to efficiently adapt in the rapidly changing environment. Cultural differences can also pose a challenge for marketers in emerging economies. The chapter provides recommendations on how to deal with cultural perceptions.

The diaspora market is a critical aspect of the EEs discourse that has not attracted adequate attention. It is even sparse in the marketing communication literature. In discussing the power shift and the changing role of public relations, a chapter uses the Hispanic context within the American context to discuss PR in contemporary times. Global environments and market conditions are constantly changing worldwide. The change in the media landscape brought by the widespread use of social media and online platforms has also changed how markets consume media messages. An economic downturn brought by a global pandemic has also forced marketers to cut down advertising and promotional costs to guard organizational financial stability. Within the US market, the change in demographics seen through the rapid growth of minority groups, primarily Hispanics, who now hold a growing purchasing power, requires marketers to shift attention to this particular group. The Hispanic market is a key component of the emerging economies as they are part of the diaspora market. Diaspora remittances contribute a great deal to their home countries. The chapter focuses on viable and creative avenues through public relations campaigns that marketers could consider when reaching the Hispanic community in the United States and emerging economies globally as they touch upon emotions using culture, traditions, values and representation. The chapter posits that in times of change in media preferences and economic decline, the use of public relations should be seen as a powerful tool to drive positive change and influence for consumers in emerging economies.

EEs are dominated by small and medium-scale enterprises (SMEs). Sufficient attention has not been paid to this critical sector in the marketing communication literature. The chapter on "Marketing Communication Planning for SMEs in Emerging Markets" in this book provides a comprehensive framework for marketing communication program development for SMEs in emerging economies. The chapter presents a model that highlights the SME communication process, key determinants of communication program development and channel options and the effective measure of SME communication. This has become necessary as extant literature has not paid adequate attention to marketing communication developments in SMEs in developing and emerging economies. The chapter demonstrates how marketing research and intelligence gathering are core to developing and implementing an effective marketing communication strategy for SMEs in emerging economies. The contributors offer some managerial advice to SMEs on sing cost-effective channels through traditional and new media channels.

In the chapter "Communicating Corporate Social Responsibility Initiatives: A focus on COVID-19", the contributors, through a systematic review, offer exciting perspectives on how to communicate corporate social responsibility in a pandemic period. There is advocacy to adopt a strategic approach in corporate social responsibility communication. In emerging economies, the performance of CSR has been widely viewed as a philanthropic gesture, thus leading to firms not using innovative ways such as CSR communication to enhance its effectiveness and strategic benefits. This chapter adopted a semi-systematic literature review approach to understanding ways to perform CSR communication, looking closely at communications on firms' COVID-19 initiatives. Some examples of COVID-19 CSR communications in emerging economies are also provided. The chapter offers that a strategic CSR communication on COVID-19 is a function of the communication strategy (informational, reactive and deliberative), the creative message and content of message (CSR initiative, CSR fit, CSR motive and CSR impact), communication channel (advertisement, website, annual report and sustainability report, social media) and result orientation.

The chapter on "Responding to Customer Emotions during Uncertainties" demonstrates that hope can be communicated effectively in turbulent periods. A feeling of possibility has a strong effect on how a person may endure a situation as possibility is embedded in hope and uncertainty. In marketing communications, brands inspire some form of hope in terms of what the brand can do. This chapter evaluates and shares insights from a marketing campaign that inspired hope and spurred a nation in an uncertain situation. During the global coronavirus pandemic, tourism customers and travelers were uncertain about attaining their goals and needed "possibility" communicated to mitigate the negative emotions of not being able to achieve a positive goal-congruent outcome. The South African Tourism responded to the ominous mood and frightful psychological state created by the pandemic and communicated hope, which galvanized the nation. The brand identified that the country needed to act collectively and instead of seeking capitalistic transactions. The focus was on seeking out and delivering the true intangible value of customer well-being through coordinated, customer-centric marketing communications. The chapter shares insights into how brands can create value even in uncertain and harsh conditions.

The practice of marketing communication in smaller firms in EEs generally has received mixed reactions among staff and clients alike. The chapter on the perception of IMC investigates the opinions of staff and customers of selected Rural and Community Banks (RCBs) in Ghana. Using a multi-stage sampling technique, the chapter reveals a positive but low perception of marketing communications. The chapter recommends, among others things, that management of RCBs and other businesses operating in EEs should put in place training and research programs that seek to enhance the effectiveness of marketing communications both internally and externally. It recommends periodic surveys and training on marketing communications effectiveness with deep participation of all internal customers.

Despite the growing importance of advertising recounted in literature, there is little understanding of firm-level management issues and challenges affecting the performance of firms in the advertising industry. The chapter on "Exploring Drivers of Performance in Advertising Firms in Ghana: A Perspective of Attribution Theory" provides a qualitative perspective of some key management issues affecting advertising sector performance in EEs. Through an in-depth interview approach, the chapter shows that the factors are associated with the human practices, technological advancement and managerial process of the firms. It concludes that managerial practices have instead not helped the growth of advertising firms in the Ghanaian context.

The purpose-driven marketing trend became popular in 2018 because consumers have increasingly become engaged in political and social causes debates on social media. However, COVID19 has provided brands with another kind of communication challenge they have to deal with. By meaningfully responding and interacting with their target audiences on social media about important COVID19-related topics and issues, consumers could better understand brands' reason for existence. In the chapter on "Using Social Media Communication to Enact Brand Purpose During A Global Health Pandemic", a general inductive approach is followed to illustrate how a leading South African brand executed its brand purpose with social media brand communication on two social media platforms during the first 5 months of the pandemic. The chapter showcases how the brand aligned consumer priorities with core brand values. It also demonstrates how the brand focused on the future and shared helpful information for principle-driven solutions and support. The findings from this chapter can serve as a heuristic for other brands on how to represent their purpose on social media.

Point-of-purchase advertising is a standard marketing promotional tool in influencing consumer purchase behavior within the retail store environment. Marketers use point-of-purchase promotions in an attempt to gain consumers' attention and influence their purchases in emerging markets. However, the efficacy of point-of-purchase materials in emerging markets remains unexplored. The chapter on "Aesthetics Response to Point-of-Purchase Advertising and Purchase Intentions of Groceries" uses the stimulus-organism-response theory to examine shoppers' evaluation of point-of-purchase material advertising and their purchase intentions. The findings imply the need to design point-of-purchase materials that have higher levels of aesthetic features. Marketers in the retail sector must attempt to include many aspects of aesthetic features in developing marketing promotions in emerging markets.

The penultimate chapter evaluates social media usage in Indonesia and Malaysia. High social media penetration in Indonesia (60% of its population) and Malaysia (81% of the population) has compelled businesses to adopt social media marketing strategies for many purposes. The real-time, interactive and borderless features of social media enable companies to engage and connect with customers, share information, build brand image and retain customers. This chapter draws relevant and important insights from social media consumption in those two EE contexts from consumers and businesses. It develops a typology of social media marketing strategies for the B2C sector. The typology is based on two dimensions (engagement and commerce). It results in four social media marketing strategies (social media optimization strategy, social media engagement-focused strategy, social media commercial-focused strategy and social media early extension strategy). The chapter concludes with social media marketing implications and addresses future challenges.

1.4 Conclusion

Volume II of the Marketing Communication in Emerging Markets book offers some valuable insights for both practices, teaching and learning, and research. Through a diverse author, this volume shares lessons on communicating corporate social responsibility more effectively, affecting social media usage to enhance communication and customer interactions, and how to enact brand purpose through social media communication. This book discusses the shifting nature of the power of public relations even in the social media era. It provides some critical lessons on marketing communication planning for small businesses with little or no marketing communication budget. The book discusses the link between communication and firm performance using different cases and empirical examinations. The practice and theory-focused nature of this book makes it a valuable tool for practitioners, students and research scholars.

References

Belch, G. E., & Belch, M. A. (2004). *Advertising and promotion: An integrated marketing communications perspective* (6th ed.). McGraw-Hill/Irwin.

van Ruler, B., & Verčič, D. (2005). Public relations and communication management in Europe: Challenges and opportunities. *Comunicação e Sociedade, 8*, 179–191.

2

Traditional and Contemporary Notions of Marketing Communications

Genevieve Bosah

2.1 Introduction

Marketing communications are the means by which firms attempt to inform, persuade, incite and remind consumers—directly or indirectly—about the brands they sell (Keller, 2009). Perhaps no area of marketing has seen more dramatic changes over the years than marketing communications. Marketing has also evolved rapidly and is affected significantly by technology (Muñiz & Schau, 2007). Finne and Grönroos (2017) mentioned that traditional marketing is an umbrella that includes various advertising channels that are being used daily. These channels are applied to older media. The marketing communication and advertising field in particular, as it is currently understood, operates under a modernist paradigm (Venkatesh, 1996), as shown in Fig. 2.1. This chapter will

G. Bosah (✉)
University of Hertfordshire, Hatfield, UK
e-mail: g.bosah@herts.ac.uk

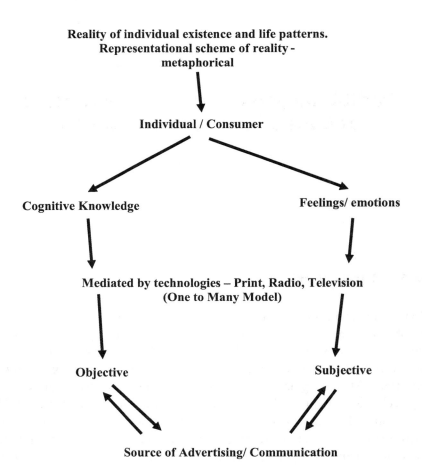

Fig. 2.1 Modernist Paradigm

explore core theories while focusing on modernism and cognitive models which best describe the current phenomenon.

Modernism is a cultural/philosophical position that regards human subjects in cognitive terms instead of viewing them in semiotic or symbolic terms. The channels that are being part of traditional media include; film, television, radio, billboards, face to face, purchase of point and newspapers. All these forms of marketing have numerous benefits, and it enables the business to prosper and grow. As Finne and Grönroos

(2017) mentioned, these modes increase the reach and frequency and appear to be more visually appealing.

Another theoretical framework of marketing communications is presented by Keller (2009), as shown in Fig. 2.2. The figure shows a marketing communication tetrahedron with the consumer at the top of the tetrahedron. The life span of traditional marketing is entirely defined. For instance, magazines were regarded as having the longest life span. Whereas, newspapers were reported to have a shorter life span as it was picked up daily and left to commute and picked by any other person. However, times have changed, Duffett (2017) mentioned that face-to-face communication is still considered one of the most significant interactions and marketing notion. The Central Marketing Institute's

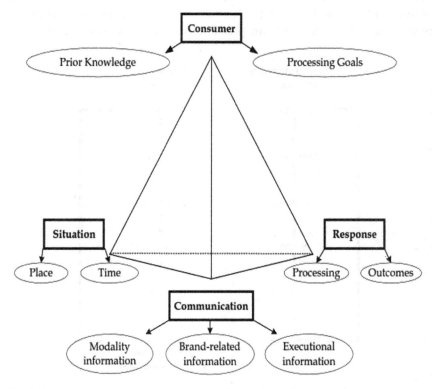

Fig. 2.2 Marketing communication tetrahedron

report claimed that face-to-face interactions are considered the leading method in conversion rate. Word of mouth is also part of the traditional marketing umbrella and is regarded as an effective strategy. Figure 2.3 provides the marketing and communication process by Duncan and Moriarty (1998).

In the present era, emphasis is laid on social bonds, which is characterized by individualism. Moreover, the impact of individualism can be felt by everyone in society. Due to the use of technology, people feel more isolated than ever. The use of technology is so extensive that it makes it difficult for people to interact with one another. Hence, postmodern society is inflicted with the disease of social suspension and individualism (Grossmann & Santos, 2020). Therefore, to reach a wider audience has become a challenge for marketers. In the current business environment, marketers have to adapt themselves rapidly. As mentioned earlier, marketing is now shifted from product-oriented to a customer-oriented

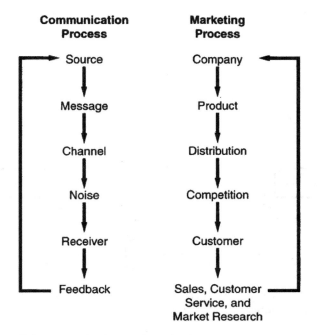

Fig. 2.3 Parallel communication and marketing process

approach. Hence, the major challenge for marketers is to reinvent themselves. Also, they need to focus on relationship management. Another challenge that marketers face is that there are no particular guidelines or discipline set for the marketing of the products (Hoeckesfeld et al., 2020). The following sections discuss traditional marketing and theories of traditional marketing, the theories of traditional marketing communications are also discussed.

2.2 Traditional Marketing

Duffett (2017) stated that traditional marketing describes products' marketing only to increase the firms' profits. He further mentions that the traditional marketing concept is a narrow concept that was evolved around the push marketing strategy. During the seventeenth century, the mass and media communications came into being, and it became more comfortable for the people to spread their message to large groups all at once. At that time, the aim of advertising was only to appeal to mass audiences. The push marketing strategy is how the sellers execute various marketing strategies to force consumers to purchase their products, hence increasing their sales and profits.

2.2.1 Theories of Traditional Marketing

One of the theories that is widely used is Ansoff's Matrix. According to this theory, a product falls under four categories depending on the market conditions and its release. One of the types of this theory is about new products and new markets. This is, in other term, defined as the diversification stage. In this stage, the businesses try to introduce diversity in the product portfolio. The aim of diversification is to eradicate the monotonous and appeal to the audiences differently. It is quite a known fact that with time the consumers' needs and preferences change. Hence, in his report, Robinson stated that this is where the firms must change their products portfolio. For instance, one of the famous company Apple that was facing loss but with the help of Steve Jobs, they developed and introduced new gadgets in the market, which gained popularity, and it became a hit in the market. With this new diversion, they use the opportunity to expand their product line and introduce tablets and laptops (Balmer, 2017).

2.2.2 Traditional Marketing Mix

In his book, Kotler (2003) has mentioned a tool widely used by marketers and scholars to evaluate marketing strategies. This tool is known as marketing mix, which is the amalgamation of four Ps: price, product, promotion and place. The aim and purpose of this tool are to provide marketers with a way through which they can generate a positive response in the target market. In addition to this, this tool can be easily adjusted to meet the challenges of the changing dynamics of the marketing environment. The following paragraphs explain these four Ps.

Product: The product is defined as a tangible and intangible good and services developed and designed to fulfil the customers' needs and desires. The marketers in order to design the good have to understand the needs of customers, and for that reason, they utilize a different array of tools. This enables them to create a demand for the products and easily attract them to purchase it. Every product has a life cycle, and with this help of the life cycle, the marketers get a better understanding of the product's position and performance in the market. Hence, with this, they quickly bring changes accordingly and meet the challenges of the market. As time evolves, it has been seen that it impacts the preferences of the consumers as well. Thus, the marketers keep track of the product's performance and diversify and modify it according to the needs (Quesenberry, 2020).

Price: As defined by Kotler, Price is the payment for the products and services consumers acquire or purchase. It plays a vital role in appealing to consumers. It is related to the product's value that the customer is ready to pay. For instance, if the consumers perceive the product's value as high or low, they end up not purchasing it. This is why marketers need to know their target market to determine the price accordingly. For instance, in one study about Walmart, they have goods for every type of consumer. They have placed branded and both unbranded products for their customers to purchase the products from one place easily. In addition to this, the price can impact and be impacted by other variables, for instance, the distribution plan, value chain cost and mark-ups. Furthermore, in his report, Duffett (2017) has mentioned that the consumers have become more competitive to the prices these days. Before purchasing any item, they compare the goods and quality prices with other substitute products.

Place: One of the factors that play an imperative role in attracting the consumers towards the product is that they need to be placed at the right time and at the right place. The prices of the goods first impact the placement of the products. Second, how the channel partners are playing a role in the placement of the products. It has also come to notice that it may increase the product's price when too many distributors are involved. The product placement is also needed to complement the other marketing strategies to attract the target market and incur sales in the long run (Quesenberry, 2020).

Promotion: The strategies that are being part of marketing communications fall under this category. The promotion strategies include direct mailing, sales promotions, advertising on print media and televisions and public relations. The promotional strategies serve many benefits to the companies. One it helps in attracting the customers. Second, it helps the customers to stick loyal to the brand and third, it retains them for a more extended period of time. Different organizations utilize effective solutions to promote their items, for instance, visually appealing images in magazines and newspapers with different sales promotions. Like in traditional marketing, television and magazines were a ubiquitous mode of promotion as they helped the business reach more people and attract more consumers (Moravcikova et al., 2017).

2.2.3 Theories of Traditional Marketing Communications

This section will present three theories of traditional marketing communications. It is important for scholars to understand these theories and the synergy between them. These theories are part of integrated marketing communications (IMC).

Interactive Communication Theory: According to Schultz (1993), there is a significant importance of communication foundation of interactive communication theory. Schultz noted that "If we think for a moment about traditional marketing, we begin to realize that almost all the marketing techniques and approaches that we have used over the years are essentially some form of communication."

This theory focuses on interactive communications, which is from the source to the receiver and vice versa. This idea of an on-going dialogue between marketers and consumers is one of the most important paradigm shifts. This has changed in recent years with more emphasis on social media and word of mouth. This exchange between the marketers and consumers is both a communication and a business process (Duncan et al., 1997).

Communication strategy in marketing takes a whole new meaning where the aim is to have an engaging conversation with customers as opposed to targeting them with a persuasive message (Moriarty & Schultz, 2012). This shift results in making a customer a participant as opposed to just a target in a dynamic ongoing communication network.

Perceptual Integration Theory: This section presents the perceptual integration theory and communication effects, which is explained by Lane Keller (2001) as "communication effects are what consumers saw, heard, learned, thought, felt, and so on while exposed to a communication." Keller also added that marketing communications' role is to contribute towards establishing the brand in the memory of the consumers and also establishing unique associations with it. Researchers have shown that even though brands may have strategies for defining the brand images and positioning, but mostly these images exist in the mind of consumers as subjective impressions, for example Starbucks. According to Moriarty and Schultz (2012), brands exist in the consumers' minds only through the process of conceptual integration. All this perceptual integrity leads to the notion of consumer-based brand equity.

Reciprocity Theory: Another critical element in integrated marketing communications is reciprocity. The idea of reciprocity can be traced back to the Greek philosopher Aristotle, where the idea is that all the communication must result in a win–win situation for the consumer and the marketer. In traditional marketing theory, the marketers build value in the product and customers extract that value when they buy and use the product. So if the consumer perceives the value to be greater than the cost of purchasing then it will result in customer likely repurchasing the product.

In today's world, the communication relationship is based complex communication network, and this has evolved into a system where both the marketer and consumer receive value from the communication activity for it to be continued. Moriarty and Schultz (2012) explain that for this relationship to continue and be maintained, the buyer and seller should both benefit from it, as if the value is tilted too far on one side, one of the parties will withdraw and the relation will fail. Consumers have lots of choices available today, reciprocity has and will become significant in understanding customer–stakeholder–brand–marketer relationships. All these concepts are built around the concept of stakeholders and the connected relationship theories (Moriarty & Schultz, 2012).

2.2.4 Advantages of Traditional Marketing Communications

Every business wants to grow and expand, and they aim at maintaining a sustainable relationship with their clients. One of the widely used tools used by many marketers is advertising, although, with time, different methods are being used, one of the oldest methods is still widely used. Some of the advantages of traditional marketing communication are discussed as follows:

More Reach to Local Audiences: As mentioned in the report by Moravcikova et al. (2017), if the customers are local, they should opt for a radio ad. As statistics reveal, radio was one of the most useful marketing media employed, and it was one of the quickest ways to convey the message. Furthermore, it did not take a long time in airing the ad over the local radio station.

Storing and Recycling of the Promotional Materials: One of the benefits of using traditional methods is that the materials are available in the physical form regarding flyers, posters, and magazines. In other words, they are hard copies, which can be read and taken anywhere with you, unlike online material, which requires either connection or any other electronic gadgets. Furthermore, Robinson mentions that these promotional materials can easily be reused and recycled (Vieira et al., 2019).

Easy to recall and process: One more advantage of traditional marketing is that these hard copies are easy to recall. A study done by the Canadian entity stated that paper marketing was more straightforward for customers to process. Simultaneously, it was easy to make them remember the information (Meyer, 2009). It mentioned that the participants who participated in the test showed that they could recall the advertisement in the print form on posters or newspapers compared with the one published digitally (Serafinelli, 2018).

2.3 Contemporary Marketing Communications

In the last few decades, there has been considerable discussion in the marketing literature about describing and defining marketing in the contemporary environment (Coviello & Brodie, 2001). In the book by Jaffe (2005), Don Shultz notes that

> *Media advertising, as we have known, practised, and worshipped it for the past sixty or so years, is in trouble. Big trouble. And it's not going to get well. Ever.* (Pilotta & Schultz, 2005, p. xi)

For many, the commonly accepted view of marketing has been that offered by the American Marketing Association (1985), which defines marketing to be:

...the process of planning and executing the conception, pricing, promotion, and distribution of ideas, goods, and services to create exchange, and satisfy individual and organizational objectives.

The most significant change in contemporary times is that marketing now focuses on the retention of customers rather than attracting new customers (Du et al., 2021). Marketing was considered as a business function during the First World War and even during the Second World War. This was the time when Protector and Gamble and Unilever developed the concept of product and brand management. Between the 1950s and 1960s, the audience started taking an interest in the concept of marketing. Also, the concept of transaction marketing began to gain pace.

Furthermore, the rise in disposable income and penetration of new technology stimulated the growth of marketing. During that time, the companies' primary challenge was to increase their production activities and find ways to market their products. In the past, the American industry had to face huge losses because their focus was not on marketing activities; instead, they also ignored the sector which had unfulfilled demand. Later, in the 1970s after the oil crises, there was a decline witnessed in the disposable income, which again became a challenge for the companies. Moreover, high inflation also changed the perception of people. The concept of conventional marketing has been evolved and seems deficient in the current business environment. The companies find themselves in a different environment, as seen in the 1950s and 1960s.

In her book, Rachel Carson also mentioned the fact that there was a decline witnessed in the manufacturing sector, which led to an increase in the rise of the service sector (Carson, 2002). The above discussion makes it clear that traditional forms of marketing are now being challenged. The demands of customers are increasing due to the sophistication of the market. Globalization has also led to an increase in the demand of customers. Moreover, the availability of ample information has also made customers more aware of the products. There are different approaches used in contemporary marketing. Relationship marketing, industrial marketing and business marketing are examples of contemporary marketing. The focus of contemporary marketing is on society and consumers.

2.3.1 Digital Marketing Communications

The Internet and other technologies have profoundly affected the way we do business and resulted in Internet marketing, also known as e-marketing (Strauss & Frost, 2008). Koiso-Kanttila (2004) introduces the concept of digital content marketing or the marketing of products in which both the entity and the delivery of the product are digital; such digital content is an increasingly important part of the commercial landscape. The idea behind contemporary marketing is to fill the gaps, which are caused by traditional marketing. Rowley (2008) presents the difference between traditional and digital media, as shown in the table below (Table 2.1).

Contemporary marketing is also called personalized marketing as it tries to alter the products according to customers' needs (Pridmore & Zwick, 2011). According to Rowley (2008), a multi-faceted approach to

Table 2.1 Comparison between traditional and online media

	Traditional media	Online
Space	Expensive commodity	Cheap, unlimited
Time	Expensive commodity for marketers	Expensive commodity for users
Image creation	Image is everything Information is secondary	Information is everything Image is secondary
Communication	Push, one-way	PutL. interactive
Call to action	Incentives	Information [incentives!
Audience	Mass	Targeted
Links to further information	Indirect	Direct/embedded
Investment in design	High	Low, allows change
Interactivity	Low	Ranges across a spectrum from low to two-way dialogue

understanding customer value is required, she also reports that there is a need to embrace the consumption values that shape consumer's experiences, and the values that underlie their decision-making processes, and how each of these develops and evolves.

As discussed in previous sections, traditional marketing ways are the most recognizable form of marketing. Digital marketing, on the other hand, is the marketing of products or services, which uses digital channels to reach customers. Kannan (2017) has noted that digital marketing has evolved from just marketing products and services using digital channels to the process of using digital channels to attract and shape customers preferences. He also added that it can be used to promote brands, retain customers and increase sales. Idrysheva et al. (2019) have presented a detailed comparison between traditional and digital marketing as shown in the table below (Table 2.2).

In this digital age that we live in, communication is a fundamental condition for our social coexistance. The way people communicate on Internet depends on the relationship between the parties, and this relation can affect the channel used (Shumate & O'Connor, 2010). With the recent advancement in web technologies such as Web 2.0, this creates a two-way communication between customers and businesses, hence increasing their communication and interaction (Ahmad et al., 2016).

2.3.2 Social Media and Digital Marketing Communications

Communication through digital channels such as social media networks has largely two types, "from the business to the consumer", i.e. B2C and the other is user-generated content, i.e. UGC. B2C is the definitive case of viral marketing promotions, while UGC can also be an excellent promotion technique if the business does something unusual. Yadav et al. (2015) have described the example of McDonald's promotional strategy whereby it gave 5–10 dollars gift vouchers to 100 users who register at a McDonald's restaurant. This campaign on social media results in 33% increase in signups while McDonald only spent less than 1000 dollars.

Table 2.2 Comparison of traditional marketing and digital marketing

Traditional marketing	Digital marketing
Traditional marketing includes print, television, mail and telephone	Digital marketing includes Internet advertising, electronic marketing, and marketing, social media, text messaging, partner marketing, search engine optimization
No interaction with the audience	Interaction with the audience
The results are easy to measure	The results are pretty much easy to measure
Advertising campaigns are planned for a long time	Advertising campaigns are planned in a short time
Expensive and time-consuming process	A fairly cheap and fast way to promote products or services
Success of traditional marketing strategies-if the firm can reach a large local audience	The success of a digital marketing strategy is considered if a firm can reach a specific number of local audiences
One campaign for a long time	Campaigns can be changed with ease and innovations can be implemented within any campaign
Limited client access due to limited number of client technologies	Wider reach to the client due to the use of various technologies
Round-the-clock year-round exposition is impossible	Round-lhe-clock year-round exposition is possible
There is no way to go viral	Opportunity to go viral
One way to talk	Two ways to lalk
Responses can only occur during business hours	Response or feedback can occur at any time

Source Idrysheva et al. (2019)

Social media and mobile marketing (DSMM) have brought a significant and constant transformation in marketing (Müller et al., 2018). DSMM combines various digital technologies, which influence research and practice of marketing. In the context of B2C, DSMM does not have a vital role currently, where the marketers only focus on brand image, but Järvinen et al. (2012) have noted that it has significant potential. In a recent paper by Jacobson, Gruzd and Hernández-García (2020), the authors have raised the issue of using publically available data on social media sites such as Twitter and Facebook. Marketers can have access to user-generated content such as a public post on Twitter and a public Facebook post but they do not have access to data, which is privately shared by individuals on social media.

According to Leeflang et al. (2014), the digitalization of marketing has led to serious issues for marketing executives. As the digital world is rapidly evolving, the digital markets are also rapidly changing beyond the control of the executives. As a result of this complex environment where the marketing executives work, they have become aware of the changes and how to deal with them efficiently. The study by Leeflang et al. (2014) through interviews and discussions with marketers shows that the digital marketing tensions can be divided into three main categories, business strategy and customer understanding; operations and execution of market entry and third, organization and opportunities.

2.4 Co-Creation

One of the theories included in contemporary marketing is called co-creation (Gummesson & Mele, 2010). Gratification is used to bridge the gap between businesses and customers. For instance, blogs are written to provide customers with useful information to attract them towards the brand. Most of the contemporary research literature uses terms like shared value and relationship marketing. Another term recently used by several researchers such as Muñiz and Schau (2007) is customer evangelism, which is also a form of co-creation.

2.4.1 Shared Values

Another famous theory that is used in contemporary marketing is called shared value (Camilleri, 2017). In this theory, the companies focus on the market they wish to enter and decide on the shared values. Tesla is an example of a company that uses contemporary marketing. Electric charging stations are established by the company in Asia, Europe and North America. This way the company has managed to attract more consumers. Moreover, B2B companies create an event where companies with similar backgrounds are invited and can discuss various offers.

2.4.2 Relationship Marketing

Kotler (2012) has defined relationship marketing as the process in which emphasis is laid on the cultivation and strengthening of bonds with all the stakeholders and customers. The focus of marketing activities on campaigns which are related to response marketing. The idea behind such activities is to increase the satisfaction level of customers. The rise in relationship marketing is due to the increase in technology use. The Internet has opened avenues for communication. The most significant benefit that companies attain by using relationship marketing is that they can encash customers' loyalty. Prior and Keränen (2020) claim that relationship marketing helps increase customer loyalty and allows businesses to have a positive image. Jabbar et al. (2020) suggest that customer loyalty helps align management strategies. The profitability of the business is likely to increase. Relationship marketing also helps in the customer retention process.

2.4.3 Customer Evangelism

In recent years, consumer-generated content has been on the rise in digital platforms (Gretzel, 2006). Such content has been generated by fans of all the big brands (Muñiz & Schau, 2007). Such customer evangelism goes by many names, including "folk ads" (O'Guinn, 2003), "open source" branding (Garfield, 2005), "homebrew ads" (Kahney, 2004) and "vigilante marketing" (Ives, 2004). The term vigilante marketing is preferred as it most accurately captures the phenomenon. Merriam-Webster defines a vigilante as "a self-appointed doer of justice." Consumers creating such content are acting as self-appointed promoters of the brand and often have firm convictions regarding what is right and wrong for it. Muñiz and Schau (2007) define vigilante marking as.

unpaid advertising and marketing efforts, including one-to-one, one-to-many, and many-to-many commercially oriented communications, undertaken by brand loyalists on behalf of the brand.

2.4.4 Business Marketing

Business marketing is also known as industrial marketing and is also another contemporary form of marketing (Havaldar, 2005). The current technology revolution has allowed business marketing to flourish with commercial businesses tend to opt for this approach. The focus of this type of marketing is to increase sales for customers. This type of marketing activity also leads to close alignment of brands. Business marketing helps companies to formulate long-term strategic goals. It allows companies to use available resources (Nwankwo & Gbadamosi, 2010). Another factor that has led to an increase in business marketing is the entrepreneurial revolution. This helps entrepreneurs to remain adaptable and aggressive. Moreover, they become in the position to untap the markets. Marketing practitioners and scholars have started to abandon the marketing mix approach as it does not justify the interaction and information exchanges between the consumers and the marketers (Andersen, 2001). As discussed in Sect. 2.3, the traditional marketing is moving towards a more integrated communications network. The emphasis is now on "profitable relationships" (TR Duncan, 2002).

2.4.5 Social Marketing

Another approach that is used for marketing is called social marketing (Prior & Keränen, 2020). There is a difference between social and commercial marketing. The significant difference between the two is that the former involves more customer involvement. Though, the major difficulty in implementing social marketing is that resistance is faced by customers. Hence, marketers need to be extra careful while designing a social marketing campaign. Rossiter and Percey have suggested four steps to implement the marketing campaign (Kover & Abruzzo, 1993). In the first step, the focus is on identifying the target audience. In the second step, action objectives are set. Third, communication objectives are set. Finally, media and creative strategy is formulated. The idea behind social marketing is that marketers do not develop the product; instead, they try to solve customers' problems (Melas, Foret, & Hesková, 2020).

2.4.6 Transaction Marketing

Another form of contemporary marketing is called transaction marketing. Wal-Mart and Carrefour are examples of companies that have transaction marketing (Lindgreen et al., 2004). Their strategy is to use low prices to attract customers as they, customers, prefer such marketing where they do not have to search for deals. The basic idea behind this type of marketing is to promote interpersonal relationships (Cluley, 2020).

2.4.7 Consumerism

Lately, society is stuck in a state of near no availability of space and time to distant itself from the massive attacks of information, via any advertising tool relating to consumerism (Hasyim, 2017). The term is widely used in literature about marketing in recent decades. Researchers use consumerism technology to assess the consumption behaviour of the customers (Han & Yoon, 2015). Consumption has an effect on the social and economic issues of the country. Hence, businesses need to take consumers seriously, or else it will lead to a rise in irrelevant markets. Developed countries are making full use of consumerism approach, and its adverse effect can be felt on developing nations (Stearns, 2006).

2.4.8 Examples of Contemporary Marketing Communications

In a recent study by Vodrey (2020), a case of contemporary marketing is presented where a large company in France was losing out its market share due to competition prevalent in the market. Hence, they decided to switch towards ready to eat meals. Also, the company initiated a database marketing system. In addition to this, the company hired external marketing agencies to provide the material in order to communicate with their clients. This material was then distributed to respective customers. The company used contemporary means of marketing technique and invested minimum amount. This amount was relatively cheaper than what the company would have invested in the traditional method. This marketing campaign was designed to target the unmet segment. The study reports that the results of this campaign were positive. The company managed to increase its sales and profits by using contemporary marketing strategies. Hence, from the above-mentioned case, it is revealed that contemporary marketing allowed company to personalize their messages according to the needs of customers.'

Another example of contemporary marketing communications is EasyJet and Ryanair use of these strategies. These companies developed a low-cost marketing strategy to attract customers. They have installed software through which customers can book their appointment through the Internet. Moreover, if there is more space on the plane then customers get a low price. Other companies are also using the Internet to reduce their cost and offer maximum benefit to customers. The above is an example of how companies generate an engaging dialogue with their customers. In addition to this, this relationship is also known as transactional (Vrontis & Christofi, 2020).

2.5 Conclusion

Many factors have contributed to the changes in marketing practice. Initially, the concept of marketing was to attract more customers, but now the focus is on the retention of customers. Hence, in this report, there was a thorough discussion on contemporary as well as traditional notions of marketing. Furthermore, different theories of traditional and contemporary are deliberated in this report. As mentioned earlier, there has been an addition to the four Ps with three more Ps. The idea behind this addition is to ensure the needs and wants of customers remain satisfied. In addition to this, the focus of marketing is to build a long-term relationship with all the stakeholders (Jabbar et al., 2020). The above discussion has made it clear that both contemporary and traditional marketing have their pros and cons. In the former, the focus of the companies is to attract the customers to the products rather than the brand. Contemporary marketing communications assist in building a strong relationship with customers.

The current chapter attempted to understand both the traditional as well as contemporary notions of marketing communications. As discussed in this chapter, the digital age not only brings a lot of opportunities for marketers but also challenges for communication practitioners. The digital channels allow businesses to collect, register, analyze and use consumer information for better targeting the customers with tailored messages. With the advent of internet technology, the communication process has become interactive and offers real-time dialogue between customers and brands. This helps businesses to analyze and quickly adapt to the consumers' feedback and to restructure dynamically its communication to the new situation.

This presents an opportunity for all practitioners and economies to manage this flow of information between the organization and the online environment. In recent years, this feedback can be automated by using an automatic software application. A well-organized information system can also transmit the analysis of the online communication process to the top management, which can take the relevant decisions regarding the core values of the corporation and the general strategy of the firm.

Finally, culture has become an important factor in effective marketing communication. Contemporary communication managers seek to understand the cultural nuances of their market before developing their marketing communication strategy. Cultural difference can create psychological and physical barriers in emerging economies. Managers in emerging economies must consider this as a significant issue when they use digital technology, i.e. social media to promote their brands as this would require a lot of attention on the nuances of emerging market cultures where the businesses operate. It is important to localize the communication elements to elicit the required response from the market. Involving local and indigenous knowledge will assist marketers to shoot down any problem which may occur due to misconceptions or assumptions about the culture and the audience behaviour.

References

Ahmad, N. S., Musa, R., & Harun, M. H. M. (2016). The impact of social media content marketing (SMCM) towards brand health. *Procedia Economics and Finance, 37*, 331–336.

Andersen, P. H. (2001). Relationship development and marketing communication: An integrative model. *Journal of Business & Industrial Marketing, 16*(3), 167–182.

Balmer, J. M. (2017). Explicating corporate brands and their management: Reflections and directions from 1995. In *Advances in corporate branding* (pp. 22–46). London: Palgrave Macmillan.

Camilleri, M. A. (2017). Unlocking corporate social responsibility communication through digital media. In *Communicating corporate social responsibility in the digital era* (pp. 17–34). Routledge.

Carson, R. (2002). *Silent spring*. Houghton Mifflin Harcourt.

Cluley, R. (2020). The politics of consumer data. *Marketing Theory, 20*(1), 45–63.

Coviello, N. E., & Brodie, R. J. (2001). Contemporary marketing practices of consumer and business-to-business firms: How different are they? *Journal of Business & Industrial Marketing, 16*(5), 382–400. https://doi.org/10.1108/08858620110400223.

Du, R. Y., Netzer, O., Schweidel, D. A., & Mitra, D. (2021). Capturing marketing information to fuel growth. *Journal of Marketing, 85*(1), 163–183.

Duffett, R. G. (2017). Influence of social media marketing communications on young consumers' attitudes. *Young Consumers, 18*(1), 19–39.

Duncan, T. (2002). *IMC: Using advertising and promotion to build brands*. McGrawHill.

Duncan, T., & Moriarty, S. E. (1998). A communication-based marketing model for managing relationships. *Journal of Marketing, 62*(2), 1–13.

Duncan, T., Duncan, T. R., Tom Duncan, K., Moriarty, S. E., & Moriarty, S. (1997). *Driving brand value: Using integrated marketing to manage profitable stakeholder relationships*. Irwin Professional Publishing.

Fahn, C. W. (2020). Marketing the prosthesis: Supercrip and superhuman narratives in contemporary cultural representations. *Philosophies, 5*(3), 11.

Finne, Å., & Grönroos, C. (2017). Communication-in-use: Customer-integrated marketing communication. *European Journal of Marketing., 51*(3), 445–463.

Garfield, B. (2005). Listenomics. *Advertising Age, 76*(41), 1–35.

Gretzel, U. (2006). Consumer generated content–trends and implications for branding. *E-Review of Tourism Research, 4*(3), 9–11.

Grönroos, C. (2004). The relationship marketing process: Communication, interaction, dialogue, value. *Journal of Business & Industrial Marketing, 19*(2), 99–113.

Grossmann, I., & Santos, H. C. (2020). Individualistic cultures. In *Encyclopedia of personality and individual differences* (pp. 2238–2241).

Gummesson, E., & Mele, C. (2010). Marketing as value co-creation through network interaction and resource integration. *Journal of Business Market Management, 4*(4), 181–198.

Han, H., & Yoon, H. J. (2015). Hotel customers' environmentally responsible behavioral intention: Impact of key constructs on decision in green consumerism. *International Journal of Hospitality Management, 45*, 22–33.

Hasyim, M. (2017). The metaphor of consumerism. *Journal of Language Teaching and Research, 8*(3), 523–530.

Havaldar, K. K. (2005). *Industrial marketing: Text and cases*. Tata McGraw-Hill Education.

Hoeckesfeld, L., Sarquis, A. B., Urdan, A. T., & Cohen, E. D. (2020). Contemporary marketing practices approaches in the professional services industry in Brazil. *Revista Pensamento Contemporâneo Em Administração, 14*(1), 56–75.

Idrysheva, Z., Tovma, N., Abisheva, K.-Z., Murzagulova, M., & Mergenbay, N. (2019). *Marketing communications in the digital age*. Paper presented at the E3S Web of Conferences.

Ives, N. (2004). Unauthorized campaigns used by unauthorized creators to show their creativity become a trend. *New York Times*, pp. 23, C3

Jabbar, A., Akhtar, P., & Dani, S. (2020). Real-time big data processing for instantaneous marketing decisions: A problematization approach. *Industrial Marketing Management, 90*, 558–569.

Jacobson, J., Gruzd, A., & Hernández-García, Á. (2020). Social media marketing: Who is watching the watchers? *Journal of Retailing and Consumer Services, 53*(C), 1–12.

Jaffe, J. (2005). *Life after the 30-second spot: Energize your brand with a bold mix of alternatives to traditional advertising*. Wiley.

Järvinen, J., Tollinen, A., Karjaluoto, H., & Jayawardhena, C. (2012). Digital and social media marketing usage in B2B industrial section. *Marketing Management Journal, 22*(2), 102–117.

Kahney, L. (2004). Home-brew iPod ad opens eyes. *Wired News*.

Kannan, P. (2017). Digital marketing: A framework, review and research agenda. *International Journal of Research in Marketing, 34*(1), 22–45.

Keller, K. L. (2009). Building strong brands in a modern marketing communications environment. *Journal of Marketing Communications, 15*(2–3), 139–155.

Koiso-Kanttila, N. (2004). Digital content marketing: A literature synthesis. *Journal of Marketing Management, 20*(1–2), 45–65.

Kotler, P. (2003). *A framework for marketing management*. Pearson Education India.

Kotler, P. (2012). *Kotler on marketing*. Simon and Schuster. https://books.google.com/books?hl=en&lr=&id=iHWxeT7X5YYC&oi=fnd&pg=PT7&dq=Kotler+on+marketing&ots=ei4RuZ9CLO&sig=cJgOtpoGl908MAzt_qn13ISoXqw.

Kover, A. J., & Abruzzo, J. (1993). The Rossiter-Percy Grid and emotional response to advertising: An initial evaluation. *Journal of Advertising Research, 33*(6), 21–28.

Lane Keller, K. (2001). Mastering the marketing communications mix: Micro and macro perspectives on Integrated Marketing Communication programs. *Journal of Marketing Management, 17*(7–8), 819–847. https://doi.org/10.1362/026725701323366836.

Leeflang, P. S., Verhoef, P. C., Dahlström, P., & Freundt, T. (2014). Challenges and solutions for marketing in a digital era. *European Management Journal, 32*(1), 1–12.

Lindgreen, A., Palmer, R., & Vanhamme, J. (2004). Contemporary marketing practice: Theoretical propositions and practical implications. *Marketing Intelligence & Planning., 22*(6), 673–692.

Melas, D., Foret, M., & Hesková, M. (2020). *Importance of quality of life and social indicators in contemporary marketing*. Paper presented at the Proceedings of FEB Zagreb International Odyssey Conference on Economics and Business.

Meyer, P. (2009). *The vanishing newspaper: Saving journalism in the information age*. University of Missouri Press.

Moravcikova, D., Krizanova, A., Kliestikova, J., & Rypakova, M. (2017). Green marketing as the source of the competitive advantage of the business. *Sustainability, 9*(12), 2218.

Moriarty, S., & Schultz, D. (2012). Four theories of how IMC works. *Advertising Theory, 3*, 491–505.

Müller, J. M., Pommeranz, B., Weisser, J., & Voigt, K.-I. (2018). Digital, social media, and mobile marketing in industrial buying: Still in need of customer segmentation? Empirical evidence from Poland and Germany. *Industrial Marketing Management, 73*(1), 70–83.

Muñiz, J. A. M., & Schau, H. J. (2007). Vigilante marketing and consumer-created communications. *Journal of Advertising, 36*(3), 35–50. https://doi.org/10.2753/joa0091-3367360303.

Nwankwo, S., & Gbadamosi, A. (2010). *Entrepreneurship marketing: Principles and practice of SME marketing.* Routledge.

O'Guinn, T. C. (2003, December). *(Brand) community support for the (Brand) orchestra.* Presentation to Marketing Science Institute Conference on Brands, Orlando, FL.

Olaniran, B. A. (2018). Social media as communication channel in emerging economies: A closer look at cultural implications. *Journal of Advances in Management Research, 15*(2), 130–145.

Pilotta, J. J., & Schultz, D. (2005). Simultaneous media experience and synesthesia. *Journal of Advertising Research, 45*(1), 19–26.

Popkewitz, T. (2001). *Cultural history and education: Critical essays on knowledge and schooling.* Routledge.

Pridmore, J., & Zwick, D. (2011). Marketing and the rise of commercial consumer surveillance. *Surveillance & Society, 8*(3), 269–277.

Prior, D. D., & Keränen, J. (2020). Revisiting contemporary issues in B2B marketing: It's not just about artificial intelligence. *Australasian Marketing Journal (AMJ), 28*(2), 83–89.

Quesenberry, K. A. (2020). *Social media strategy: Marketing, advertising, and public relations in the consumer revolution.* Rowman & Littlefield Publishers.

Rowley, J. (2008). Understanding digital content marketing. *Journal of Marketing Management, 24*(5–6), 517–540. https://doi.org/10.1362/026725708x325977.

Schultz, T. (1993). *Lauterborn, integrated marketing communications.* NTC books.

Serafinelli, E. (2018). *Digital life on Instagram: New social communication of photography.* Emerald Group Publishing.

Shumate, M., & O'Connor, A. (2010). The symbiotic sustainability model: Conceptualizing NGO–corporate alliance communication. *Journal of Communication, 60*(3), 577–609.

Stearns, P. N. (2006). *Consumerism in world history: The global transformation of desire*. Routledge.

Strauss, J., & Frost, R. (2008). *E-marketing*. Prentice Hall Press.

Venkatesh, A. (1996). New visions of information technology and postmodernism: Implications for advertising and marketing communications. In *The information superhighway and private households* (pp. 319–337). Springer.

Vodrey, S. P. R. (2020). *Revisiting the contemporary flow of influence in political marketing*. Carleton University,

Vrontis, D., & Christofi, M. (2020). *Contemporary issues in management and marketing research*. Sage.

Yadav, M., Joshi, Y., & Rahman, Z. (2015). Mobile social media: The new hybrid element of digital marketing communications. *Procedia-Social and Behavioral Sciences, 189*, 335–343.

3

Power Shift: Analyzing the Changing Role of Public Relations in the Marketing Mix

Ligia A. Trejo

3.1 Introduction

In a global business environment defined by continuous economic declines, marked by change of preference in media channel consumption, and continued change in demographics, marketers are forced to review best avenues to promote products, services, and/or organizations that will allow continued market share. During these changing times, consumers look more for interactivity and connection (Naumovska & Blazeska, 2016). For this reason, public relations as part of the marketing mix have evolved from being thought of as "any non-paid communication between the firm and its constituencies" (Robinson, 2006, p. 249) and as a supporting agent for promotional activities to having a more active role in attracting market consumers. Thus, the power that public relations convey during changing business environments should be based on its

---

L. A. Trejo (✉)
Florida International University, Miami, FL, USA
e-mail: Ltrej003@fiu.edu

ability to convey credibility, trust, and the provision of an intimate level of communication that influences consumer's perspectives (Naumovska & Blazeska, 2016). Public relations activities, unlike other elements in the marketing mix, should also display interaction and messaging of encouragement, participation, and awareness. These activities will likely help build brand awareness (Naumovska & Blazeska, 2016) and create brand loyalty, thus positioning public relations at an advantage over all the other elements in the marketing mix.

Because public relations is about nurturing good relationships (Robinson, 2006), building positive perceptions, credibility, and trust (Naumovska & Blazeska, 2016), digital media and social media provide a greater opportunity for the development of public relations activities as it provides a platform in which organizations and consumers can have continued interaction, presenting opportunities for the relationship forming and community involvement. Digital media offers an ad-free space that is preferred by the public (Naumovska & Blazeska, 2016; Robinson, 2006), giving public relations an ideal platform to develop and distribute content related to organizational initiatives, product launching, and social responsibility. Moreover, digital and social media provide an advantage for public relations practitioners in that it allows the reach of a wider audience through newsletters, blogs, alerts, and other public relation-related material in a faster and more cost-efficient way (Place et al., 2016).

Similar to the change in preference in media channel consumption, the world economic decline has also forced marketers to find creative avenues to gain and maintain market share as marketing budgets decreased (Picard, 2011). It is widely known that the more popular and traditional marketing tools like advertising require large expenditures that include media planning and media selling activities as well as production costs (D'Angelo, 2015; Naumovska & Blazeska, 2016). Moreover, the large sums of expenditures invested in advertising campaigns do not necessarily guarantee that the message will reach the targeted audience especially given the amount of message clutter in an "over advertised society" (Naumovska & Blazeska, 2016, p. 180). This has created room for public relations to become a more accepted tool for marketing practices (Nakra, 1991), partly because of its cost efficiency (Elrod & Fortenberry, 2020; Howard, 1989), as it eliminates costs associated with media planning and media buying activities and of other marketing promotional activities that potentially impact an organization's financial bottom line in a negative way.

In this chapter, we will also look at the importance of adaptation of marketing plans to the change in the demographic landscape tailoring marketing campaigns to specific emerging markets. Particularly in the United States, marketers have shifted their attention to minority groups such as the Hispanic population because of its rapid growth and purchasing power and the potential economic possibilities they represent (Korzenny & Korzenny, 2012; Llopis, 2012). We will look at some examples developed by marketers in the United States aimed at attracting this particular group.

Taken together, the main purpose of this chapter is to reflect on successful public relations strategies used for marketing purposes that could be used as benchmarks by marketers trying to gain and maintain market share in emerging economies operating in a constantly changing global environment. In the first section, we explain the importance of public relations in the marketing mix, through its stance in Integrated Marketing Communications (IMC). Second, we will touch upon the change in media consumption preferences and why public relations has an advantage over other elements in the IMC when using digital media, providing examples of successful public relations campaigns made viral through digital and social media. Third, the chapter will discuss the benefits of using public relations campaigns during economic declines as "free publicity" (Nakra, 1991, p. 43). Fourth, the chapter will look at the change in the demographic landscape in emerging economies seen through the Hispanic population in the United States—a forceful economic engine and important target for marketers. We will draw on examples of public relations campaigns used by marketers in the United States that have successfully attracted this particular segment. Finally, the chapter will provide managerial implications with key information for marketers looking to gain and/or maintain market share in emerging economies emphasizing the use of public relations initiatives for marketing purposes especially under changing business landscapes.

3.2 Public Relations Role in Integrated Marketing Communications

Public relations, defined as "a strategic communication process that builds mutually beneficial relationships between organizations and their public" (Public Relations Society of America [PRSA], n.d., "About public relations" section, para. 3), is known to be used to "harmonize external and internal relationships" (Naumovska & Blazeska, 2016, p. 179), and often seen as a tool to communicate internal and external changes and as a channel of communication that is particularly powerful when dealing with disaster and crisis management (Robinson, 2006; Smith & Place, 2013). Public relations as a marketing tool is part of Integrated Marketing Communications (IMC), a concept with the primary role of combining elements found in the marketing promotional mix to maximize marketing efforts to transmit a unified and cohesive message to promote and sell a product or service. Nonetheless, the concept known as Integrated Communications (IC) has been argued to be a more "holistic" (Smith & Place, 2013, p. 170) approach to IMC and positions public relations as the governing element of all aspects of communications found in the marketing promotional mix (Smith & Place, 2013).

The difference between IMC and IC is argued to be that IMC includes all elements in the marketing promotional mix, including those that are clear marketing concepts, aimed to persuade instead of informing, whereas IC deals with communication concepts that do not have a marketing core, but instead fall within the field of communications, which are meant to inform rather than sell. As an element in IMC, public relations is mostly utilized to create initial awareness about a new product or service. It is a form of anticipating what is to come, serving as a starting point for all other promotion mix elements to follow (Miller & Rose, 1994). Through its power of publicity and image building, "public relations can help reposition products, revitalize old ones, open new markets, and strengthen advertising claims" (Nakra, 1991, p. 43). In a changing global environment, public relations has shifted its power to be regarded as an indispensable element in the marketing mix. It is no longer being regarded as a tool used only for the mere utility of gaining publicity and image building but is seen as a vehicle that continuously has helped in the acquisition of market share (Nakra, 1991). Furthermore, a new outlook of public relations as the primary element of IC that bridges relationships between organizations and the public through transparent and trusting communication efforts give leverage to the only element in the IMC that can create long-lasting brand loyalty through credibility and trust, thus helping the overall and long-term financial stability of the organization. This provides a great advantage to public relations as a marketing tool over other elements in the marketing promotional mix as it gives marketers and organizations a comprehensive tool to communicate and maintain relationships with consumers despite changes in the global landscape changes.

3.3 Emerging Media: Digital Platforms and Social Media

Digital media, specifically social media, has revolutionized the way the public consume media. The fast connectivity, interactivity, and large reach have rapidly become a popular communication channel for masses. Moreover, its fairly inexpensive use allows people to easily connect at all times, cutting through time, space, culture, and gender (Gesualdi, 2019). In a changing media space, traditional one-way media outlets have decreased popularity among publics that look to interact with others in a shared space. Nonetheless, the increased use of social media and other digital platforms has forced marketers to try to find ways to market products in non-traditional media spaces and consider social and digital media to be new channels that enable brand management (Gesualdi, 2019). A leading factor created by social media is found through the ability of forming relationships through a two-way form of communication that allows for interactivity between organizations and the public as they share and learn about product preferences, product complaints, and overall information surrounding a particular product (Briones et al., 2011). The two-way communication form gives marketers an opportunity to discuss products, services, and/or organizations in an instant and attentive manner given with a personable flair that results in great value creation and allows for the development of positive perceptions of a product and/or organization. The management of public perceptions is a core function of public relations (Naumovska & Blazeska, 2016), considering public relations "attempt to define reality for the target consumers" (Naumovska & Blazeska, 2016, p. 179). Through posting of messages and individual interactions on online media platforms, public relations professionals are able to build and manage product perceptions (Berry & Wilson, 2020). The use of social media sites such as Facebook, Twitter, and Instagram by marketers allows for informal and at-large communication between consumers and brands while generating knowledge about a product and gives higher potentiality of positive buzz and perceptions over a product or service. Moreover, the interactivity function of social media platforms allows participants to share their experiences and perceptions of products that result in free publicity. The concept of free publicity is often achieved through "user-generated content" (Wright & Hinson, 2009, p. 3), when users upload personal videos and content endorsing or commenting about given products and services, thus becoming consumers to be "ambassadors for a brand" (Robinson, 2006, p. 249). These activities often influence a network's purchasing decision and are the reason why word of mouth created by free publicity is considered to be "a dream of most marketers" (Robinson, 2006, p. 249). Importantly, the foundation of purchasing decisions through word of mouth relies on trusting observations and experiences that allow for recommendations of products (Robinson, 2006).

The emergence and popularity of digital media give public relations professionals an advantage over marketing professionals as it relates to professional skills and job requirements (Park & Ki, 2017). Public relations professionals use digital platforms, probably with more frequency than marketing professionals do (Place et al., 2016). In a new digital era, public relations professionals can distribute their work, both written material and visual, through digital platforms primarily due to the quickness of delivery and accessibility of the platform. Communications that involve the launching of new products, crisis management, press conference videos, and publicity stunts (Alexandrescu & Milandru, 2018) are rapidly dispersed through the use of digital platforms and can be captured by masses at once and instantly despite geographical location and time. In the same way, public relations professionals use their communication skills for the promotion of a product or service, thus giving public relations professionals a lead when marketing products, services, and/or organizations through digital platforms compared with counterparts in marketing professions.

It is, therefore, clear that social media gives marketers and public relations professionals the ability to instantly communicate and interact with consumers and shares news and ideas on products and services. Additionally, social media presents a platform to share viewpoints on societal and environmental issues that affect consumers worldwide. Nonetheless, the proper usage of messaging and sensitivity to issues is crucial to attain the right publicity and light surrounding a product or service and organizations (Kumar et al., 2017). In a time when marketers are looking to build relationships with consumers, negative reviews and comments about a product are factors that likely prevent the attainment of marketing goals. It is imperative for marketers to understand that the handling of both positive and negative reviews can either help or destroy loyalty and following (Kumar et al., 2017). Given the ability to deal with crisis moments and ability to convey trustworthy and credible messaging, public relations professionals also have an advantage over marketing professionals in this sense (Place et al., 2016; Smith, 2010).

Public relations professionals are expected to deal with crisis moments and handle publicity. Therefore, connecting with the public through the attention of issues that affect communities and, thus communicating shared values and standpoints can come with much ease. Moreover, communication activities that convey positive and truthful messaging as well as compelling stories about victory, positivism, and self-reflection can encourage consumers to engage with a brand and assist in the development of long-term brand reputation (Kumar et al., 2017). Public relations messaging done right can easily and effectively bring attention to products, services, and/or organizations, creating brand loyalty, awareness, and following (Berry & Wilson, 2020). Moreover, the challenge is creating content that appeals to the public. To connect with the public, marketers must create engaging, creative and innovative content.

The success of an online public relations campaign is only as effective and engaging as the content that is produced for online media (D'Angelo, 2015). Furthermore, the ability to consume media content without commercial breaks, in an uninterrupted medium, also makes social media and other digital platforms a more appealing medium to go to when looking for entertainment. This capability is one that can present challenges for the integration of elements such as advertising spots, but this also gives public relations an opportunity to engage with the public through the development and delivery of creative and innovative content that could live in a digital space without commercial interruptions. Creative content developed and delivered is, thus, one that has to be dynamic, accessible, engaging, and of special interest to the public, keeping in mind that this content is to be shared with networks of friends and family and has the potential of creating buzz over a product, service and/ or an organization. Marketers and public relations professionals must also acknowledge that as consumers become more empowered, informed, and technically savvy, they are also likely to be able to more easily disperse negative or positive word of mouth (Nath & Bell, 2016). This requires an understanding of how and why consumers are gathering and sharing information that influences them (Wright & Hinson, 2009).

Moreover, public relations has been largely known to be the communication method used as means to inform employees about organizational news that include internal organizational changes, news about products, and crisis management (Howard, 1989). Externally, they communicate product information, generate product awareness, share organizational news, and aim to create an overall positive public image surrounding products and organizations (Nath & Bell, 2016; Robinson, 2006; Smith, 2010). Nonetheless, public relations activities that serve the purpose to advocate, educate, and bring a positive light to audiences more than just inform about news of products and organizations, often create valuable links with the public as they touch upon emotion and issues that matter most to their consumers and their everyday lives. Through the communication of positive, credible, and truthful messages, public relations initiatives are able to instill trust that positively influences purchase decision and builds brand awareness (Naumovska & Blazeska, 2016).

The ability conveyed to instill trust and positive influence can also be used to incite social responsibility and create awareness. A great example of how social media can be used to create awareness through viral connectivity, and interaction was one created by The Amyotrophic Lateral Sclerosis (ALS) with the "The Ice Bucket Challenge." This initiative was created for fundraising purposes and awareness of ALS. The "challenge" created worldwide buzz and immediate popularity as people all over the world uploaded videos in their social media accounts, thus creating free user-generated content. Uploaded videos showed participants having a bucket of ice-cold water poured over them, as they challenged someone else in their network to do the same. This campaign engaged people from all walks of life and included participation by well-known figures including athletes, politicians, and celebrities among others, creating a successful campaign elevating awareness for the condition as well as monetary donations for the association. Indeed, it was reported that the campaign raised more than $100 million for the association, attracting more than 3 million donors worldwide (Sutherland, 2016).

Another good use of creative content to engage and inform the public is presented by Lyft. Widely known as a company to engage in social responsibility initiatives, Lyft uses their social media accounts and company website to inform the public using uplifting messages and narratives of positivism during uncertain and unstable times. Through the use of blogs, social media postings, and website content, Lyft has been able to promote their commitment to making positive impact by lifting each other up. The content in their social media accounts, both user-generated and company-generated, presents a very positive image of a company that is interested in the welfare of a community. Social media postings include messages from drivers, corporate employees, and consumers sharing stories of experiences with Lyft, often bringing attention to events and issues that affect the community and the world. Their website can be described as very interactive and user-friendly, thus engaging and of great appeal for users. The website also contains a section dedicated to the support of underserved communities, stating their alliances and partnerships with non-profit organizations to help serve a community better. In addition, their efforts through the promotion of social responsibility messaging garnered positive publicity and image, allowing for brand association with positive causes. Moreover, the company also presents content in the form of short videos found on their YouTube channel with several stories featuring different real-life scenarios that include episodes such as a driver's first experience as a Lyft driver as well as undercover appearances of sports and entertainment celebrities, some of them representing minorities, as is the case of Red Sox star athlete David Ortiz, as Lyft drivers. Some participants take advantage of the opportunity to promote charities, while others promote movies, concerts, and upcoming events, among others (Lyft, 2020). Content gives viewers relevant and entertaining information that immediately associates the brand with social responsibility initiatives, sponsorships, and minority representation.

Other organizations that use social media to promote more global social responsibility messages include TOMS shoes, promoting donation of shoes for children in need, and Coca-Cola promoting their Clean Water Project (Chu & Chen, 2019). Chu and Chen (2019) further suggest that some organizations create online pages dedicated to social responsibility and awareness projects through which the public is able to obtain information on the project and create a user following. Through these kinds of activities involving social responsibility through the use of social media, organizations are able to develop brand awareness through consumer engagement and brand affinity (Amaladoss & Manohar, 2013; Chu & Chen, 2019) that creates free publicity.

Through the examples above, it is clear that the use of social media and other digital platforms provides great avenues for marketing communications activities. However, the usage of digital platforms in emerging economies can be hindered by many challenges. These include inadequate business practices and lack of human and technological infrastructure (Coleman et al., 2016; Schultz et al., 2016). Additionally, government regulations, internet access, cultural forms, and religious beliefs can also present challenges in emerging economies (Coleman et al., 2016; Schultz & Malthouse, 2017). However, despite the challenges mentioned above, emerging markets present a high use of mobile devices as a tool for communication (Coleman et al., 2016; Schultz & Malthouse, 2017), which gives marketers an opportunity to promote products and organizations through creative and visually engaging content that can be easily accessed through mobile devices. Moreover, this can present an opportunity for public relations through social responsibility and social awareness campaigns that not only create a positive image for an organization and affinity with a brand but also provide free publicity that is often given by word of mouth and community interaction and is an aspect that every marketer aims to have (Robinson, 2006) especially during global financial uncertainty. In the following section, we will further see why public relations as a promotional tool is to be considered during economic declines. Later, in the chapter, we will see how marketers in the United States tap into emotions through representation to attract the Hispanic population, thus, creating a positive brand image and affinity with this particular group.

3.4 Public Relations in Economic Declines and Marketing Constraints

The economic instability that is marked by a financial recession and high unemployment levels leaves less access to resources forcing organizations and marketers to guard themselves in order to maintain financial stability while keeping market presence and market share. Organizations are forced to cut down budgets (Naumovska & Blazeska, 2016; Picard, 2011) furloughing or laying-off workforce and placing scarce and available financial and human resources to attend most significant organizational priorities. Moreover, research shows that marketing expenditures decline as world economies decline (Picard, 2011), especially given the low priority marketing activities can have in organizations facing financial instability. Research by Kantar media shows media planning and media selling-related expenditures in the United States decreased 19.1% in the first half of 2020 compared with the first half of 2019 (Goetzen, 2020). The financial situation calls for organizations as well as marketing professionals to seek cost-efficient and creative ways to engage with the public while adapting to the current organizational as well as global economic state.

The element of free publicity, as mentioned in the previous section, can be easily attained through public relations campaigns through digital platforms and often requires minimal cost. Also, as mentioned in the section above, digital media provides a more cost-efficient alternative to media consumption (Olotewo, 2016) and also provides a channel for ad-free content. Some of the cost-efficient public relations activities that can primarily be developed in an online space include blog posts, social media, and digital content, which incur minimal costs that are often related to staffing (Berry & Wilson, 2020). Furthermore, public relations campaign allows for savings on media planning and media selling activities as well as production costs incurred by advertising (D'Angelo, 2015; Elrod & Fortenberry, 2020; Nakra, 1991; Naumovska & Blazeska, 2016). In addition to this, advertising activities are most effective through more traditional media spaces such as television and radio, and not largely as impactful through digital platforms (Naumovska & Blazeska, 2016). Furthermore, the high cost required to produce and allocate advertising spots through traditional media does not guarantee that advertising spots will be seen by audiences (Robinson, 2006), especially given the decline in audience numbers, traditional media channels have experienced in recent years (Maheshwari & Koblin, 2018).

In order to build a relationship with consumers and brand awareness during a health pandemic that has affected communities worldwide from financial, emotional, and physical standpoints, Lyft again provides a great example of an organization using uplifting and encouraging messages to connect with communities. Through their digital accounts, they use messages to promote unity and community welfare as well as inform and educate audiences about the risks that a health pandemic can have on the overall global environment. Additionally, as a business, they use this platform to inform their consumers about business operations advising on procedures taken to safeguard clients and employees. Their messages convey social responsibility as well as awareness of a global health pandemic that affects everyone. Messages include user-generated content posted by Lyft drivers and employees as well as company-generated content featuring healthcare workers, drivers, and many other professionals that risk their lives to serve a community.

Activities like this generate free publicity through the interaction of thousands of followers that continuously post uplifting comments, giving the organization a positive outlook and publicity. Public relations messaging requiring minimal costs could include online publicity and social responsibility campaigns similar to one provided by Lyft. Campaigns on social responsibility and awareness that appeal to emotions are some of the ways that marketers are able to create relationship with consumers and brand affinity (Amaladoss & Manohar, 2013; Chu & Chen, 2019). Social media campaigns that touch upon emotions, such as ones done by Lyft and the ALS foundation, can be done at a minimal cost yet have the potential of virality that results in free publicity. In the next section, we focus on the Hispanic population of the United States and see how marketers have used emotions through culture and representation to attract this particular group.

3.5 Public Relations and Emerging Demographic Landscapes: Hispanics in the United States

The Hispanic population in the United States has shown constant growth during the past two decades, reaching approximately 61 million in 2019 (Lopez et al., 2020). From the years 2000–2010, the Hispanic population represented the largest minority growth in the United States (Johnson & Lichter, 2016) and has become an "engine of demographic and social change unfolded evenly across the United States" (Johnson & Lichter, 2016, p. 706). They are predicted to have a 93.5% growth by 2060 (Vespa et al., 2020). Moreover, the importance of the attraction to this specific population for marketers is attached to their increasing spending power, which is reported to be $1.5 trillion, larger than the GDP of Australia (Ridley, 2019; Vann, 2020; Weeks, 2019), representing a 212% growth (Vann, 2020; Weeks, 2019).

The cause of Hispanic population growth is attributed to a "combination of domestic migration, immigration, and fertility" (Johnson & Lichter, 2016, p. 706). From 2010–2019, growth in the Hispanic population accounted for more than half (52%) of the total population growth in the United States, reaching a record 60.6 million, equivalent to 18% of the total U.S. population (Krogstad, 2020). It is anticipated that the Hispanic population, as it rapidly becomes an important demographic in the United States ethnic population, will "reshape racial and ethnic relations as well as the future of the country" (Johnson & Lichter, 2016, p. 709). Its fast growth has allowed this group to become a main driver of the nation's purchasing power. It is estimated that one out of every six Americans in the United States is of Hispanic descent (Weeks, 2019) making them an important target for marketers.

With immigration to the United States greatly declining in the past years, mostly due to strong immigration laws that make it harder to immigrate to the United States, the growth of the Hispanic population in the United States can be attributed to the number of American born Hispanics (Korzenny, & Korzenny, 2012). The new Hispanic generations, second and third generations, are bi-cultural and bi-lingual and are no longer engaged in Spanish-only content. The rapid shift in demographics requires marketers to focus attention on this particular group that not only views themselves as Hispanic but also as American. However, like their parents and grandparents, they are very well engaged through content that is self-reflective and acknowledges family struggles, as well as the portrayal of family values and heritage (Korzenny & Korzenny, 2012; Zuniga & Torres, 2015). The Hispanic community is said to have the youngest median age among all minorities in the United States that can be justified through the larger birth-rate number compared with the non-Hispanic demographic (Johnson & Lichter, 2016). This growing demographic now has higher purchasing power, in part due to higher education and higher paying jobs (Korzenny & Korzenny, 2012). Moreover, this generation is more technologically savvy, giving a strong platform to social media and other digital channels.

The Hispanic culture is one that is driven by frequent interpersonal communication and the building of relationships. Moreover, the use of social media presents a vehicle for constant connection and frequent communication with friends and family in the motherland (Goodrich & Mooij, 2014), especially for those who are foreign born. Studies done by PwC (2016) show more social activity by Hispanics than by any non-Hispanics as it provides a good means to stay connected with family abroad as well as creates a sense of social community that is strongly valued. Furthermore, Hispanics are more likely to engage in other online activities such as shopping, reading, and entertainment (Li & Tsai, 2015). Therefore, understanding the overall increase of usage of digital media by Hispanics should be of great importance for marketers. As such, they should take advantage of this generally cost-efficient medium and develop content that appeals to Hispanics through careful, insightful, and relevant information that appeals to them both emotionally and psychologically. This will likely help in the creation of trusting emotions, which allows for brand engagement and loyalty.

Trust is another important factor highly regarded by Hispanics (Llopis, 2012). Trusting recommendations can often lead to the influence of purchased decisions. Opinions from trusted family and friends matter deeply to Hispanics. They often acquire knowledge of products and services through word of mouth. Word of mouth is a very important and common method of promotion that is especially relevant in emerging markets (Atsom et al., 2012). People in emerging economies give high importance to affiliations and relationships, whether it is family, community, or social groups (Schultz & Malthouse, 2017). Furthermore, social media provides a great platform for sharing through word of mouth that influences not only immediate family and friends but also larger networks (Robinson, 2006).

Similar to many other emerging markets, the Hispanic community is not homogenous (Bang et al., 2016; Korzenny & Korzenny, 2012). There are many subcultures that make up the Hispanic population. Generalizing is a big mistake that marketers need to be aware of as this can result in negative impacts on brand engagement (Korzenny & Korzenny, 2012). For example, Hispanics from Mexico may not have the same driving forces as Hispanics from Cuba as their immigration stories are vastly different. Therefore, their process of acculturation may be also different. One factor that indeed could be the same for the majority is the expatriation experience of having to leave all behind in hopes to find a better life in estranged lands. Nonetheless, their love for family, traditions, and culture is prevalent throughout (Korzenny & Korzenny, 2012). Learning about what makes subcultures different and showing respect and interest in this community's culture will make them more likely to respond positively to the intended brands (Carufel, 2020). Targeting the Hispanic community in the United States, marketers must also learn to understand what drives the purchasing power and loyalty of this community. Understanding their culture, for example, can translate into developing brand loyalty and following (Carufel, 2020) and trust. To gain acceptance with this population, marketers must learn to develop messages that include strong appeal to heritage, family values, and representation. The Hispanic community is especially drawn to initiatives that include self-reflection (Zuniga & Torres, 2015), instilling pride and gratification. Hispanics like to see themselves represented through brands (Garrido, 2019). Because of this, marketers should use activities, especially through public relations, that elevate Hispanic achievements and show representation that instills emotional bonds with this segment of the population. Garrido (2019) explains that brands should look to empathize with Hispanic societal problems. Hispanics greatly value brands that participate and engage in trying to solve matters that affect them socially. Therefore, understanding Hispanic culture and issues that affect them socially are crucial to developing content and messages that will evolve into trust in brands.

Due to the value Hispanics find in heritage, culture, tradition, and representation (Zuniga & Torres, 2015) public relations campaigns developed through narratives rooted in these aspects allow for the development of emotional connections and trusting relationships. A good example of a successful public relations campaign targeted toward the Hispanic population was done by Toyota in 2017 through the "Juntos Somos Imparables" or "Together we are Unstoppable" campaign (Garrido, 2019). The kick-off event campaign included appearances in various Hispanic events across the nation, including the showcase of their newly developed state-of-the-art headquarters in Texas. The campaign was developed to represent and celebrate the livelihood of Hispanic immigrants in the United States touching upon inspiration and resilience. The core of the campaign dealt with traits and messages resembling struggles endured by Hispanics in the United States as they assimilated to a new culture yet maintained their traditions and values alive. Attendees had an option to participate in the engraving of license plates that marked their experiences as immigrants reaching the "American dream" and these were displayed in murals throughout. Words engraved emphasized resilience, sacrifice, resonating struggles when dealing with factors such acculturation, representation, and discrimination—all important aspects that face Hispanics in the United States. The delivery of the campaign resembled one of gratitude toward a community that showed loyalty to the Toyota brand among many other brands. Indeed, for nearly a decade, Toyota had been known to be the best-selling automotive brand among Hispanics in the United States (Toyota Newsroom, 2015). As a value of representation and showcasing Hispanics that have thrived despite their own acculturation struggles, Toyota used Hispanic journalist Neida Sandoval as an ambassador, making her a symbol of what Hispanics are able to achieve as immigrants in the United States. Here, she shared her own story of acculturation and perseverance as an immigrant in the United States. This resonated very well with many and also gave them a sense of pride through representation. The results of the campaign showed an increase in 30% brand consideration and 41% in brand perception (Schermer, 2017). Building upon events and initiatives that involve Hispanic representation and acknowledgment, it is not a surprise that Toyota has been a continued preferred brand among Hispanics in the United States (Garrido, 2019).

The Super Bowl is perhaps the most widely watched sports event in the United States. Super Bowl 54 held in Miami had an extra appeal, especially for an emerging yet important market. Colombian rock star Shakira and Hispanic American Jennifer Lopez were showcased in the halftime show of what could be the most important televised event of the year in the United States regardless of language. It marked the first time that two Hispanic performers headlined an event of this magnitude. A highly awaited spectacle, the yearly event carries out millions of dollars in ad revenues and is usually marked by the presence of English-speaking performers, catered mainly to the American-born population, which are known to be the primary followers of the sport. Nonetheless, the occasion had a Hispanic flair, taking advantage of the stage being in Miami, a city where the Hispanic population is a majority. This was widely accepted by the Hispanic population as it gave them representation on a worldwide stage. Furthermore, the performance by Jennifer Lopez with children in cages reflected issues currently affecting Hispanic immigrants at the border between the United States and Mexico. The show created instant worldwide buzz and gave a reflection of the importance of Hispanic ethnic contribution to the United States. This production, and the decision to showcase two important Hispanic performers, is a way that organizations, in this case, the NFL, Pepsi, as well as entertainment group ROC Nation, tried to reach out to connect with Hispanic consumers (Kaufman, 2020; Vann, 2020).

3.6 Managerial Implications

In this chapter, we learned that public relation, at the core of IC strategies, is a valuable element in an evolving business landscape due to its purpose of communicating and informing. The advantages public relation has over other elements in the marketing promotional mix include its cost-efficiency and its ability to convey trusting and credible messages that foster relationship building with a specific target demographic. Although this chapter is specific to the Hispanic population as an emerging economic powerhouse in the United States, whose consistent growth and purchase power have created a shift of focus for marketers looking to acquire and maintain market share, it can also apply to other global emerging economies where marketers try to gain and maintain market share. Moreover, because some of these elements often present challenges for marketers when introducing products and services (Coleman et al., 2016; Paul, 2019; Schultz & Malthouse, 2017) marketers should strive to understand the driving forces to build effective relationships with consumers. For instance, embracing the digital and social media to create creative content that could be of relevance to a community may help obtain the brand loyalty and awareness marketers look for. In doing so, marketers should pay attention to issues that matter to these segments and create messaging that provides emotional comfort, encouragement, and pride in times of global uncertainty. Additionally, marketers should be constantly learning about changes in demographic, economic, and technological developments that may influence and alter brand attraction as well as loyalty. This may include a constant review of demographic data that can aid in the development of relevant marketing strategies to reach emerging markets with ease.

As discussed in the chapter, emerging markets, as seen through Hispanics in the United States, place a great value in relationship building. In order to build effective relationships, marketers looking to target emerging economies should seek to develop strategies that foster culture, traditions, relationships, and representation. Specific to Hispanics, strong relationships can be achieved by learning and understanding about the differences found in the sub-cultures that make up the Hispanic population as not all Hispanics in the United States share the same cultural expressions (Korzenny & Korzenny, 2012). It can also be attained through campaigns with representation, showcasing, and collaborating with prominent Hispanic personalities that reflect pride and achievement in the community. A similar approach can be used with other emerging economies globally. For example, organizations should learn about aspects related to cultures, traditions, and representation while having sensitivity and understanding of different traditions, values, and societal standards (Coleman et al., 2016) and use those aspects to foster strong relationships with their consumers. To do this, marketers must understand drivers, motives, and necessities that the public crave and look for in a product. Marketers should also understand that consumers look for reassuring messages that comfort them in times of crisis (Reid, 2020) and learn that emerging markets, similar to Hispanics in the United States, are not homogenous. Therefore, careful review and tailoring of messaging for respective markets is a necessity.

Other potential strategies for marketers in emerging economies may also include the implementation of public relations initiatives as part of their corporate strategies (Amaladoss & Manohar, 2013) because public relations allows for "direct engagement with the public" (Place et al., 2016, p. 9). They can achieve this by leveraging on the cost-efficient channel of communication presented through social media and other digital platforms that provide instant and larger reach. Finally, through the use of digital media, marketers may consider creating a space to interact with others in a network as it cultivates a sense of belonging (Chu & Chen, 2019) and potential connections with brands.

3.7 Conclusion

The marketing mix consists of several elements that are used in order to sell a product, service, or organization. IMC is a method used by marketers to maximize these elements, integrating them to deliver a unified message. Furthermore, the concept of IC accentuates public relations as a primary driver of all communication efforts among elements in the marketing promotional mix. Despite being constantly used interchangeably by authors, there has been a denoted difference between both concepts (IMC and IC) that rest on the primary use of marketing core elements in the IMC, and the primary use of communication elements in the IC. Furthermore, the power shift of public relations in the marketing mix is emphasized by its ability to communicate credible and trusting messages that allow for the fostering of long-lasting relationships with constituents. Nonetheless, it is clear that under optimal circumstances, the best strategy is to incorporate all elements in the marketing mix and promote a service, product, and/or an organization as professed by IMC. It has been argued that none of the marketing promotional mix elements can be used solely when implementing marketing communication plans (Naumovska & Blazeska, 2016). However, changing times require adaptability. In changing environments in which media channel preference has moved to a more interactive and faster medium, when organizations are forced to cut down budgets and costs to protect business financial bottom-lines, and also where ethnic minorities have significantly become a power economic engine, marketers must learn to adapt and create best avenues to promote products, services, and/or organizations in order to keep market share. Traditionally, public relations has been often seen as a tool to communicate internal change to both internal and external parties and as a method to communicate positive company and product images. Nonetheless, public relations has changed its position in the marketing mix as it is increasingly being used as a promotional method due to its effectiveness to create and foster long-term relationships through two-way communication lines that not only serve the purpose of selling a product but also can be used to inform, educate, and advocate for community-related programs. Moreover, the emergence and fast-growing popularity of digital platforms and social media provide an interactive and instant way to communicate with consumers. This provides an advantage for public relations professionals as it compares to their marketing counterparts. This is due to several factors. First, public relations professionals have a particular skill set that requires constant use of social media and digital platforms to create and distribute communication. Second, public relations has the power to inform and educate the public in the midst of chaotic environments and global conditions. Through the effective development and delivery of prompt and timely messages that can be easily shared through social media and other digital platforms, public relations communication can serve the purpose of informing about products and also can be used to emotionally connect with the public that need positive reinforcement through critical times. Third, the interactive two-way communication form presents marketers and consumers a way to engage and openly react to certain products, services, and/or organizations. The use of public relations as a promotional tool is of importance when building relationships by conveying credibility and trusting messages (Naumovska & Blazeska, 2016) that can draw communities to organizations, products, and services; thus, creating strong bonds with communities, especially those seeking representation and visibility.

There are several similarities between Hispanics as an emerging market in the United States and consumers in emerging markets globally that should be considered by marketers. First, the creation of bonds is particularly important to Hispanics in the United States who are often drawn to look for representation and have emotions rooted in their culture, heritage, and family values. This is also true for consumers in emerging economies globally. Second, the increase in purchase power by emerging markets including Hispanics in the United States dictates that marketers must learn what drives, motivates, and the social and cultural differences of particular target groups to be able to understand and market to them better. Third, trust is also of great importance for these groups. Creating trusting relationships with brands can potentially create free publicity through word of mouth that is known to highly influence a network's purchasing decision (Robinson, 2006).

In summary, marketers must adapt to marketplace conditions. In times of economic recession, demographic shifts, and when digital media has quickly gained popularity, marketers seek more cost-efficient yet creative and innovative channels to gain and maintain market share. To carry out and achieve marketing objectives, a rearrangement and repositioning of elements in the marketing mix is needed. This rearrangement leads to the placement of communication elements such as public relations at the core of the marketing strategies. In an era where the public seeks connection and affinity through relationships, marketers have a fundamental tool in public relations as it provides a two-way form of communication that can result in earned trust and credibility. The power shift of public relations to a more central position has to do with its great potential to connect with the public on an emotional and psychological level, a characteristic that differentiates public relations from all other elements in the marketing mix. Nonetheless, public relations professionals must acknowledge the importance of public relation messaging and the power it conveys as it relates to the management of relationships and connections. Moreover, connections with emerging markets as seen through the Hispanic market in the United States require a deep understanding of their culture and their ethnicity as a whole. A deep notion of what drives them, empowers them, and motivates them can be seen as a display of interest for their culture, allowing for deep connections and loyalty. Finally, marketers must know that the world will always be changing, and so will the marketing strategies. This means adjusting, adapting, and prioritizing marketing mix elements that will allow continued market value and representation.

References

Alexandrescu, M. B., & Milandru, M. (2018). Promotions as a form of communication of the marketing strategy. *Management and Economics, 4*(92), 268–274.

ALS Association. (n.d.). *Ice bucket challenge dramatically accelerated the fight against ALS.* https://www.als.org/stories-news/ice-bucket-challenge-dramatically-accelerated-fight-against-als. Accessed 31 October 2020.

Amaladoss, M. X., & Manohar, H. L. (2013). Communicating corporate social responsibility-A case of CSR communication in emerging economies. *Corporate Social Responsibility and Environmental Management, 20*, 65–80. https://doi.org/10.1002/csr.287.

Atsom, Y., Kuentz, J. F., & Seong, J. (2012). *Building brands in emerging markets*. McKinsey & Company, Marketing and Sales. https://www.mckinsey.com/business-functions/marketing-and-sales/our-insights/building-brands-in-emerging-markets. Accessed 30 August 2020.

Bang, V. V., Joshi, S. L., & Singh, M. C. (2016). Marketing strategy in emerging markets: A conceptual framework. *Journal of Strategic Marketing, 24*(2):104–117. https://doi.org/10.1080/0965254X.2015.1011200.

Berry, T., & Wilson, D. (2020). Public relations marketing. *Business Know-How.* https://www.businessknowhow.com/marketing/prmarketing.htm Accessed 26 June 2020.

Briones, R. L., Kuch, B., Liu, B. F., & Jin, Y. (2011). Keeping up with digital age: How the American Red Cross uses social media to build relationships. *Public Relations Review, 37*, 37–43. https://doi.org/10.1016/j.pubrev.2010.12.006.

Carufel, R. (2020). *Targeting U.S. Hispanics-what this influential audience wants from brands and content, Agility PR Solutions*. https://agilitypr.com/pr-news/publicrelations/targeting-u-s-hispanics-what-this-influential-audience-wants-from-brands-and-content/. Accessed 5 August 2020.

Chu, S., & Chen, H. (2019). Impact of consumers' corporate social responsibility-related activities in social media on brand attitude, electronic word-of-mouth intention, and purchase intention: A study of Chinese consumer behavior. *Journal of Consumer Behavior, 18*, 453–462. https://doi.org/10.1002/cb.1784.

Coleman, L. J., Manago, S. M., & Cote, L. (2016). Challenges and opportunities for social media in emerging markets. *Journal of Marketing Development and Competitiveness, 10*(3), 26–31.

D'Angelo, M. (2015). The changing world of marketing communications. In W. W. Carney & L. Lymer (Eds.), *Fundamentals of public relations and marketing communications in Canada* (pp. 133–154). University of Alberta Press.

Elrod, J., & Fortenberry, J. L. (2020). Public relations in health and medicine: Using publicity and other unpaid promotional methods to engage audiences. *BMC Health Research, 20*(1), 2–7 https://doi.org/10.1186/s12913-020-05602-x.

Garrido, M. (2019). Why brands need to find ways to connect with Hispanic consumers. *Adweek*. https://www.adweek.com/brand-%20%20marketing/why-brands-need-to-find-ways-to-connect-with-hispanic-consumers/. Accessed 2 November 2020.

Gesualdi, M. (2019). Revisiting the relationship between public relations and marketing: Encroachment and social media. *Public Relations Review, 45*(2), 372–382. https://doi.org/10.1016/j.pubrev.2018.12.002.

Goetzen, N. (2020). US Media spending dropped by nearly one-fifth year over year in H12020. *BusinessInsider*. https://www.businessinsider.com/us-media-spending-dropped-by-one-fifth-yoy-2020-9. Accessed 31 October 2020.

Goodrich, K., & Mooij, M. D. (2014). How social are social media? A cross-cultural comparison of online and online purchase decision influences. *Journal of Marketing Communications, 20*(1/2), 103–116. https://doi.org/10.1080/13527266.2013.797773.

Howard, C. M. (1989). Integrating public relations into the marketing mix. *Vital Speeches of the Day, 56*(3), 93–96.

Johnson, K., & Lichter, D. (2016). Diverging demography: Hispanic and non-hispanic contributions to U.S. population redistribution and diversity. *Population Research and Policy Review, 35*(5), 705–725. https://doi.org/10.1007/s11113-016-9403-3.

Kaufman, M. (2020). JLo, Shakira shake Hard Rock stadium with high-energy, Latin Super Bowl halftime show. *Miami Herald*. https://www.miamiherald.com/sports/nfl/super-bowl/article239888908.html. Accessed 3 November 2020.

Korzenny, F., & Korzenny, B. A. (2012). *Hispanic marketing: Connecting with the new Latino Consumers* (2nd ed.). Routledge.

Krogstad, J. M. (2020). *Hispanics have accounted for more than half a total U.S. population growth since 2010*. Pew Research Center. https://www.pewresearch.org/fact-tank/2020/07/10/hispanics-have-accounted-for-more-than-half-of-total-u-s-population-growth-since-2010/. Accessed 31 October 2020.

Kumar, V., Choi, J. B., & Greene, M. (2017). Synergistic effects of social media and traditional marketing on brand sales: Capturing the time-varying effects. *Journal of the Academy of Marketing Science, 45*(2), 268–288. https://doi.org/10.1007/s11747-016-0484-7.

Li, C., & Tsai, W. S. (2015). Social media usage and acculturation: A test with Hispanics in the U.S. *Computers in Human Behavior, 45*, 204–212. https://doi.org/10.1016/j.chb.2014.12.018.

Llopis, G. (2012). Earn the trust of Hispanic consumers and your brand will dominate. *Forbes*. https://www.forbes.com/sites/glennllopis/2012/04/02/earn-the-trust-of-hispanic-consumers-and-your-brand-will-dominate/?sh=6a7916ca42ad. Accessed 2 November 2020.

Lopez, M. H., Krogstad, J. M., & Passel, J. S. (2020). *Who is Hispanic?* Pew Research Center. https://www.pewresearch.org/fact-tank/2020/09/15/who-is-hispanic/. Accessed 15 October 2020.

Lyft. (2020). *Undercover Lyft*. [Video file]. https://www.youtube.com/playlist?list=PL-04sKrMar6Nnjw-94V1zSjpgEDahng1X&app=desktop. Accessed 2 October 2020.

Nakra, P. (1991). The changing role of public relations in marketing communications. *Public Relations Quarterly, 36*(1), 42–45.

Nath, P., & Bell, M. (2016). A study of the structural integration of the marketing and PR functions in the C-suite. *Journal of Marketing Communications, 22*(6), 626–652. https://doi.org/10.1080/13527266.2014.933443.

Naumovska, L., & Blazeska, D. (2016). Public relation based model of integrated marketing communications. *UTMS Journal of Economics, 7*(2), 175–186.

Maheshwari, S., & Koblin, J. (2018). Why traditional TV is in trouble. *The New York Times*. https://nyti.ms/2Gc7kBC. Accessed 30 October 2020.

Miller, D. A., & Rose, P. B. (1994). Integrated communications: A look at reality instead of theory. *Public Relations Quarterly, 39*(1), 13–16.

Olotewo, J. (2016). Social media marketing in emerging markets. *International Journal of Marketing Research, 2*(2), 10–19. https://doi.org/10.5455/IJOMR.2016254411.

Park, H., & Ki, E. J. (2017). *Current trends in advertising, public relations, integrated marketing communication and strategic communication education*. Public Relations Journal Special Issue: Public Relations Practices in Asia. https://prjournal.instituteforpr.org/wp-content/uploads. Accessed 14 October 2020.

Paul, J. (2019). Marketing in emerging markets: A review, theoretical synthesis and extension. *International Journal of Emerging Markets, 15*(3), 446–468. https://doi.org/10.1108/IJOEM-04-2017-0130.

Picard, R. G. (2011). Effects of recessions on advertising expenditures: An exploratory study of economic downturns in nine developed nations. *The Journal of Media Economics, 14*(1), 1–14.

Place, K., Smith, B., & Lee, H. (2016). Integrated influence? Exploring public relations power in Integrated Marketing Communication. *Public Relations Journal, 10*(1), 1–35.

Public Relations Society of America. (n.d.). *About public relations*. https://www.prsa.org/about/all-about-pr. Accessed 2 November 2020.

PWC Consumer Intelligence Series. (2016). *Always connected—US-based Hispanic consumers dominate mobile, entertainment, and beyond*. https://www.pwc.com/us/en/services/consulting/library/consumer-intelligence-series/hispanics.html. Accessed 2 November 2020.

Reid, A. (2020). Best practices for marketing during and after COVID-19. *Entrepreneur*. https://www.entrepreneur.com/article/349535. Accessed 2 December 2020.

Ridley, A. (2019). Minority groups in U.S. have combined buying power of $3.9 trillion. *WUGA.org*. https://www.wuga.org/post/minority-groups-us-have-combined-buying-power-39-trillion#stream/0. Accessed 5 August 2020.

Robinson, D. (2006). Public relations comes of age. *Business Horizons, 49*, 247–256. https://doi.org/10.1016/j.bushor.2005.09.005.

Schermer, J. (2017). *Toyota's juntos somos imparables salutes Latino achievement at Hispanicize 2017*. [video file]. http://jeffschermer.com/toyota-juntos-somos-imparables Accessed 31 October 2020.

Schultz, D. E., & Malthouse, E. C. (2017). Interactivity, marketing communication, and emerging markets: A way forward. *Journal of Current Issues & Research in Advertising, 38*(1), 17–30. https://doi.org/10.1080/10641734.2016.1233152.

Schultz, D., Chu, G., & Zhao, B. (2016). IMC in an emerging economy: The Chinese perspective. *International Journal of Advertising, 35*(2), 200–215. https://doi.org/10.1080/02650487.2015.1014775.

Smith, B. G. (2010). Beyond promotion: Conceptualizing public relations in Integrated Marketing Communications. *International Journal of Integrated Marketing Communication, 2*(1), 47–57.

Smith, B. G., & Place, K. R. (2013). Integrating power? Evaluating public relations influence in an integrated communication structure. *Journal of Public Relations Research, 25*, 168–187. https://doi.org/10.1080/1062726X.2013.758585.

Sutherland, K. E. (2016). Using propinquital loops to blend social media and offline spaces: A case study of the ALS Ice-Bucket challenge. *Media International Australia Incorporating Culture and Policy, 160*(1), 78–88. https://doi.org/10.1177/1329878X16651138.

Toyota kicks off "Juntos Somos Imparables" series in Texas to salute Latino achievement at NALEO 34th annual conference. (2017). *Latinx Newswire*. https://www.latinxnewswire.com/toyota-kicks-off-juntos-somos-imparables-series-texas-salute-latino-achievement-naleo-34th-annual-conference/. Accessed 31 October 2020.

Toyota Newsroom. (2015). *Toyota celebrates milestone as no. 1 automotive brand in Hispanic market for 10 years*. https://pressroom.toyota.com/toyota-celebrates-10-year-milestone-hispanic-market/. Accessed 2 November 2020.

Vann, L. (2020). 2020 will be the year of the Hispanic. *Hispanic Online Marketing*. https://www.hispaniconlinemarketing.com/2020/01/2020-will-be-the-year-of-the-hispanic/. Accessed 29 October 2020.

Vespa, J., Medina, L., & Armstrong, D. M. (2020). *Demographic turning points for the United Stated: Population projections for 2020 to 2060*. U.S. Census Bureau. https://www.census.gov/content/dam/Census/library/publications/2020/demo/p25-1144.pdf. Accessed 27 June 2020.

Weeks, M. (2019). Minority markets see economic growth. *UGA Today*. https://news.uga.edu/multicultural-economy/. Accessed 30 October 2020.

Wright, D., & Hinson, M. (2009). An updated look at the impact of social media on public relations practice. *Public Relations Journal, 3*(2), 1–27.

Zuniga, M. A., & Torres, I. M. (2015). Demographics and ethnic minority lifestyles. In A. Jamal, L. Penaloza, & M. Laroche (Eds.), *The Routledge companion to ethnic marketing* (pp. 185–210). Routledge, Taylor & Francis Group.

4

Marketing Communication Planning for SMEs in Emerging Markets

Bright Senanu and Thomas Anning-Dorson

4.1 Introduction

Integrated marketing communication (IMC) has attracted practitioner and research attention since its conceptualization between the late 1980s and early 1990s. Since then, countless attempts have been made at conceptualizing studies around its different themes and issues. Consequently, three key themes have dominated IMC scholarship since 2000. These themes include: (1) IMC and internal marketing issues and corporate communications; (2) IMC and branding, brand equity, identity and outcomes; (3) IMC and media planning, media measurement, and integration/synergy of multiple media (Kliatchko & Schultz, 2014). The

---

B. Senanu (✉)
Ghana Institute of Journalism, Accra, Ghana

T. Anning-Dorson
School of Business Sciences, University of the Witwatersrand, Johannesburg, South Africa

current chapter presents discussions on the third theme with a particular focus on SMEs in emerging economies context.

In the cluttered, fragmented, deregulated, global, dynamic, and competitive marketplace, a conscious, and comprehensive methodology towards the development and implementation of marketing communications is considered crucial (Cacciolatti & Fearne, 2013). IMC is considered as integral to strategy and operational successes in the increasingly complicated business and communications environment (Keller, 2016). Characteristically, an effective IMC planning in today's business environment is one that comprises of a relatively large number of the many growing communication tools that are interconnected yet with delineated strategic communication roles to assist the consumer in the purchase journey. The proliferation of communication channels and tools available to both businesses and its audience does not simplify the choice of communication mix to businesses but complicates the communication function.

Amidst these complexities, it remains puzzling what processes influence the marketing managers' considerations toward selecting tools or channel options and content for an effective communication. Indeed, one fundamental yet a significant solution to the complexity is the role of research, marketing intelligence and a dedicated attempt toward identifying likely antecedents to channel choice (Kliatchko & Schultz, 2014) especially among small and medium-sized enterprises (SMEs) in emerging economies who are resource-constraint. Hence, the current chapter discusses the role and use of research by SMEs in planning their communication strategy and activities. It sheds light on the applicability of research and intelligence to planning marketing communication programs and proposes a comprehensive model to guide communication activities of SMEs in emerging economies. The chapter begins with an evaluation of the processes and methods for the selection of appropriate marketing communication strategies. It continues with discussions on the role and application of research and intelligence in the design of appropriate marketing communication programs and offers useful recommendations for SMEs in emerging economies.

4.2 SMEs and IMC Planning and Deployment in Emerging Economies

There is no uniformity in marketing considerations and practice on what works best for all. The approach differs depending on the size of the firm and customer markets and contexts (Reijonen, 2010). Hence, large and small firms cannot be considered as a homogenous group for which the applicability of marketing theory and principles should run the same. Marketing communication that is an element of the marketing theory is no exception. Its practice differs according to these delineated dissimilarities. Research in IMC, noticeably, is in a crescendo (Porcu et al., 2019; Muñoz-Leiva et al., 2015; Tafesse & Kitchen, 2017). In fact, some researchers trace back the IMC concept to the 1980s (Kliatchko & Schultz, 2014); since then, a number of studies have been conceptualized and conducted on different issues. IMC in the B2B contexts (Garber & Dotson, 2002; Garber et al., 2020), IMC in tourism marketing (Palazzo et al., 2020) and IMC in hospitality marketing (Wang et al., 2009) are few examples. These studies have provided varied insights and directions that business managers could consult in making decisions relative to general business communications. Despite these burgeoning studies with solutions and cues for business managers, gaps still exist in research and practice. For instance, the absence of a simplified yet comprehensive IMC framework that serves as a guide and supports the entire process of converting the intangibles and tangibles of firms into outcomes reduces the benefits of IMC as a capability to firms (Luxton et al., 2015). Specifically, the factors that inform and influence firms' considerations and decisions relative to IMC channel options and the prominent role of research and intelligence remain unattended to at all fronts with much deficiency in emerging economy contexts. Thus, dedicated insights from emerging economy contexts that outlines practical steps toward the implementation of IMC plans and particularly the selection and integration of channel options among SMEs are required.

SMEs by their characteristic agenda for rapid growth play significant roles in the development of economies through localized and national contributions. Their contributions include sustained job creation (Chen & Hambrick, 1995), provision of goods and services, as well as tax obligations among others (Ahmed, 2003; Kuratko, 2008). SMEs in emerging economies thrive on being flexible and agile with the owner–manager or entrepreneur being the biggest driver of success. While this characteristic may be common among SMEs, there are significant behavioral differences in the management and decision-making style of entrepreneurs and owner–managers (Cacciolatti & Fearne, 2013). The nature of developing economies is such that they are characterized by active government involvements, inefficient markets, high uncertainty, extensive business networking among other features that contest the efficacy and practicality of marketing models and theories (Xu & Meyer, 2013). Furthermore, studies have bemoaned the unstructured nature and lack of appreciation of marketing among SMEs stemming from constrained owner–manager or entrepreneur exposure, capability and marketing skills (Levy & Powell, 2005; McCartan-Quinn & Carson, 2003). Hence, under these circumstances, the capabilities of SMEs in emerging economies in making sound and practicable marketing decisions including marketing communications are curtailed.

The IMC literature in its current shape presents hierarchical models as the predominant tools for advertising and planning of full marketing communication program (Garber & Dotson, 2002). Studies (e.g., Longenecker et al., 2012; Kliatchko, 2012; Batra & Keller, 2016) have also presented various models and processes that firms can utilize to make IMC-related decisions with the majority of these literatures emanating from developed economy contexts. The applicability of these models in emerging economy contexts with specific SME complexities and constraints becomes a challenge. There is a need for context-specific models for IMC planning, decisions and implementation in which the chapter seeks to present.

4.3 An Evaluation of IMC Planning Among SMEs in Emerging Economies

Generally, among both academics and practitioners, marketing in small and medium-sized enterprises has been fragmented (Brodie et al., 1997; Gilmore et al., 2001; Gabrielli & Balboni, 2010), which is attributable to the delineated dissimilarities indicated in the earlier section. Largely, classical marketing theories and concepts often developed for large firms are the ones adopted and applied by SMEs (Chaston & Mangles, 2002). The implication is that marketing theories and concepts developed are suitable for both large and small firms. Sticking to this assumption, the IMC theory propounds an operational and strategic approach to communication through integrated activities that large firms pursue when communicating. As a result, most research in IMC focuses on quantitative approach and case studies with the focus dedicated to large organizations. Limited empirical research on IMC practice within SMEs can be readily found in literature (Fam, 2001; Low, 2000) with evidence from developing economies particularly scanty. Overall, this is a reflection of the lack of development of marketing theory suitable for SMEs (Brodie et al., 1997; Carson & Cromie, 1990; Gilmore et al., 2001).

The characterization of SMEs in developing economy contexts has remained largely consistent. Resource and capability constraints, competition from established brands among others remain a dominant feature (Ndubisi & Agarwal, 2014). There is a lack of empirical findings on how SMEs go about planning and deploying these scarce resources and capabilities to achieve performance (financial and non-financial). Specifically, in communicating value, little evidence is available in the literature on how SMEs from emerging economies plan and select marketing communication mix. As marketing theory and IMC concepts are continuously being developed with large organizations in focus, practical value communication strategies and processes designed for small businesses remain scanty. Marketing theory and small business texts such as Longenecker et al. (2003) and Kotler and Armstrong (2010) together with empirical studies (see Gabrielli & Balboni, 2010; Garber et al., 2020; Garber & Dotson, 2002) have attempted to highlight applicable methods businesses engage in when communicating value with an underlying emphasis on large businesses.

Longenecker et al. (2003) designed a marketing communication framework for small businesses that is almost identical to those in the literature for larger firms. The authors presented a small business communication channel that follows a personal communication theory and is identical to the larger firm theory found in the literature. It outlines the source, message, channel options and the identification of the receiver(s) as the steps involved in small business communication process. The channel options are the promotional mix elements available to small businesses. They consist of a blend of nonpersonal, personal, and special forms of communication techniques used in promotional campaigns. The particular combination of the various promotional methods—advertising, personal selling, and sales promotional tool id determined by many factors (Longenecker et al., 2003). Figure 4.1 depicts the generic communication channel for small businesses inspired by a personal communication theory that uses nonpersonal and personal mediums to communicate intentions and information (message) from a sender (source) through a channel (digital and/or traditional) to a receiver (target audience/customers). For small businesses, the source is the firm, the message is the value and promises the firm seeks to deliver to its target market, and the channel options are the mediums through which the firms can get the message across. The mediums include a combination of either of these mediums thus traditional and digital media such as newspaper, radio or television advertising, personal selling and social media.

Kotler et al. (2018) also delineate elements in the marketing communication process for businesses. Almost similar to Longenecker et al. (2003), the authors identified the sender, encoding, message, media and decoding as those key elements in the communication process. In this

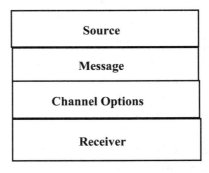

Fig. 4.1 The small business communication process (*Source* Longenecker et al. [2003])

case also, the interpretation of all the other steps in the process compared to the small business process delineated by Longenecker et al. (2003) remains constant. Encoding, however, involves putting thought into symbolic forms, thus words, symbols sound etc. into an advertisement that will convey the intended message. The decoding process is when the receiver of the message, the target audience assigns meaning to the encoded message.

Having established the elements that underpin business communications, we proceed to interrogate the crux of the section, thus an evaluation of the methods SMEs in developing economies employ in selecting their communication mixes. It is important to, however, note that the chapter endorses the delineated elements in the communication process and proceeds to argue that SMEs in emerging economies contexts are driven by entrepreneurial, owner–manager mindsets and skills with the assistance of a limited staff. As such, their communication often assumes the personal communication process and by extension the outlined business communication process by Longenecker et al. (2003). Deductively, personal communications by small firms often mean communication planned by the owner–manager/entrepreneur with little or no assistance from elsewhere. Garber and Dotson (2002) examined the selection of appropriate business-to-business integrated marketing communication mixes and drawn on the hierarchy of effects model, specifically the AIDA (awareness, interest, desire and action) model and empirically tested and confirmed its application to IMC planning in B2B settings.

Other studies (e.g., Luxton et al., 2017) provide empirical evidence that firms of larger size appear to exhibit stronger IMC capabilities and often embark on associated activities that promotes communication success. IMC capability represents the development of the firm's communication drive and the development of strategies to achieve stated brand and communication objectives. It is important to note that in SME management, the IMC capability draws on the entrepreneur/owner cultural predisposition to work cooperatively, learn and to leverage the market. It also depends on the customer-sensing capabilities of the enterprise to devise message and media strategies for their brands. Relative to marketing-related decisions, Carson and Gilmore (2000) outline *knowledge experience, judgment and communication* as core competencies required by SMEs. The rationale implies that for SME owner–managers and/or entrepreneurs to make sound marketing management decisions in the market, they must be guided by on their knowledge, experience, judgment and communication abilities. Considering the fact that the SME business environment is often dynamic, competitive and sometimes hostile, success will largely depend on how dynamic the competencies are and how agile and adaptive the business is (Quinn, 1988). As SMEs grow and develop over time through the different business stages, it requires that managerial competencies become adaptive and altered to suit each phase. Thus, managerial competencies must evolve according to the changes of the SME and the industry in which it operates. What is obvious is that SMEs are constrained on the possession of requisite IMC capabilities and customer-sensing/intelligence gathering skills that enable effective IMC planning, which is integral to a successful marketing program (Cacciolatti & Fearne, 2013). As a result, we argue that the starting point for acquiring the requisite IMC capability is the learning-oriented mindset of the SME owner–manager/entrepreneur and employees.

Learning orientation (LO) is the primary and essential attitude toward learning, i.e., the organizational and managerial attributes that facilitate the organizational learning process (Real et al., 2014). Thus, LO enables firms learn from competition and the market. Small businesses also acquire knowledge by sharing information with other companies in the same market or industry. SMEs with strong LO are able to interrogate and challenge existing practices, review the outcomes of marketing efforts such as campaigns and pursue new knowledge to enhance their performance (Unger-Aviram & Erez, 2016). To this end, SMEs must possess LO as an attribute and antecedent to developing a successful IMC strategy. Having established this prerequisite, we proceed to bring together and discuss the various methods available in the literature for the design of IMC program with focus on SMEs in emerging economies.

The crux of the IMC theory is the carefully integrated and coordinated communication channels designed to deliver clear, coherent and compelling messages about the SME brand and its products. The proliferation of online, mobile and social media channels presents enormous challenges to IMC planning and yet presents immense opportunities for

SMEs. The key challenge is to bring these continuously proliferating channels together in a synergistically organized way—the underlying principle of IMC. In selecting the appropriate IMC mixes for an SME in an emerging economy we argue that it is dependent on some antecedents. The next section discusses marketing communications, marketing objectives and the firm/product life cycle.

4.4 Marketing Communication Objectives and the Product Life Cycle

Fundamental to selecting a channel in the IMC process is the stage of the product in the Product Life Cycle (PLC) and the corresponding marketing objectives (Pelsmacker et al., 2013; Garber et al., 2020). Marketing communication objectives can be categorized into three— reach goals, process goals and effectiveness goals. The reach goals enable firms to reach target audience in an effective and efficient manner. To achieve the reach goal, a good segmentation and definition of the target audience as well as insights into their media behavior is required. Process-related goals are conditions that should be established before any communications can be effective. Primarily, all communications should dominate the immediate thought and attention of the target group, appeal to them, so that they can process and remember the encoded message. The effectiveness goal is the most important because, whereas reach goals give the exposure and the process goals provoke processing of the message, the effectiveness goals ensure the enforcement of the intended message, which is the overriding objective.

The introduction stage and its attendant SME communication objectives: An SME that is introducing a new product into the market must develop the market and its full accompaniments such that consumers will have to learn about the new product and the need it satisfies or the value it promises relative to suitable substitutes. The major communication objective at the introductory stage is to create awareness especially among early adopters and key channel members.

The growth stage and its attendant SME communication objectives: An SME key communication objective at the growth stage is to intensify awareness and communicate key brand preference. The growth stage is characterized by rising sales and profits and requires that relevant strategies be applied to other marketing functions aside communications. As awareness increases and sales and profit grow, the relevant communication objective for an SME is to defend its brand position in the market against attacks from competitors who may not be SMEs with equal resources but 'big brands' with unbridled quest for expansion and market leader strategies. Marketers will have to create brand preference by communicating and emphasizing the right product features and benefits to differentiate the brand from competitors and position it as unique.

Maturity stage and its attendant SME communication objectives: An SME brand in the maturity stage of its life cycle has to cope with strong competition in the market that is scarcely growing. Certainly, in the maturity stage, the market becomes increasingly saturated. As a result, an increase in the returns gained on one product will be reflected in a decrease in a competitor's revenues and same can be said about market share and other relative marketing performance indicators. As such SME communications strategies at this stage will focus on increasing the loyalty of consumers. Accordingly, customers should be persuaded to be less open to the advantages of competing and substitute brands. Six plausible communication objectives in the maturity stage of the PLC are outlined below;

1. Top-of-mind awareness
2. Reminding efforts and effects
3. Communicating a clear and unique value proposition that is significantly different from competitor promises and offerings
4. Saturation and less differentiation will require that key attribute such as prices especially in emerging economies where pricing is key is emphasized in communications
5. Innovation is important to garner the desired attention
6. Communication strategies should be more defensive at this stage of the PLC, thus current and acquired customers must constantly be reassured about their choice in terms of satisfaction and positive experience of the brand.

4.4.1 The Decline Stage and Its Attendant SME Communication Objective

Generally, as PLCs become shorter due to intense competition and its increasingly transient characteristic, it is assumed that firms generally shall abandon their promotional efforts and limit their associated expenditure. However, to revive the declining product and extend the life cycle of the SME's offerings, a clear communication objective can relay;

1. Important product adaptation
2. Draw attention to new uses, benefits and applications (new variants and extensions).
3. Communicate frequency of usage
4. Redefining target audience.

As indicated in Fig. 4.2 at each stage of the PLC, the target audience varies and so is the communication objective. The resultant effect is a

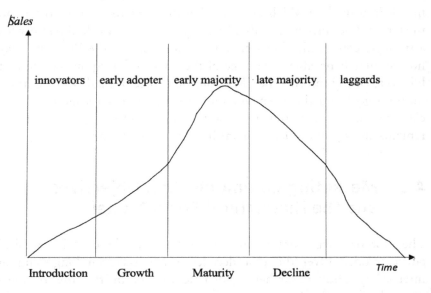

Fig. 4.2 Stages in the product life cycle (Adapted from Polli and Cook [1969])

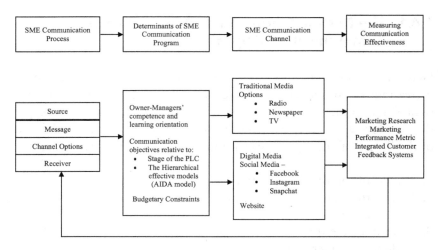

Fig. 4.3 A model for IMC (*Source* Authors' conceptualization)

variation in the IMC mixes as the product transition and travels through the PLC. Depending on the stage and its associated target audience, the firm is informed on which IMC mix has the propensity of delivering on the targeted performance goals. Different media may work differently for a strategic communication function at each stage of the PLC and may not be interchangeable. The stage of the SMEs offering on the product life cycle clearly informs the SMEs on the choice of marketing communication goal and the attendant tools to deploy. Each stage requires a clear communication strategy to derive the intended response and that remains an important determinant in selecting IMC mixes.

4.5 Marketing Communication Objectives and the Hierarchical Effect Model

The new product adoption model (NPAM) is a kind of hierarchical effects model. Over the past decades, there has been long-standing interest by both researchers and practitioners in the use of hierarchical effects models for communication planning (Garber et al., 2020; Vakratsas & Ambler, 1999). Several variants of the hierarchy of effect model have been proposed over the period, beginning with the AIDA model (Awareness, Interest, Desire, Action) (Strong, 1925). These models are built upon the assumption that consumers go through some interlinked thought and action-oriented process in arriving at a decision to purchase a product or service.

In many cases, the desired response for marketing communications is the purchase response. However, the purchase response can be derived only after a long consumer decision-making process. As a result, the SME or the marketing communicator must know which stage the target audience and buyer are in order to design messages suitable for a particular stage in the process with a probable strength to influence a transition to the next stage. The buyer readiness model is a recent variant of the hierarchical effect models. It advances that consumers typically go through awareness, knowledge, liking, preference, conviction and purchase stages. Again, the goal of marketing communication is to move target audience through the buying process. The chapter makes a case that, the consumer readiness stages can also be examined by SMEs in emerging economies in their consideration towards integrating channel options.

4.6 Budgetary Constraints

For SMEs to have loyal customer base, a strong brand and a competitive posture, its management approach should show greater creativity, focusing and leveraging on strong associations developed by the firm itself. This can be achieved through partners or strategic alliances and finding low-cost SME brand-building communication schemes to enhance the fortunes of the SME brand. Unfortunately, no mathematical formula has been advanced for calculating how much an SME can spend on IMC. Invariably, SMEs could adopt four main approaches to allocate funds for IMC purposes.

1. Allocations from percentage of sales
2. Industry benchmarking
3. Determining often through invoices how much is needed to carry out an IMC job and

4. Determining how much of revenue could be spared.

In developing economies, most SMEs lack financial resources to compete in the marketplace where local giants and multinationals corporations participate. Saddled with these constraints, cost-effective measures remain a key determinant in selecting IMC mixes. Both online and traditional IMC tools are options entrepreneurs or owner/managers of SMEs consider constituting integrated channel options. Historical antecedents suggest that the traditional options are cash-oriented and demand substantial budget in getting the message across. However, a variety of low-cost solutions and options are increasingly becoming available, which incidentally are predominant usage options for target audiences' media consumption channels. As such, it is being adopted by SMEs in emerging economies as main communication tools (Taiminen & Karjaluoto, 2015). Compared with the high prices charged by the traditional media, online, specifically, social media platforms are low cost yet effective communication tools. Scholars have recommended social media as cost-effective and efficient option that is free for consumers to join and may not have to spend to view its contents unlike the traditional and paid media (Hanna et al., 2011; Odoom et al., 2017).

Furthermore, Chaterjee and Kar (2020) presented empirical evidence that suggests that perceived usefulness, perceived ease of use, compatibility, low cost and the potentially positive effect of social media marketing on SME performance make a strong case the choice of social media tools for marketing purposes. The implication is that social media offers an important option for SMEs as they seek to deploy and effective IMC strategy. The chapter argues that cost as single factor that inhibits the usage of traditional mediums by SMEs is mitigated by the adoption of social media options. Low setup expenditure, low participatory barriers and low IT skill requirements inter alia motivate SMEs to adopt and use social media. More importantly, social media gives scope to the SMEs to communicate with their target audience or consumers at lower costs while affording them the rare opportunity of designing specific messages for their target audience (Kaplan & Haenlein, 2010; Zhang et al., 2019). Furthermore, while social commerce in developed countries is dominated by big and established brands, social commerce in emerging economies is dominant among individuals, and SMEs or players in the marketing channel like resellers. Main social media platforms predominantly used by people in emerging economies are—Facebook, Instagram and recently Snapchat (Sembada & Koay, 2019; Yuniar & Lin, 2016). As a result, the solution to the longstanding issue of budgetary constraint for SMEs in developing economies in marketing communication is the advent of social media. SMEs, thus, find social media financially expedient and effective in communicating their value propositions and have since dominated these platforms with their stores (pages), marketing their goods and services.

4.7 Marketing Research and Marketing Communication Mix Selection

Generally, research in any form provides insights, knowledge and serves as a guide in practical decision-making. Findings from research enable firms to make decisions based on scientific evidence. What is unclear, however, is the application of these findings and insights to SME decision-making. The chapter refers to academic empirical and industrial studies as the two main knowledge domains. A number of contributions have been made in the journals that are dedicated to SME and entrepreneurial studies. Despite these contributions, it is important to reiterate that gaps relative to what considerations SMEs in emerging economies make in integrating channel options scantly exist. However, as indicated earlier, possessing a learning-oriented attribute as an organization (SME) facilitates the application of these limited existing knowledge. As long as LO is evident and strongly so among SME owner/managers, they become inherently amenable to inquisitorial learning to acquire the requisite knowledge to make the right decision.

Even though the literature on IMC is rich, the focus on IMC practices and considerations particularly among SMEs in emerging economies have not received considerable attention leaving gaping gaps that militates against the performance of SMEs in these contexts. Table 4.1 shows a list of studies that cover SME communications in developing economy context. It provides directions for readers and particularly

Table 4.1 Relevant literature on SME IMC channel options and media planning

Authors & Year	Title	Context	Key findings
Taiminen and Karjaluoto (2015)	How perceived behavioral control affects trust to purchase in social media stores	Emerging economy	Ease of transaction and security facilitates trust on consumer social commerce behavior
Gabrielli and Balboni (2010)	SME practice toward integrated marketing communications	SMEs in developed economies	Found some evidence of marketing communication management among SMEs. SMEs identify a need to communicate when it is simultaneously managing relationships with different kinds of customers (final consumers, key distributors, retailers, etc.) or when it is penetrating new and unlike markets

(continued)

SMEs on key insights that facilitate their marketing communications and management.

Table 4.1 provides relevant studies that to a large extent have examined IMC practice by SMEs in developing economy context. Although not sufficient, resorting to the findings of these delineated studies provide insights and guide to SMEs in planning their integrated marketing communication strategies. These studies generally advance the importance of IMC to SMEs and provide some empirical insights into the barriers and prospects thereof. Gabrielli and Balboni (2010) provided

Table 4.1 (continued)

Authors & Year	Title	Context	Key findings
Camilleri (2019)	The SMEs' technology acceptance of digital media for stakeholder engagement	SMEs in developed economies	Digital technologies and applications were perceived as useful by SME owner–managers. Small and micro-businesses use digital media to enhance their stakeholder engagement and communicate their entrepreneurship issues
Longenecker et al. (2003)	Small Business Management: Launching and Growing Entrepreneurial Ventures		Insights on small business communication management
Chatterjee and Kar (2020)	Why do small and medium enterprises use social media marketing and what is the impact: Empirical insights from India	SMEs in developed economies	Perceived ease of use, usefulness, compatibility, cost and social media marketing are significant antecedents to SME social media marketing and performance
Odoom et al. (2017)	Antecedents of social media usage and performance benefits in small- and medium-sized enterprises (SMEs)	SMEs in emerging economy	Interactivity, cost-effectiveness and compatibility are significant antecedents to SME social media usage and performance

(continued)

Table 4.1 (continued)

Authors & Year	Title	Context	Key findings
Luxton et al (2015)	Integrated marketing communication capability and brand performance	SMEs & large enterprises in developed economies	Drawing on the resource-based view, the study confirmed IMC as a firm capability that influences both brand communication and promotional campaign effectiveness
Schultz et al. (2016)	IMC in an emerging economy: the Chinese perspective	SMEs in an emerging economy context	IMC practice is prevailing in this context although hindered by IMC training, inadequate business structures and uneven business development, lack of a customer focus culture and media restraints and censorship

empirical insights into IMC practice by SMEs but rather from a developed context. The specific gap available, therefore, is the empirical studies into factors that SMEs in developing economies consider in making choices relative to what constitutes IMC media tools as well as the impact of new media on their performance.

We further argue that findings from these studies appear not to have been fully utilized by SMEs especially those in developing economies. Authors from emerging economy context working on key concepts such as the IMC are encouraged to share findings via personal blogs, social media accounts and any means through which SMEs can have easy access. We believe that these new media applications are where the majority of business owners and entrepreneurs consume information and so sharing via such media tools becomes most effective. Authors can also share such findings through business news media, specific radio and TV shows where SMEs consume information. Aside scholarly articles, industry reports are equally good sources of some insights that can be derived to shape business decision-making. Some of these industry reports capture trends in the market with some being surveys that shed light on trends in the market.

4.8 Marketing Research and SME IMC Channel Options

Marketing communications remain one of the most difficult but critically significant components of modern marketing (Keller, 2016). The myriads of channels, the fleeting yet constant and rapid nature of advancement in technology demand that marketing decisions relative to communications shape the conduct of businesses and markets. A key approach to making almost all marketing decisions is through marketing research. SMEs in developing economies must pay attention to research no matter how basic it is to gather consumer insights needed for marketing decisions such as IMC approaches and tools. Just as there are several success stories of the implementation marketing communication programs, there are scores of instances in which poorly planned and implemented communications programs failed woefully in the market.

A crucial factor in the equation of a successfully executed marketing communication program begins with defining and understanding the target audience. Marketing research serves as the bedrock of understanding consumer needs and characteristics. As discussed earlier, SMEs are financially constrained and may not have much to spare on extensive marketing research that gives them detailed and rich data to rely on in making such decisions, but the overriding importance of firm-level research makes it imperative that a minimal level of research is conducted. Basic understanding of who the target customers are and their media consumption patterns must be clearly understood. Cost-cutting measures in research can include deploying digital data collection tools such as 'survey monkey' and Google Docs as well as engaging start-ups with research business and management research mandate in a form of barter and parallel trade exchanges. Beyond the well-intentioned, fashioned and tight communication brief with the choice of channel inspired by data, how do the SME judge the effectiveness of the communication program? Specifically, as to whether the choices are well integrated and offer the most effective and efficient solution to their communications, challenges can be determined through marketing performance metrics (O'Sullivan & Abela, 2007) and customer feedback systems, which inherently is underpinned by research principles.

The role of research integrating the right media channels to achieve communication objectives is made clear. Additionally, highlights on the need for both passive and customer feedback to confirm the efficacy and efficiency of the tools integrated are discussed. Just as all the steps leading up to engaging customers and communicating value are important, selecting the appropriate communication mix defines how effectively and efficiently SME values communicated reach its target audience.

4.9 Marketing Intelligence, Research and IMC Decisions

Generally, the collection of marketing information is predominantly possible through marketing intelligence even though information is not easy to collect and comes with some cost (Harrigan et al., 2008). Marketing intelligence involves actively scanning the marketing environment to obtain marketing information on competitors, customers and general marketplace happenings from which useful information could be obtained and used for planning, improvement and deployment of marketing activities to enhance performance (Cacciolatti & Fearne, 2013; Kirca et al., 2005). Studies (see Cacciolatti & Fearne, 2013; McCartan-Quinn & Carson, 2003) have shown that marketing in SMEs is often not structured and not fully appreciated by firm actors among other constraints like finances. This inhibits the development and full deployment of marketing strategies. Nonetheless, the enormous benefits of marketing intelligence require that SMEs constantly engage in gathering marketing intelligence in order to be abreast with all facets of the firm's operations and market happenings. Whereas marketing research involves a more focused and concentrated study to obtain customer insights connected to specific marketing decisions and considerations, SME marketing intelligence involves gathering general market information on the marketing environment, which consists mainly of competitors, customers and relevant stakeholders. Such information requires both covert and overt methodologies. For instance, an SME gathering information on prices of its competitor may employ mystery shopping to obtain such information. Other marketing intelligence techniques include observing consumers' first-hand, interrogating or examining company's own employees, benchmarking competitors' products, online research and monitoring online interactions.

For an SME in an emerging economy, marketing intelligence techniques such as monitoring social media engagements about the product category can help decipher how customers relate to their brands alongside competing brands. Such information enables SMEs to determine the impact and effectiveness of their marketing communication so as to improve on it. Hence, the objective of marketing research and intelligence in SME IMC decision is primarily to enable them to constantly gather customer feedback, general market information as well as information on specific business and/or marketing activities. Their motive here is to improve on its offering and provide superior value to customers. Empirical studies that provide insights into SME IMC-related issues presented in Table 4.1 makes a fine reference and guide for SME IMC decisions and considerations. Continuous gathering of intelligence and marketing research is required by SMEs to ultimately enhance an effective and efficient IMC channel integration.

The model above provides some guidelines in designing IMC strategy and programs tailored for SMEs in emerging economies. It begins with the steps involved in the small business communication process then to the key determinants of IMC mix. Having designed the message considering key factors like the hierarchical effect models and the stage of the product in the product life cycle, the next step is selecting the media through which the message should be transmitted. A well-defined audience predicts the precise choice of media and same rests on the financial ability to fund the communication program. The model also indicates that the choice of media is dependent on the SME/business owner's learning orientation and competence, which predicts his or her innovative capabilities. The mix remains the two media options thus the traditional and digital media. The model exposes that integrating these media options, an SMEs can have a combination of both dominant channel options (digital and traditions), i.e., Facebook, Instagram, Snapchat, newspapers, posters, radio and television. However, in emerging economies, the traditional media options especially radio and television could be quite expensive. SMEs may look toward more targeted inexpensive media outlets such as community radio stations, sponsorships, community support programs, etc. The cost-intensive nature of traditional media orients SMEs in such contexts toward using Internet-based channels such as social media as the main channel. Social media options allow SMEs to exploit the interactive features embedded in such applications like Facebook to generate valuable customer feedback on product or services, new offerings and promotional campaigns.

Furthermore, marketing research and performance metrics could determine the efficiency and effectiveness of the channel and the message as well. Depending on the outcome, the SME might choose to vary the selected media. It is important to note that electronic feedback options have enormous prospects. Sampson (1998) suggests that collecting feedback in electronic forms provides substantial advantages to data collection and use. The overarching objective of an SME is growth, which is attainable mainly through understanding the customer and providing superior value. Hence measuring the performance of the media options through performance metrics marketing research and customer feedback systems derived from digital media options remain very efficient. Key advantages include data-driven development, which enables tabulation of evaluations and other opinions gathered from customer feedback, which can also be generated into charts and trends. It is also important to indicate that a good majority of audience in emerging economies are not subscribed to social media and other digital media as Internet and smartphones' penetration are relatively low in such contexts. As a result, integrating both traditional and digital media in these contexts is likely to be a more effective option. As indicated earlier, an option to mitigating the cost factor associated with the traditional option is barter trades and an efficient inclusion of available option in the traditional media. For instance, an agribusiness into the farming and sales of fruits and vegetables can propose the supply of fruits for the staff of a radio or television station in lieu of an ad cost on their media. Also, including jingles and live presenter mention together with social media ads through influencers (earned media) and sponsored business ads could be a suitable integrated option.

4.10 Conclusion

The model synthesized can be empirically tested through sound conceptualization of relevant aspects of the concepts and issues put forth. The attempt shall validate or otherwise, the propositions made and provide empirical insights to the marketing communication planning efforts by SMEs in emerging economies. This is the foremost model that provides a simplified go-to framework that guides SMEs in emerging economies in their communication planning. Therefore, serial empirical validation of the claims authenticates it and enhances the generalization of same. We, thus, invite further studies to empirically test aspects of the model to enrich the literature on IMC planning among SMEs in emerging economies.

The chapter is dedicated specifically to the discussion on the process and considerations SMEs in emerging economies could go through to develop an SME communication program. Generally, the chapter sheds light on the likely considerations of SMEs on integrating channel options with a model illustrated as a guide toward successful integration of channel options. Summarily, the chapter outlines owner–managers competence and learning orientation, stage of offering in the PLC, the hierarchical effect models (AIDA) and budgetary considerations as key antecedents SMEs in developing economies consider in selecting and integrating channel options. The key channel options identified in the literature as being predominantly used by SMEs in emerging economies cut across the two main media that is traditional and digital media. Out of the two media categories, social media (Instagram, Facebook, Snapchat), Websites, television, radio and newspaper are the likely media options integrated by SMEs in their marketing communications. The chapter acknowledged that the marketing reality of SMEs differs significantly from large firms as a result, digitization remains a better option in terms of cost for them. However, a combination of owner–manager competence and learning orientation helps them to adjust and learn to develop a robust organization, which is customer-centered, market-driven and competitive. In conclusion, the chapter enhances knowledge on how SMEs in emerging economies should utilize and integrate media channels for effective and efficient marketing communications.

References

Ahmed, M. U. (2003). *The Economics of small-scale industries revisited*. Micro.

Batra, R., & Keller, K. L. (2016). Integrating marketing communications: New findings, new lessons, and new ideas. *Journal of Marketing, 80*(6), 122–145.

Brodie, R. J., Coviello, N. E., Brookes, R. W., & Little, V. (1997). Towards a paradigm shift in marketing? An examination of current marketing practices. *Journal of Marketing Management, 13*(5), 383–406.

Cacciolatti, L. A., & Fearne, A. (2013). Marketing intelligence in SMEs: Implications for the industry and policy makers. *Marketing Intelligence & Planning., 31*(1), 4–26.

Camilleri, M. A. (2019). The SMEs' technology acceptance of digital media for stakeholder engagement. *Journal of Small Business and Enterprise Development, 26*(4), 504–521.

Carson, D., & Cromie, S. (1990). Marketing planning in small enterprises: A model and some empirical evidence. *Journal of Consumer Marketing, 7*(3), 5–18.

Carson, D., & Gilmore, A. (2000). SME marketing management competencies. *International Business Review, 9*(3), 363–382.

Chaston, I., & Mangles, T. (2002). E-commerce in small UK manufacturing firms: A pilot study on internal competencies. *Journal of Marketing Management, 18*(3–4), 341–360.

Chatterjee, S., & Kar, A. K. (2020). Why do small and medium enterprises use social media marketing and what is the impact: Empirical insights from India. *International Journal of Information Management, 53*, 102103.

Chen, M.-J., & Hambrick, D. C. (1995). Speed, stealth, and selective attack: How small firms differ from large firms in competitive behavior. *The Academy of Management Journal, 38*(2), 453–482.

Fam, K. S. (2001). Differing views and use of integrated marketing communications-findings from a survey of New Zealand small businesses. *Journal of Small Business and Enterprise Development, 8*(3), 205–214.

Gabrielli, V., & Balboni, B. (2010). SME practice towards integrated marketing communications. *Marketing Intelligence & Planning.*

Garber, L. L., & Dotson, M. J. (2002). A method for the selection of appropriate business-to-business integrated marketing communications mixes. *Journal of Marketing Communications, 8*(1), 1–17.

Garber, L. L., Kim, K., & Dotson, M. J. (2020). The IMC mixes that trucking managers use. *Journal of Business & Industrial Marketing, 35*(12), 2067–2077.

Gilmore, A., Carson, D., & Grant, K. (2001). SME marketing in practice. *Marketing Intelligence & Planning, 19*(1), 6–11.

Hanna, R., Rohm, A., & Crittenden, V. L. (2011). We're all connected: The power of the social media ecosystem. *Business Horizons, 54*(3), 265–273.

Harrigan, P., Ramsey, E., & Ibbotson, P. (2008). e-CRM in SMEs: An exploratory study in Northern Ireland. *Marketing Intelligence & Planning, 26*(4), 385–404.

Kaplan, A. M., & Haenlein, M. (2010). Users of the world, unite! The challenges and opportunities of social media. *Business Horizons, 53*(1), 59–68.

Keller, K. L. (2016). Unlocking the power of integrated marketing communications: How integrated is your IMC program? *Journal of Advertising, 45*(3), 286–301.

Kirca, A. H., Jayachandran, S., & Bearden, W. O. (2005). Market orientation: A meta-analytic review and assessment of its antecedents and impact on performance. *The Journal of Marketing, 69*(2), 24–41.

Kliatchko, J. D., & Schultz, D. E. (2015/2014). Twenty years of IMC. *International Journal of Advertising, 33*(2), 373–390. https://doi.org/10.2501/IJA-33-2-373-390

Kotler, P., Armstrong, D., & Opresnik, M. O. (2018). *Principles of marketing.* 17., uudistettupainos. Lego.

Kuratko, D. (2008). *Entrepreneurship: Theory, process and practice.* South Western Educational Publishing.

Levy, M., & Powell, P. (2005). *Strategies for growth in SMEs.* Elsevier Butterworth-Heinemann.

Longenecker, J. G., Moore, C. W. and Petty, J. W. (2003). *Small business management—An entrepreneurial emphasis*. Thomson South-Western, Mason, OH.

Longenecker, J. G., Petty, J. W., Leslie, P., & Francis, H. (2012). *Small business management: Launching and growing entrepreneurial ventures* (16th ed.). South Western United States.

Low, G. S. (2000). Correlates of integrated marketing communications. *Journal of Advertising Research, 40*(3), 27–39.

Luxton, S., Reid, M., & Mavondo, F. (2015). Integrated marketing communication capability and brand performance. *Journal of Advertising, 44*(1), 37–46.

Luxton, S., Reid, M., & Mavondo, F. (2017). IMC capability: Antecedents and implications for brand performance. *European Journal of Marketing, 51*(3), 421–444.

McCartan-Quinn, D., & Carson, D. (2003). Issues which impact upon marketing in the small firms. *Small Business Economics, 21*(2), 201–213.

Muñoz-Leiva, F., Porcu, L., & Barrio-García, S. D. (2015). Discovering prominent themes in integrated marketing communication research from 1991 to 2012: A co-word analytic approach. *International Journal of Advertising, 34*(4), 678–701.

Ndubisi, N. O., & Agarwal, J. (2014). Quality performance of SMEs in a developing economy: Direct and indirect effects of service innovation and entrepreneurial orientation. *Journal of Business & Industrial Marketing*.

Odoom, R., Anning-Dorson, T., & Acheampong, G. (2017). Antecedents of social media usage and performance benefits in small-and medium-sized enterprises (SMEs). *Journal of Enterprise Information Management, 30*(3), 383–399.

O'sullivan, D., & Abela, A. V. (2007). Marketing performance measurement ability and firm performance. *Journal of Marketing, 71*(2), 79–93.

Palazzo, M., Vollero, A., Siano, A., & Foroudi, P. (2020). From fragmentation to collaboration in tourism promotion: An analysis of the adoption of IMC in the Amalfi coast. *Current Issues in Tourism*, 1–23.

Pelsmacker, P. D., Geuens, M., & Bergh, J. (2013). *Marketing communications: A European perspective* (5th ed.). Pearson.

Polli, R., & Cook, V. (1969). Validity of the product life cycle. *The Journal of Business, 42*(4), 385–400.

Porcu, L., del Barrio-Garcia, S., Alcántara-Pilar, J. M., & Crespo-Almendros, E. (2019). Analyzing the influence of firm-wide integrated marketing communication on market performance in the hospitality industry. *International Journal of Hospitality Management, 80*, 13–24.

Quinn, R. (1988). *Beyond rational management: Mastering the paradoxes and competing demands of high performance*. San Francisco: Jossey-Bass.

Real, J. C., Roldán, J. L., & Leal, A. (2014). From entrepreneurial orientation and learning orientation to business performance: Analysing the mediating role of organizational learning and the moderating effects of organizational size. *British Journal of Management, 25*(2), 186–208.

Reijonen, H. (2010). Do all SMEs practise same kind of marketing? *Journal of Small Business and Enterprise Development, 17*(2), 279–293.

Sampson, S. E. (1998). Gathering customer feedback via the Internet: Instruments and prospects. *Industrial Management & Data Systems, 98*(2), 71–82.

Schultz, D., Chu, G., & Zhao, B. (2016). IMC in an emerging economy: The Chinese perspective. *International Journal of Advertising, 35*(2), 200–215.

Sembada, A. Y., & Koay, K. Y. (2019). How perceived behavioral control affects trust to purchase in social media stores. *Journal of Business Research*. https://doi.org/10.1016/j.jbusres.2019.09.028.

Strong, E. K. (1925). *Psychology of selling and advertising*. McGraw-Hill.

Tafesse, W., & Kitchen, P. J. (2017). IMC–an integrative review. *International Journal of Advertising, 36*(2), 210–226.

Taiminen, H. M., & Karjaluoto, H. (2015). The usage of digital marketing channels in SMEs. *Journal of Small Business and Enterprise Development, 22*(4), 633–651.

Unger-Aviram, E., & Erez, M. (2016). The effects of situational goal orientation and cultural learning values on team performance and adaptation to change. *European Journal of Work and Organizational Psychology, 25*(2), 239–253.

Vakratsas, D., & Ambler, T. (1999). How advertising works: What do we really know? *Journal of Marketing, 63*(1), 26–43.

Wang, Y. J., Wu, C., & Yuan, J. (2009). The role of integrated marketing communications (IMC) on heritage destination visitations. *Journal of Quality Assurance in Hospitality & Tourism, 10*(3), 218–231.

Xu, D., & Meyer, K. E. (2013). Linking theory and context: 'Strategy research in emerging economies' after Wright et al. (2005). *Journal of management studies, 50*(7), 1322–1346.

Yuniar, R. W., & Lin, L. (2016). In southeast Asia, Facebook and Instagram are where people shop. Dec 6, Retrieved from *The Wall Street Journal*.

Zhang, C., Fan, C., Yao, W., Hu, X., & Mostafavi, A. (2019). Social media for intelligent public information and warning in disasters: An interdisciplinary review. *International Journal of Information Management, 49*, 190–207.

5

Communicating Corporate Social Responsibility Initiatives: A Focus on COVID-19

Kojo Kakra Twum and Richard Kwame Nimako

5.1 Introduction

The success of firms largely depends on their responsible behaviour to society (Bravo et al., 2012; Hammann et al., 2009). The responsibility of firms towards stakeholders made up of employees, customers, society, shareholders, investors, governments, etc., enhances societal well-being and firm social and financial performance. The responsibility towards various stakeholders can be achieved by engaging in Corporate Social Responsibility (CSR). In today's socially conscious market environment, corporations across the world have placed corporate social responsibility very high on their agenda (Du et al., 2010). CSR is defined by the European Commission (2001) as "a concept whereby companies integrate social and environmental concerns in their business operations

K. K. Twum (✉) · R. K. Nimako
Department of Business Administration, Presbyterian University College, Abetifi, Ghana
e-mail: twumkojo@presbyuniversity.edu.gh

and in their interaction with their stakeholders on a voluntary basis". Therefore, CSR enables firms to respond to a multiplicity of social and environmental concerns such as pandemics.

He and Harris (2020) assert that probably the COVID-19 pandemic represents one of the most significant environmental changes in modern marketing history, which could potentially have a profound impact on CSR, consumer ethics, and basic marketing philosophy. The COVID 19 pandemic, in the view of He and Harris (2020), has led to the following:

- businesses are being put to the test to show their commitment to ethical business conduct and CSR. This is because the pandemic has led to financial strains, thus may lead to firms reducing long-term financial commitments and pushing for short-term financial gains even through fraud and misconduct.
- many firms have also been observed using CSR initiatives to provide support for society during the pandemic. One profound evidence of the assistance offered by firms is the turning of their manufacturing plants to produce ventilators, hand sanitisers, protective equipment, etc. In Ghana, for example, alcoholic companies such as Kasapreko and Adonko have produced hand sanitisers to support the fight against COVID-19.

In an editorial in the Journal of Advertising, Taylor (2020) posits that one area that needs attention during the COVID 19 pandemic is the use of effective CSR appeals. This is against the background that consumers expect firms to be involved in various appeals such as consumer safety, donations to charity, employee welfare, honouring first respondents, etc. To ensure the effectiveness of CSR during the COVID-19 pandemic, Taylor (2020) proposes that issues of concern must focus on company/message fit, trust in the advertiser, and authenticity. The effectiveness of CSR communications during the COVID-19 pandemic is, therefore, crucial. Lessons can be learned from the study of Du et al. (2010), who identified two main issues affecting the effectiveness of CSR communication are:

- the level of awareness of a company's CSR activities among its external stakeholders (e.g. consumers) or even among its internal stakeholder (e.g. employees) is typically low, hence constituting a key stumbling block in the company's quest to reap strategic benefits from its CSR activities. The phenomenon where CSR is hardly known by consumers, therefore, leading to a moderate effect of CSR on purchase decisions. However, consumers have a higher expectation for firms to involve in CSR.
- the next key challenge of CSR communication is how to minimise stakeholder scepticism. While stakeholders claim they want to know about the good deeds of the companies they buy from or invest in, they also quickly become concerned about the CSR motives when companies aggressively promote their CSR efforts.

Managing firms CSR communications in times of COVID-19 is very challenging. There is a need to base CSR decisions and actions on a sound strategy, which appreciates the adoption of a strategic CSR communication approach. A strategic CSR communication process includes designing the CSR message and deciding the CSR communication channel, and ensuring CSR communications achieve the expected outcomes by ensuring the attainment of contingency factors such as minimising CRS scepticism. To address these issues, a semi-systematic literature review, which reviews how scholars have applied different conceptualisations to understand a phenomenon (Snyder, 2019), was adopted. This chapter first explains CSR communications and CSR communication strategies. The chapter also provides some evidence of CSR communication during the COVID-19 pandemic by firms in emerging economies. The rest of the chapter focuses on how organisations can perform strategic CSR communication during the COVID-19 pandemic by explaining the development of an effective CSR message and CSR communication outcomes.

5.2 CSR Communication

CSR communication provides information about a firm's identity that are not only fundamental and enduring, and distinctive (Du et al., 2010). A firm can, therefore, distinguish itself through the information it provides to the target audience regarding its involvement in sponsorship of social causes. As a result, CSR communication is basically about communicating CSR (Golob et al., 2013). CSR communication, according to Golob et al. (2013, p. 178), the following views explain the concept of CSR communication: first it "is about using promotional techniques that are directed at informing about companies' CSR and actively supporting CSR-based brand identity and reputation" and second, it is "conceived as a means to influence stakeholders' perception of organisations in terms of the resources of information (specific contents, media, channels or rhetorical arsenals) they use to inform stakeholders about their CSR policies and activities".

There are two epistemological foundations providing the basis for CSR communications, which are the functionalistic approach and constitutive approach (see Table 5.1). The functionalistic approach leads to a view about CSR communication as a democratic communication, which may represent diverse and conflicting views of stakeholders. This form of communication does not expect to result in a consensus where stakeholders must suppress their views and expectations to arrive at an agreement. The approach used here does not aim to seek the consent of all stakeholders. The focus is on providing CSR activities to stakeholders.

Table 5.1 Two approaches to CSR communication: Functionalistic and constitutive approach

Characteristics	Functionalistic approach to CSR communication	Constitutive approach to CSR communication
Conceptualisation interaction	Messaging	Interaction
Objective	Transparency	Co-creation
Metaphor	Conduit	Connectness
Channel	Monological	Dialogical
Perspective	Sequential	Holistic

Source Golob et al. (2013)

The constitutive approach emphasises viewing CSR communication as a holistic activity that takes into account the views and concerns of other stakeholders. CSR communication must reflect all the elements that constitute the organisation.

The two epistemological approaches to CSR communication seem to form the basis for the various CSR communication strategies. The elements of the functionalistic approach are evident in the information CSR communication strategy, while the constitutive approach suits the deliberative (involving) CSR communication strategy. The discussion on CSR communication strategies by Morsing and Schultz (2006) and Etter (2014) below help to cement the assumption that CSR communication is based on these two epistemological approaches discussed earlier. Morsing and Schultz (2006) identified three CSR communication strategies that can be performed through a number of tasks.

5.2.1 Stakeholder Information Strategy

Organisations provide information about their CSR decisions and actions to stakeholders. To do this, a one-way public communication approach is adopted. This approach leads to stakeholders asking or looking for information about what organisations have done to respond to a social event. This approach may also create a situation where stakeholders such as employees, customers, shareholders, etc. may either support or oppose the CSR initiative due to the lack of collaboration. The communication strategy, therefore, will be to design appealing concept messages that will gain the acceptance of stakeholders.

5.2.2 Stakeholder Response Strategy

Organisation demonstrates to their stakeholders that their concerns are integrated into responsible behaviour. The CSR communication approach is directed towards soliciting actions by stakeholders in response to organisations decisions. These initiatives are to address the concerns that might arise from top management decisions. This approach in the COVID-19 era might be to resolve management actions that might cause a negative impact on stakeholders. Organisations must provide timely communications to reassure stakeholders during difficult times. For instance, organisations can use various communication mediums to detect the response of their stakeholders to organisations actions during the pandemic. A stakeholder response CSR strategy will be to address important issues stakeholders would like organisations to focus on.

5.2.3 Stakeholder Involvement strategy

The organisation invites and establishes a dialogue with stakeholders, who, therefore, become involved in CSR messages. This seems to be similar to the deliberative CSR approach, as explained by Seele and Lock (2015). In the COVID-19 era, organisations are collaborating with their stakeholders to find solutions to the problems posed by the pandemic. Collaborations with international and government agencies, NGOs, customers, employees can lead to CSR activities that are created from negotiations. The CSR communication strategy, therefore, is a two-way approach to bring about mutual understanding through dialogue.

5.3 Etter's Three Strategies of CSR Communication on Twitter

The study of Etter (2014) on classifying the CSR communication strategies used by firms on Twitter also identified three main strategies. Based on the classification of Morsing and Schultz (2006), careful analysis of these CSR communication strategies proposed by Etter (2014), namely, broadcasting strategy, reactive strategy, and engagement strategy, lead to the conclusion that there are three main CSR communication strategies. The broadcasting strategy, which is an informational approach, seeks to disclose to a firm's diverse stakeholders its CSR initiatives. This is a one-way communication effort, which might seek to create awareness among the general public about a firm's CSR efforts. The second strategy is the reactive approach (responding to stakeholders' interests).

Table 5.2 Three CSR communication strategies on Twitter

Twitter CSR communication	Description
Broadcasting strategy	This approach is basically a one-way communication, from the firm to target audience. The main aim is to provide information on CSR actions to target audience on Twitter
Reactive strategy	This approach entails responsive CSR communication behaviour. This CSR communication on Twitter is to respond to questions and remarks from stakeholders
Engagement strategy	This is a two-way communication. There is regular dialogue with stakeholders relating to CSR activities on Twitter. Apart from disseminating CSR information, corporate executives show interest in interacting with stakeholders

Source Adapted from Etter (2014)

This CSR communication approach emanates from CSR decisions of firm managers to address the expectations, interests, and pressure. A third strategy is a deliberative approach where firm managers enter into dialogue with stakeholders to inform how CSR actions can be implemented. This is a two-way communication approach, which implies that stakeholders like employees, shareholders, NGOs, government agencies, etc., have the opportunity to be part of CSR activities and their communications (Table 5.2).

5.4 Reporting of CSR Activities During COVID-19 Pandemic

The use of CSR communications to inform stakeholders about firm's CSR activities during the COVID-19 pandemic is evident. The following online stories (see Table 5.3) report the contribution of firms in emerging markets towards the fight against COVID-19. These reports are mainly about firm donations. Some initiatives are also about cause promotions, providing education about COVID-19. There are also

Table 5.3 COVID-19 CSR reportage in emerging economies

Nestle: https://www.nestle-cwa.com/en/media/pressreleases/allpressreleases/cocoa-chocolate-industry-donates-835000-help-farmers-fight-covid-19?	Cocoa, chocolate industry donates $835,000 to help farmers fight COVID-19
Nestle—Cote d'Ivoire https://www.nestle.com/media/news/nestle-cote-ivoire-donates-ventilators-covid-19	Nestlé Côte d'Ivoire donates ventilators to assist critical COVID-19 patients
MTN Ghana https://mtn.com.gh/personal/covid-19/	Y'ello! As part of our efforts to support our customers during the COVID-19 Pandemic, we have zero-rated a number of educational sites to help students continue to study using online resources. Please note that these websites have a daily cap of 500 MB
Newmont https://www.newmont.com/operations-and-projects/health-and-safety/default.aspx#:	On April 9th, 2020, Newmont announced the establishment of a US$20 million fund to help host communities, governments and employees combat the COVID-19 pandemic. The Newmont Global Community Support Fund (the Fund) builds upon other local contributions and efforts that the Company has implemented in March
Vodafone: https://www.vodafone.com/covid19/news/vodafone-ghana-foundation-helps-frontline-workers-against-covid-19	Vodafone Ghana Foundation helps support frontline workers in the fight against COVID-19
MTN https://www.mtn.com/blog/covid-19/	MTN Irancell sends awareness messages on COVID-19 via SMS
ABSA https://www.facebook.com/AbsaUganda/videos/covid-19-education-yaya-toure/661460744404193/	ABSA Bank Uganda using Yaya Toure to provide public education on COVID-19
30 Different companies https://www.businessinsider.com/companies-donating-proceeds-coronavirus-relief-2020-3?IR=T	Companies donating percentage of their proceeds to COVID-19
Zhejiang https://www.ilo.org/empent/whatsnew/WCMS_740657/lang--en/index.htm	Zhejiang Communication Construction Ltd in China is using employees to disinfect work environment against COVID-19

(continued)

Table 5.3 (continued)

ABSA https://www.facebook.com/AbsaGhana/videos/to-support-you-and-help-reduce-the-economic-impact-of-covid-19-we-are-offering-t/162410311599070/	ABSA Bank Ghana provides banking support to customers, e.g. 2% reduction in lending rate on qualified personal and SME loans

instances where organisations' employees volunteer to assist in fighting the pandemic.

5.5 Managing CSR Communications

There are a number of important activities that need to be performed to ensure CSR communication achieves its intended purpose. These activities are crucial in ensuring the attainment of effective CSR communication. Based on the study of Du et al. (2010), the following activities must be performed:

5.6 Designing CSR Communication Message Decisions

5.6.1 Message Content

The CSR message is involved with the actual social initiative a firm has been involved in or involving in. From the marketing communication process, the message represents the actual information and impressions that the sender (firm) wishes to communicate (Pickton & Broderick, 2005). This aspect of the communication process entails the ways in which the message is created, the various elements that make up the message, the interpretation of the message by recipients, and the possible issues that could lead to misinterpretation of the message (Fig. 5.1).

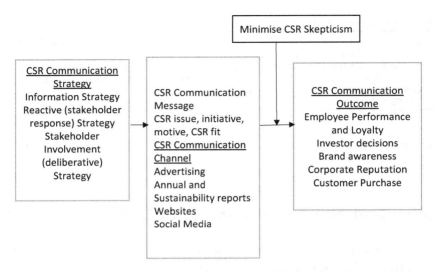

Fig. 5.1 Strategic CSR communication framework (*Source* Adapted from Du et al. [2010])

The communication of CSR initiatives must is intentional to ensure that the right response is elicited. Firms that seek to communicate their CSR activities must take note of the following:

Firms must reduce the concepts relating to CSR activity during the pandemic to a set of symbols that can be sent to the target audience. Symbols are artificial signs that are created for the purpose of providing meaning (e,g words). The words used in communicating CSR activities must be understood and meaningful to everybody. It is important to consider the background of the target audience in communicating CSR initiatives. Various target audiences have different backgrounds and may understand CSR messages differently. For instance, on the website of the Ministry of Health, Ghana, the communication of the receipt of COVID-19 relief items from the Jack Ma Foundation touched on issues such as the commitment of the Chinese government to help countries fight the virus, and the measures put in place to ensure the medical equipment were of superior standard (see https://www.moh.gov.gh/jack-ma-foundation-donates-again/) (http://gh.china-embassy.org/eng/sgxw/

t1772386.htm). This CSR communication took the opportunity to address the perception of substandard medical equipment that has been supplied to other countries to fight COVID-19. Also, the communication of this CSR initiative was supported by a picture of the Chinese and the Ghanaian delegations at a ceremony at the airport. This makes the message very believable and also aids in easy understanding by the target audience.

Pickton and Broderick (2005), citing McGuire's information processing model (1976), explain that the process an individual goes through to convert communication messages into useful knowledge. Table 5.4 presents the stages of the information process from the exposure stage to knowledge retention. The understanding of how CSR communications influence target audience knowledge based on the McGuire information processing model is presented below.

Table 5.4 Stages of information processing

Stage	Activity	Implications for CSR communication
Exposure	Target audience must have proximity to the message	CSR communications must be exposed to target audience
Attention	The target audience must be aware of the message and make effort to process it	CSR communications must have the ability to attract target audience
Comprehension	The target audience must be able to understand the message	CSR communications must be very clear and unambiguous
Acceptance	The target audience must absorb the message into their existing belief and knowledge leading to persuasion	CSR communication must will lead to target audience accepting the message leading to new set of belief and knowledge
Retention	The target audience store messages in their long term memory	CSR communication messages must be easily recalled

Source Adapted from Pickton and Broderick (2005)

The implication of the creation of content (message) in CSR communication during pandemics is that the effectiveness of marketing communications depends on the effectiveness of the message and not the number of media the communication is placed. Pickton and Broderick (2005) propose that at this stage of the communication process, much emphasis must be given to high-impact communications.

5.7 The CSR Initiative

To ensure CSR communications provide the needed results, organisations must emphasise some important issues in their CSR messages. Du et al. (2010) propose that issues relating to commitment to a cause, the level of impact of the firm's CSR initiatives on the cause, the motive for engaging in a particular cause, and the fit (the congruity between the cause and the company).

5.7.1 The CSR Commitment

In relation to the proposition by Du et al. (2010), the commitment to fighting COVID-19 can be demonstrated through a number of CSR initiatives. Kotler and Lee (2005) propose the following:

- **Corporate Philanthropy**—making direct contributions to a charity or cause, usually in the form of grants or donations. In relation to COVID-19, this social initiative appears to be the dominant one since there is an urgency to provide health equipment, PPEs, etc. Organisations in emerging economies have been reported donating to support the fight against COVID-19 (see Table 5.3). In emerging economies, corporate donations are seen as reactive support to respond to an emergency. The infrastructure challenges and inadequate logistics make this CSR initiative very impactful. A report by Hinson and Newman (2020) indicates that donations are the most common form of CSR initiatives in the fight against COVID-19.

- **Cause Promotions**—supporting social causes through paid sponsorships of promotional efforts. Cause promotion initiatives by organisations during the COVID-19 will be to sponsor awareness campaigns on preventive measures. In Table 5.3, MTN, a telecommunication company, uses their SMS infrastructure to create awareness on COVID-19 by sending messages to customers. It is expected that organisations that have easy communication access to the general public, such as television and radio stations, telecommunication companies, and technology companies, may take advantage of their resources to educate people about COVID-19. In the era of new media, organisations can use their social media platforms, which have many followers, to educate them on COVID-19. An example is ABSA Bank Uganda using their Facebook account to educate people on COVID-19 (see Table 5.3).
- **Corporate social marketing**—supporting behaviour change campaigns. This form of CSR involves initiatives that cause a change in behaviour. The fight against COVID-19 involves people performing new behaviours such as washing hands, using sanitisers, wearing a mask, etc. Organisations can promote certain behaviours among the general public and their employees. Many firms are communicating about "working from home".
- **Cause-related marketing**—donating a percentage of revenues to a specific cause based on product sales during an announced period of time. Organisations have reported the allocation of a certain percentage of their proceeds to support COVID-19. This, however, is tied to the sales revenue the organisation makes during the announcement of the initiative. This initiative has, however, not been implemented by firms. A reason could be that the pandemic is a form of an emergency that firms have to respond to. Also, basing COVID-19 support on sales of firm products may also raise issues of ethical business practices since firms may not want to be seen as taking advantage of the situation.
- **Community volunteering**—providing volunteer services in the community. Organisations during the COVID-19 pandemic have organised their employees to involve themselves in initiatives. An example is Zhejiang Communication Construction Ltd, which

trained their employees to disinfect their work environment against COVID-19. Also, Renault, an automobile company, provided support for its employees to manufacture health equipment (https://www.thisistherealspain.com/en/latest-news/corporate-volunteering-corporate-talent-takes-on-covid-19/).

To ensure a strategic benefit from CSR communications, the extent of commitment to the CSR cause will play a crucial role. The selection of initiatives to be involved must be innovative. Just as in commercial marketing, where marketing communication effectiveness may be determined by the product quality, CSR communication efforts may yield the desired results based on the kind of CSR commitments. It has been argued that each CSR initiatives have some corresponding strategic benefits. For instance, the involvement in community volunteering affects employee job satisfaction, the attraction of qualified workforce and improves the corporate image. On the other hand, corporate philanthropy increases brand awareness and reputation among customers.

5.7.2 CSR Motives

The motive of organisations' involvement in specific CSR initiatives is a challenge due to stakeholder scepticism (Du et al., 2010). Therefore, the question of whether firms in their CSR communications must emphasise altruistic motives, intrinsic motives or clearly indicate their business motive (Du et al., 2010).

Skarmeas and Leonidou (2013) propose the following relationship between CSR motives and CSR scepticism:

- Egoistic-driven motive—consumers are likely to question and doubt CSR efforts when they attribute the retailer's social involvement to blatant self-centred reasons. Thus, egoistic-driven motives relate positively to CSR scepticism.
- Value-driven motive—this forms CSR engagements based on pure ethical, moral, and societal standards leading to customers believing the firm is acting on genuine concern to help society. Value-driven motives relate negatively to CSR scepticism.

- Strategy-driven motive—this epitomises the business case for CSR. Firms engage in CSR in order to attain goals underlined by their survival and promoting the initiatives to create a win–win situation. Customers, therefore, may understand it as legitimate since businesses need to achieve economic objectives, but on the other hand, customers may also perceive firm actions as driven by profit. Strategy-driven motives relate positively to CSR scepticism.
- Stakeholder-driven motive—these are formed from pressure from stakeholders such as employees, stockholder, and society for firms to respond to the demands. This creates a negative image of firms since stakeholders view their involvement in CSR as a means to avoid punishment. Stakeholder-driven motives relate positively to CSR scepticism.

In another study by Rim and Kim (2016), the reasons that account for consumer scepticism of CSR are disbelief of CSR messages and CSR activities, distrust of management and CSR outcomes, CSR motivation, and cynicism towards business. To enable businesses and researchers to measure the level of CSR scepticism, some measurement scales have been proposed by Rim and Kim (2016).

Disbelief of CSR messages and CSR activities—Sceptics of firm's CSR messages doubt whether the messages and activities are truthful and believable. The disbelief may be caused by the lack of alignment between firm's CSR activities and core business. Also, conspicuous CSR advertising that seems to hype the CSR initiative.

Distrust of management and CSR outcomes—the perception of distrust of a firm manager's ability to introduce successful social changes will lead to scepticism towards the firm's CSR. This perception emanates from the notion that the "business of business is business" and, therefore, firms lack the ability to bring about improvements in society. Also, CSR scepticism arises from the inability of firms to show tangible outcomes of some CSR activities.

CSR motivation—The motive for engaging in CSR determines whether stakeholders will believe the initiative or will be sceptical. Intrinsic (altruistic) motivation, which is related to firm's sincere objective to engage in a social cause, while extrinsic (egoistic) motivation relates to a firm's motive to support a social cause because it seeks to improve reputation and performance. The scepticism is formed when there is a discrepancy between the CSR activity and the profit-maximising objective of the business (extrinsic motivation).

Cynicism towards Business—Consumer cynicism, which is a personal trait developed through continuous distrust for business in a market system, can create scepticism towards CSR. Cynics have a higher likelihood to doubt a firm's CSR activities, thus leading to scepticism.

5.7.3 Reducing CSR Scepticism

From a strategic CSR communication point of view, firms must emphasises the specific motive that informs their involvement in a particular CSR in order to reduce the impact of scepticism. The indication of CSR motives relating to egoistic and value-driven motives will lead to a more positive impact of a firm's legitimacy. On the other hand, a CSR communication that stresses a strategic and a stakeholder-driven CSR motive is likely to reduce the level of scepticism. In the view of Du et al. (2010), the motive underlying a particular CSR initiative must be made clear in communications. CSR communication must emphasise both the social and strategic benefits of CSR to stakeholders. This will go a long way to enhance the credibility of the business. Lee (2020) cites an experimental stimuli study by Forehand and Grier (2003) experimental stimuli, "It is hoped that this program will help alleviate a major problem in our society and simultaneously expand the market for the company's software products" (p. 352).

Apologies and responsibility acceptance attract less negative reactions than denials, excuses, and justifications (Lee, 2020). Taking responsibility for firm actions that impact negatively on the environment and society through CSR communication is a first step to indicate the willingness to help. The acceptance of criticisms and working towards using CSR actions to resolve them go a long way to gain acceptance and legitimacy. Firms must practice responsible behaviour they communicate with their target audience.

Also, the use of some specific sources of communication has been found to reduce scepticism. Lee (2020) recommends the use of public sources. Public sources of CSR information such as confessions, journalistic endeavours by neutral individuals, etc., can be a way to reduce scepticisms. The CSR activities during the COVID-19 pandemic that are communicated by independent individuals, other than firm managers will be believable as the message is coming from an independent source. Organisations can involve public media organisations to verify CSR claims relating to what the firm has been able to do. Public media and confessions can be a major source to verify the CSR claim, hence reducing CSR scepticism.

A study by Newman and Trump (2019) proposes that the CSR scepticism can be reduced when CSR messages are promoted by the gender and gender-related characteristics of the company's CSR spokesperson. Firms must consider the role of gender, as gender-related characteristics influence the interpretation of CSR information. For instance, females may view CSR claims promoted by a male spokesperson as assertive (an agentic characteristic associated with men), leading to a negative reaction. On the other hand, males will react favourably to this same message. The implication for firms is that CSR target audience that is female might be targeted with CSR messages presented by a female spokesperson.

5.7.4 The CSR Fit

To ensure CSR communication has a strategic impact, Du et al. (2010) propose that there must be a CSR fit, which is the perceived congruence between an organisation and its CSR activities (Du et al., 2010). de Jong and van der Meer (2017) explain that a high CSR fit exists when there is a clear relationship between an organisations core business and its CSR activities.

During the COVID-19 pandemic, due to the urgent need for firms to respond, most of the CSR initiatives are embarked on are in line with the firm's core businesses. In the telecommunication sector in Ghana, firms providing mobile money services (banks, telecommunication firms) with the Bank of Ghana decided not to charge customers for mobile money transactions of a certain amount (graphic.com.gh). Also, telecommunication firms like MTN and Vodafone provided free internet data for university students. Vodafone Ghana is providing free E—learning access to students in many educational institutions during the COVID-19 pandemic (https://vodafone.com.gh/explore-vodafone/free-e-learning/).

The communication of these CSR initiatives, which are aligned to firm's businesses, will have a better communication impact since the target audience will perceive the initiatives as believable. The target audience can readily associate the CSR initiative with a firm's core business, therefore, indicating reducing scepticism. In communication CSR, a clearer natural fit between a firm's business and CSR activity will enable stakeholders to react positively to an organisation's CSR activities.

5.8 Communication Channel Decision

The second big question to address in CSR strategic communication is the kind of communication channel to use. CSR activities can be communicated using web-based communications, advertising, annual reports, and a combination of the various media options (Golob et al., 2013). In the view of El-Bassiouny et al. (2018), the common contemporary CSR communication tools in emerging economies include corporate annual reports, websites, and social media. Other online sources from news agencies also provide CSR information (Twum et al., 2020). However, advertising is still an important form of CSR communication. The channels for communicating CSR are discussed below.

5.8.1 CSR Advertising

Advertising remains a way of creating conscious associations in the minds of consumers regarding a firm's responsible behaviours. Despite the preference of non-traditional media in CSR reporting, Freire and Loussaief (2018) still recommend the use of advertising (television broadcast, newspaper articles) since it remains an important channel in the consumers' mind. Information and results relating to CSR are mainly made known through annual and environmental reports. Corporate annual reports and environmental reports serve stakeholders such as employees, shareholders, NGOs, etc. and are not focused on providing CSR information to consumers. However, firms need to communicate their CSR to consumers.

CSR advertising is the use of advertising channels such as television, print media (newspaper, magazine) and outdoor advertising (billboards). A good example of CSR advertising on television broadcasts is short documentaries on their social initiatives to protect the environment and promote community welfare. In developing economies, companies in extractive industries use television documentaries to showcase their operations. An example is the use of print advertising to acknowledge and thank employees for their efforts to make the bank succeed (Pomering & Dolnicar, 2009).

5.8.2 Corporate Annual and Sustainability Reports

Organisations' annual reports are communication tools used to voluntarily disclose non-financial information for various stakeholders. Firm's annual reports have become a source for identifying CSR activities since non-financial disclosures are now becoming a major part of annual reports. In annual reports, CSR disclosures are usually reported in the sustainability section, which involves issues such as health, safety, and the environment. A study by Abugre and Nyuur (2015) found that annual reports are an important channel for reporting CSR among Ghanaian firms. COVID-19 activities will form a major part of firm's sustainability report.

5.8.3 Corporate Websites

Corporate websites are the common channel to disclose CSR information. Firms can do this by either having a separate website for their CSR activities or communicate CSR on their existing corporate websites. The first option is very simple to do when organisations already have separate entities registered to manage their CSR. An example is the MTN Ghana Foundation, a registered organisation responsible for the CSR initiatives of MTN in Ghana. A study by Nyarku and Hinson (2017) found that from 2010 to 2014, commercial banks in Ghana reported CSR activities on their websites, which leads to a conclusion that CSR reporting is a common practice by firms in Ghana. Similarly, in the telecommunication sector, Abukari and Abdul-Hamid (2018) found that company websites are fast becoming a medium for CSR communications. COVID-19 CSR activities have been widely reported on company websites. Some evidence of these reports on company websites is presented in Table 5.3.

5.8.4 Social Media

Communication CSR using social media is the key to attaining strategy objectives. The changing communication landscape due to the emergence of new forms of media demands that CSR communications must also be done through these new channels. The advent of the internet has led to a shift from mass media communications to a more direct form of communication with stakeholders. Social media platforms including Facebook, Google+ , Instagram, Linkedin, Twitter, and YouTube are common means of CSR communications. New media communication such as Twitter, Facebook, YouTube, etc., enables the target audience to be updated on organisations CSR activities on a regular basis. Unlike mass media, where firms periodically pay to communicate CSR messages, social media communications can present an opportunity for firms to send out CSR messages on a daily basis, as and when the firm embarks on such initiatives.

5.9 Typology of CSR Communication Tools

Seele and Lock (2015) identified two main typologies of CSR communication tools. These are instrumental CSR and deliberative CSR.

Table 5.5 CSR communication tools typology

	Instrumental (corporate)	Deliberative
Published communication	*CSR website* *CSR Report* *CSR brochure*	*Social Media*
Unpublished communication	*CSR strategy paper* *Internal compliance handbook* *Code of conduct*	*Stakeholder roundtable* *Stakeholder dialogue* *Internal—employees* *External: NGOs, advocacy groups, special interest groups*

Source Seele and Lock (2015)

5.9.1 Instrumental CSR

CSR-related obligations must create opportunities for the attainment of strategic objectives such as attracting new customers and markets, increase sales, positive brand image. Instrumental CSR is meant to achieve strategic objectives and is usually published on company websites, CSR report, and brochures, advertisements, etc. On the other hand, unpublished communications that are strategy-based (see Table 5.5) may include CSR strategy paper, internal compliance handbook, code of conduct. The COVID-19 CSR initiatives will best be classified under instrumental CSR.

5.9.2 Deliberative CSR

These CSR obligations are dedicated to meet the expectations of all stakeholders. This approach is more related to political CSR, which uses participation, discourse, transparency, and accountability with interested parties. To address the needs and expectations of stakeholders, firms adopt communication options such as roundtable discussions and dialogue, NGO engagement, etc. Most of these engagements are not published.

5.10 CSR Communication Outcomes

CSR communication must translate into the attainment of firm outcomes. The CSR communication outcome determines whether firm communication efforts are effective. These outcomes are explained below.

5.10.1 Brand Awareness

CSR has the ability to affect brand awareness through CSR reporting (Mattera et al., 2012). A consensus among researchers and practitioners is that for CSR initiatives to translate into brand awareness; there is the need to embark on communicating these initiatives to stakeholders. Andreu et al. (2015) argue that CSR awareness is very important since consumers must first have knowledge of the CSR initiatives of an organisation. Subsequently, the awareness of organisations CSR will translate into an awareness of the organisations brand, which becomes the first step in building brand equity. The CSR communications during the COVID-19 pandemic will first and foremost provide publicity, making the general public and consumers to be aware of their brands.

5.10.2 Corporate Reputation

Corporate reputation is the integrated perspective of corporate identity, corporate image, and corporate reputation (Barnett et al., 2006). The reputation of an organisation is formed through the identity (the perception of employees and managers of the firm) and image (perception of external stakeholders about a firm). Gotsi and Wilson (2001) define corporate reputation as a "stakeholder's overall evaluation of a company over time. This evaluation is based on the stakeholder's direct experiences with the company, any other form of communication and symbolism that provides information about the firm's actions and/or a comparison with the actions of other leading rivals". This definition emphasising on the effect of *any form of communication* that provides information on firm's actions that make CSR communication an important factor affecting corporate reputation. Fombrum (2005) explains that firms take up CSR initiatives by following the guidelines of various standards in an attempt to strengthen their reputation.

The objective of firms to enhance their reputation informs the involvement in CSR. The perception of how ethical a firm is can be formed through CSR actions, thus leading to improved firm reputation relating to their ethical behaviour. The involvement of firms in helping their stakeholders during the COVID-19 pandemic, apart from creating awareness about the company, will also create a perception of an ethical company. The reputation of firms that have been involved in COVID-19 CSR initiatives is likely to be positive among employees, customers, and the general public.

5.10.3 Consumer Purchase

The effect of CSR on consumers' purchase behaviour has formed a central part of the debate on the business case for firms to involve in CSR actions. The question is, therefore, about whether firms investing their resources in CSR will gain benefits in terms of the likelihood of a purchase from consumers. A critical question one can also ask is that, will consumers avoid buying from firms that have been reported to engage in unethical practices?

Öberseder et al. (2011) explain that CSR may not be on top of the list of factors (i.e. price, quality, brand, country of origin, or service) that determine consumer purchase decisions but found that there are some peripheral factors that have an impact of the likelihood of considering CSR as a purchase criterion. These factors are:

- ***Consumer's Perception of the Credibility of CSR***—A general knowledge of the credibility of firm's CSR can be achieved when there is a fit between a company's CSR and its core business. In the same vein, customers will view COVID-19 CSR initiatives that are aligned to the company's core business a credible. A good example is the initiatives including additional data, free access to online earning resources, free access to health and government information, waiving overcharge

fees, etc., rolled out by telecommunication companies (ITU, 2020). Telecommunication firms that communicate these kinds of CSR initiatives are likely to generate purchase responses from consumers.
- ***The Image of the company***—The image of an organisation can be formed through CSR activities. A positive perception of the image of a firm evokes the association that the organisation is socially responsible. The notion is that consumers will have a favourable reaction to CSR when the image they have for the organisation is positive. The implication of CSR COVID-19 communication on consumer purchases can be influenced by the image consumers have about the organisation.
- **Influence of peer groups**—The social influence from friends, colleagues, and family to buy from socially responsible organisations is a way that can affect the effectiveness of CSR. Based on the CSR perception of people classified as "important others" or "referent group", consumers can be persuaded to purchase from socially responsible firms. Therefore, the effect of COVID-19 CSR communication on consumer purchase decisions can be through other individuals. Positive word-of-mouth, that is, communication emanating from other individuals apart from firm managers, could be valuable.

5.10.4 Customer Loyalty

Corporate social responsibility influences customer loyalty through the improvement of trust and satisfaction (Martínez & del Bosque, 2013). The benevolent trust in the view of Martínez and del Bosque (2013) is formed through the perception that a firm cares, concerning, and is honest. The link between CSR and the formation of benevolent trust is that customers will perceive that the firm has consumer's well-being and interest at heart based on the analysis of their socially responsible activities. Customer satisfaction with the product and actions of a firm can lead to a commitment to a firm. The firms that make their customers satisfied through their social interventions are likely to make these customers committed to the firm, leading to their continuous use of products and recommendations.

5.10.5 Employee Productivity and Loyalty

The influence of CSR on employee loyalty though having little empirical support, is possible when the CSR initiatives are of interest to the employees. CSR initiatives which are employee-centred initiatives such as paying social securities for employees, paying wages that enhances the welfare of employees, transparent internal relationship, improving the working environment, ineffective safety measures, etc., must be the focus on firms attempting to enhance employee affective commitment (Zhu et al., 2014). It is worth noting that money-related changes are not very effective in enhancing affective commitment, while personal relation initiatives seem to be more effective (Zhu et al., 2014). Du et al. (2015) also acknowledge that CSR initiatives that are demanded by employees address their developmental job needs. Similarly, Sánchez and Benito-Hernández (2015) explain that CSR initiatives that have the potential of contributing to productivity are those that address internal issues affecting employees.

The implication of this in designing CSR initiatives during the COVID-19 pandemic is that employees can be targeted with some innovative initiatives. Interventions such as changes in wages, flexible working schedules, health insurance, etc., are crucial in times of pandemic to ensure they stay committed. These CSR initiatives are usually communicated internally. Employees are likely to improve their performance with the existence of initiatives that promote their welfare and work needs.

5.10.6 Investor Decisions

One question that demands an answer is whether CSR disclosures are relevant to investors. To address this, Verbeeten et al. (2016) took a look at how the type of CSR disclosure (social and environmental) influences investors. The influence of social CSR disclosures occurs due to it has been used as an indication of the human capital of a firm, which has the potential of improving firm performance (Verbeeten et al., 2016). The implication for CSR communication is that investors are interested in specific CSR activities, and the ability to disclose to them such initiatives will affect their investment decisions positively. On the other hand, tailor-specific CSR disclosures to satisfy a particular investor group may come as an expense to another group, hence, the need to work out a trade-off (Verbeeten et al., 2016). The implication of this to COVID-19 CSR communications is that disclosures must target investor stakeholders. CSR initiatives that are communicated must be explained in terms of how they affect share price and firm performance. This demands that CSR disclosures relating to COVID-19 must also be directed at investors.

5.11 Conclusion

The CSR communication strategy adopted by firms determines how the other aspects of the CSR communication activities are conducted. For firms seeking to provide information about their CSR activities, an informational approach is appropriate. This approach is a one-way communication format that seeks to maximise the use of mass media and other new media channels to reach out to as many target audiences as to create awareness of CSR activities. A reactive CSR communication strategy demands that firms must understand through surveys and intelligence gathering, the interests, and expectations of stakeholders and must come up with CSR communications that satisfy these expectations. A deliberative CSR communication strategy is a two-way communication approach with firms and their stakeholders involved in CSR communication efforts.

Firms in communicating their CSR activities during pandemics such as COVID-19 must ensure their communication efforts, follow the strategic CSR approach that incorporates a creative CSR message. Also, the effectiveness of CSR messages is determined by the kind of CSR initiative. Organisations can decide to initiative corporate philanthropy, corporate social marketing, cause promotions, community volunteerism, and cause-related marketing. Any of these CSR initiatives have unique strategic importance. However, to ensure effective CSR communication during a pandemic, firms must ensure there is a fit between the initiative and their core business. The scepticism of stakeholders about a firm's CSR communications can affect the expected effect of CSR negatively. CSR scepticism can be minimised by communicating CSR motives, ensuring there is a fit between firm business and CSR actions, communicating exactly CSR practices that have been implemented, using public sources of information, and taking into gender-related characteristics of the target audience.

The effectiveness of CSR communications can also be enhanced through the careful use of communication channels. This study suggests that CSR communication is more effective by using organisational websites, annual and sustainability reports, and social media. However, CSR advertising still remains a common option for organisations since consumers still rely on television and print media for information. For effective CSR communications, multiple communication channels can be used to reach out to target audience with different needs. The efficacy of each communication channel can add up to how CSR actions influence consumers.

Firms in emerging economies embarking on CSR can achieve strategic objectives through positive consumer's responses, employee satisfaction, and investor acceptance. CSR communications can improve brand awareness, corporate reputation, customer purchase intentions and advocacy, employee performance, investor investment decisions, etc. This has implications for CSR communications during COVID-19. Firms that are able to follow an effective communication approach in communicating their response to the pandemic are likely to achieve expected outcomes.

References

Abugre, J. B., & Nyuur, R. B. (2015). Organizations' commitment to and communication of CSR activities: Insights from Ghana. *Social Responsibility Journal, 11*(1), 161–178.

Abukari, A. J., & Abdul-Hamid, I. K. (2018). Corporate social responsibility reporting in the telecommunications sector in Ghana. *International Journal of Corporate Social Responsibility, 3*(1), 2.

Andreu, L., Casado-Díaz, A. B., & Mattila, A. S. (2015). Effects of message appeal and service type in CSR communication strategies. *Journal of Business Research, 68*(7), 1488–1495.

Barnett, M. L., Jermier, J. M., & Lafferty, B. A. (2006). Corporate reputation: The definitional landscape. *Corporate Reputation Review, 9*(1), 26–38.

Bravo, R., Matute, J., & Pina, J. M. (2012). Corporate social responsibility as a vehicle to reveal the corporate identity: A study focused on the websites of Spanish financial entities. *Journal of Business Ethics, 107*(2), 129–146.

de Jong, M. D., & van der Meer, M. (2017). How does it fit? Exploring the congruence between organizations and their corporate social responsibility (CSR) activities. *Journal of Business Ethics, 143*(1), 71–83.

Du, S., Bhattacharya, C. B., & Sen, S. (2010). Maximizing business returns to corporate social responsibility (CSR): The role of CSR communication. *International Journal of Management Reviews, 12*(1), 8–19.

Du, S., Bhattacharya, C. B., & Sen, S. (2015). Corporate social responsibility, multi-faceted job-products, and employee outcomes. *Journal of Business Ethics, 131*(2), 319–335.

El-Bassiouny, N., Darrag, M., & Zahran, N. (2018). Corporate Social Responsibility (CSR) communication patterns in an emerging market. *Journal of Organizational Change Management, 31*(4), 795–809.

Etter, M. (2014). Broadcasting, reacting, engaging–three strategies for CSR communication in Twitter. *Journal of Communication Management, 18*(4), 322–342.

European Commission. (2001). *Directorate-General for Employment*. Promoting a European Framework for Corporate Social Responsibility: Green Paper. Office for Official Publications of the European Communities

Fombrun, C. J. (2005). A world of reputation research, analysis and thinking—building corporate reputation through CSR initiatives: Evolving standards. *Corporate Reputation Review, 8*(1), 7–12.

Forehand, M. R., & Grier, S. (2003). When is honesty the best policy? The effect of stated company intent on consumer skepticism. *Journal of Consumer Psychology, 13*(3), 349–356. https://doi.org/10.1207/S15327663 JCP1303_15.

Freire, N. A., & Loussaïef, L. (2018). When advertising highlights the binomial identity values of luxury and CSR principles: The examples of louis vuitton and hermès. *Corporate Social Responsibility and Environmental Management, 25*(4), 565–582.

Golob, U., Elving, W. J., Nielsen, A. E., Thomsen, C., Schultz, F., Podnar, K., & Elving, W. J. (2013). CSR communication: Quo vadis? *Corporate Communications: An International Journal, 18*(2), 176–192.

Gotsi, M., & Wilson, A. M. (2001). Corporate reputation: Seeking a definition. *Corporate Communications: An International Journal, 6*(1), 24–30.

Graphic.com.gh. https://www.graphic.com.gh/business/business-news/coronavirus-it-is-now-free-to-send-gh-100-and-below-via-mobile-money.html.

Hammann, E. M., Habisch, A., & Pechlaner, H. (2009). Values that create value: Socially responsible business practices in SMEs–empirical evidence from German companies. *Business Ethics: A European Review, 18*(1), 37–51.

He, H., & Harris, L. (2020). The impact of Covid-19 pandemic on corporate social responsibility and marketing philosophy. *Journal of Business Research, 116*, 176–182.

https://mtn.com.gh/personal/covid-19/.

https://vodafone.com.gh/explore-vodafone/free-e-learning/.

https://www.businessinsider.com/companies-donating-proceeds-coronavirus-relief-2020-3?IR=T.

https://www.facebook.com/AbsaGhana/videos/to-support-you-and-help-reduce-the-economic-impact-of-covid-19-we-are-offering-t/162410311599070/.

https://www.facebook.com/AbsaUganda/videos/covid-19-education-yaya-toure/661460744404193/.

https://www.ilo.org/empent/whatsnew/WCMS_740657/lang--en/index.htm.

https://www.mtn.com/blog/covid-19/.

https://www.nestle.com/media/news/nestle-cote-ivoire-donates-ventilators-covid-19.

https://www.nestle-cwa.com/en/media/pressreleases/allpressreleases/cocoa-chocolate-industry-donates-835000-help-farmers-fight-covid-19.

https://www.newmont.com/operations-and-projects/health-and-safety/default.aspx.

https://www.thisistherealspain.com/en/latest-news/corporate-volunteering-corporate-talent-takes-on-covid-19/.

https://www.vodafone.com/covid19/news/vodafone-ghana-foundation-helps-frontline-workers-against-covid-19.

ITU (2020). *First overview of key initiatives in response to Covid-19.* https://www.itu.int/en/ITU-D/RegulatoryMarket/Documents/REG4COVID/2020/Summary_Key_Covid19_Initiatives.pdf.

Kotler, P., & Lee, N. (2005). Best of breed: When it comes to gaining a market edge while supporting a social cause, "corporate social marketing" leads the pack. *Social Marketing Quarterly, 11*(3–4), 91–103.

Lee, K. (2020). Consumer skepticism about quick service restaurants' corporate social responsibility activities. *Journal of Foodservice Business Research, 23*(5), 417–441.

Martínez, P., & Del Bosque, I. R. (2013). CSR and customer loyalty: The roles of trust, customer identification with the company and satisfaction. *International Journal of Hospitality Management, 35*, 89–99.

Mattera, M., Baena, V., & Cerviño, J. (2012). Analyzing social responsibility as a driver of firm's brand awareness. *Procedia-Social and Behavioral Sciences, 58*, 1121–1130.

Morsing, M., & Schultz, M. (2006). Corporate social responsibility communication: Stakeholder information, response and involvement strategies. *Business Ethics: A European Review, 15*(4), 323–338.

Newman, K. P., & Trump, R. K. (2019). Reducing skepticism about corporate social responsibility: Roles of gender and agentic-communal orientations. *Journal of Consumer Marketing, 36*(1), 189–196.

Nyarku, K. M., & Hinson, R. E. (2017). Corporate social responsibility reporting of banks operating in Ghana. *African Journal of Business Ethics, 11*(2).

Öberseder, M., Schlegelmilch, B. B., & Gruber, V. (2011). "Why don't consumers care about CSR?": A qualitative study exploring the role of CSR in consumption decisions. *Journal of Business Ethics, 104*(4), 449–460.

Pickton, D., & Broderick, A. (2005). *Integrated marketing communications*. UK: Pearson Education.

Pomering, A., & Dolnicar, S. (2009). Assessing the prerequisite of successful CSR implementation: Are consumers aware of CSR initiatives? *Journal of Business Ethics, 85*(2), 285–301.

Rim, H., & Kim, S. (2016). Dimensions of corporate social responsibility (CSR) skepticism and their impacts on public evaluations toward CSR. *Journal of Public Relations Research, 28*(5–6), 248–267.

Sánchez, P. E., & Benito-Hernández, S. (2015). CSR policies: Effects on labour productivity in Spanish micro and small manufacturing companies. *Journal of Business Ethics, 128*(4), 705–724.

Seele, P., & Lock, I. (2015). Instrumental and/or deliberative? A typology of CSR communication tools. *Journal of Business Ethics, 131*(2), 401–414.

Skarmeas, D., & Leonidou, C. N. (2013). When consumers doubt, watch out! The role of CSR skepticism. *Journal of Business Research, 66*(10), 1831–1838.

Snyder, H. (2019). Literature review as a research methodology: An overview and guidelines. *Journal of Business Research, 104*, 333–339.

Taylor, R. C. (2020). Advertising and COVID-19. *International Journal of Advertising, 39*(5), 597–589. https://doi.org/10.1080/02650487.2020.1774131.

Twum, K. K., Kosiba, J. P., Abdul-Hamid, I. K., & Hinson, R. (2020). Does corporate social responsibility enhance political marketing? *Journal of Nonprofit & Public Sector Marketing*, 1–31. https://doi.org/10.1080/10495142.2020.1798850.

Verbeeten, F. H., Gamerschlag, R., & Möller, K. (2016). Are CSR disclosures relevant for investors? Empirical evidence from Germany. *Management Decision, 54*(6), 1359–1382.

Zhu, Q., Yin, H., Liu, J., & Lai, K. H. (2014). How is employee perception of organizational efforts in corporate social responsibility related to their satisfaction and loyalty towards developing harmonious society in Chinese enterprises? *Corporate Social Responsibility and Environmental Management, 21*(1), 28–40.

6

Ithemba Lila Nyuka (Hope is Rising): Responding to Customer Emotions During Uncertainties

Kelebogile Makhafola and Thomas Anning-Dorson

6.1 Introduction

Communication plays an important role in the process of onboarding, engaging, and retaining customers (Ball et al., 2004; Hennig-Thurau, 2000). Connecting with customers and its effect on business success has been an age-old truth about customer management. Brands that stay in-touch with their customers thrive even in difficult market conditions. One sure way of staying connected with your customers is through the proper management of customer communications. Communicating with your customers is key to the customer engagement management process as it determines the extent to which brand loyalty is stimulated (Eger

---

K. Makhafola
Maruapula Brand, Randpark Ridge, Johannesburg, South Africa

T. Anning-Dorson (✉)
School of Business Sciences, University of the Witwatersrand, Johannesburg, South Africa

& Mičík, 2017; Zephaniah et al., 2020). Brands that constantly engage their clients have a higher conversion rate, improved customer experience, and deliver the eventual customer satisfaction. Communication allows the customer to know what is happening and what to expect; and how a brand can fulfill her needs. Customer-centric communication helps to deal with customer anxieties, queries, doubts and facilitate the creation of an emotional bond with the brand (Bruhn & Schnebelen, 2017; Finne & Grönroos, 2017; Lee, 2017). Brands that fail to communicate simply lose the competitive battle for the customers' share of mind and heart, and ultimately the share of wallet.

Effective communication becomes a key weapon in challenging times (Reynolds & Quinn, 2008) where there is the need for people to adapt. Changes are all around us and sometimes, these changes create major uncertainties. Brands, corporate entities, and even nations suffer from these changes that are sometimes unimagined and not prepared for. Natural disasters, wars, health pandemics are examples of unimagined changes that come to affect lives and alter our normal way of behavior. Businesses and brands also suffer from such surprising turn of events. During such uncertain periods, communication becomes an important tool to deal with the emotional and psychological effects that may be suffered by the victims. Effective communication influences psychological well-being of the affected; and help them adjust, manage and cope with the emotional consequences. It also helps them to contextualize their experiences, draw meaning from their current circumstance and develop coping mechanisms. The charge for brands and corporate entities in crisis periods is how to respond to the infinitely complicated challenges their diverse stakeholders have to deal with. Finding the right balance between taking tough decisions, and communicating the complexities associated with such decisions a key problem in crisis management. While substantial body of knowledge has been devoted to the role of communication in managing stakeholders (see Zephaniah et al., 2020; Al Nahyan et al., 2019; Finne & Grönroos, 2017; Bruhn & Schnebelen, 2017; Heino & Anttiroiko, 2016), there is a lot more to learn from how brands adapt their communications to deal with crisis.

Understanding how brands and corporate entities manage their communications with their clientele in crisis periods offers key insights into both practice and academic literature.

Furthermore, the extent to which communication drives value has not received adequate attention in literature, especially in crisis periods. Literature is replete with cases and empirical research on how brands can increase sales, compete and build loyalty (see Koponen et al., 2019; Porcu et al., 2019; Othman et al., 2021). Yet, little is known about how communication can drive customer and stakeholder value, especially during crisis periods. The current study documents how a tourism brand managed its communications with its stakeholders in a health pandemic period where customers could not have access to the wonderful experiences the brand delivers. This chapter provides an analysis of how the South African Tourism drove stakeholder value in a global pandemic period where customers could not derive the core value being offered by responding to the relevant customer emotions and concerns brought by travel restrictions.

6.2 Background, Approach and Theoretical Framework

The coronavirus pandemic (COVID-19) put all brands—private corporate and state agencies and even nations into a difficult situation of managing their communications in order to inspire confidence and hope for the future. Key sectors such as the global tourism and hospitality industries suffered greatly as they came to a halt during the height of the pandemic. The restriction on movement through various levels of lockdown meant that tourism came to a standstill while the hospitality firms suffered momentously. While there is a gradual easing of the restrictions in different countries, the telling effect on these two sectors has not seen any appreciable improvement at least for now (at the time of writing this chapter).

The pandemic affected the economic prospects of almost all countries as global travel and in some cases, local movements were halted. In the desolate period of the pandemic, different cooperate entities and sectors suffered immensely. Nation brands built around tourism were also not spared as such countries shut their borders to prevent importation of the virus while restricting movement internally. Africa's tourism was not spared. The tourism industry in Africa is estimated to contribute 7% to GDP and employs about 24.6 million people, which accounts for almost 7% of employment in Africa (Richardson, 2020). Countries such as Mauritius, Seychelles, Kenya, Namibia, Ghana, Ethiopia, The Gambia etc. suffered from the restriction on global travels. For example, a country like Ghana that had a successful 2019 in terms of international arrivals through its "Year of Return" to commemorate 400th anniversary of Transatlantic slave trade suffered greatly in 2020 with its "Beyond the Return" campaign.

In South Africa, which second to Egypt in terms of tourism industry in Africa, the industry contributes up to 9.1% of total employment—1.5 million people—and 7% to GDP. Internal tourism is big in South Africa and contributes significantly to the industry's performance. According to the OECD, SA's domestic tourism trips in 2018 totaled 17.7 million, compared with 10.5 million international tourist arrivals (OECD, 2020). This explains the critical nature of domestic tourism to the economy. South Africa under the hard lockdown (between March and July 2020) restricted all forms of travels except essential services. In these periods, internal tourism came to a complete stop couple with the closure of borders. This compounded the effect of the pandemic on the economy as tourism destinations including parks within the cities were deserted. The South African Minister of Tourism, Mmamoloko Kubayi-Ngubane, in her July budget speech indicated that a potential 75% decline in revenue for 2020; 438,000 tourism jobs at risk; $2.8 billion lost in 3 months (Richardson, 2020). This further brought about psychological effect on all citizens. These grim and frightful figures and ominous outlook called for an action to inspire hope for the future. Understanding the possible disenchantment that was to hit the people, South African Tourism designed a marketing campaign in response to the effect of the pandemic on the industry.

This paper documents some of the key successes of the campaign and shares lessons which other brands can learn from. The approach is to share insights gathered from the entity through its online platforms, news publications, social media communications and reactions among others. The authors monitored the campaign from the beginning of the launch, which was in March (when the country went under lockdown) through July 2020. This analysis appraises the efforts of innovative marketing where there is little to no options to serve ones' customers with practical products or services and still be willing and able to deliver valuable benefits to customers. We highlight the ways to reflect true brand value in the midst of immeasurable internal and external challenges.

The paper takes theoretical inspiration from the appraisal theory to explain how goal fulfillment is shaped by the environment and the hopelessness or otherwise of a person in the situation she finds herself in. The goal-congruency dimension from the appraisal theory explains the extent to which the environment is or is not conducive to goal achievement. In a good-natured environment, "goal congruent" means that a favorable outcome could occur. In a harsh or frightening environment, "goal congruent" means that a negative outcome could be avoided or solved. Environments appraised as goal congruent (incongruent) are evaluated as good or desirable (bad) and evoke positive (negative) emotions. A feeling of possibility has a strong effect on how a person may endure a situation as possibility is embedded in hope and uncertainty. MacInnis and De Mello (2005) fittingly put it in the following words: "a person does not hope for something that is uncertain per se but for something that is possible even though it is uncertain" (p. 2).

In the marketing communication tradition, brands in their communications attempt to inspire some form of hope in terms of what the brand can do. Rossiter and Percy (1991, p. 103) suggest that "all ads make a 'promise' and thereby invoke hope—whether this hope be for termination of a negative state (negative reinforcement) or for onset of a positive state (positive reinforcement)". In other words, because hope is evoked when a goal-congruent outcome is uncertain but possible, varying the hope that consumers feel should be influenced by marketing activities that affect appraisals of possibility and/or the extent to which they yearn for the goal-congruent outcome. According to MacInnis and De Mello (2005), hope is a positively valenced emotion evoked in response to an uncertain but possible goal-congruent outcome. A person feels hopeless when she is certain that what is expected will not happen. Whenever goal-congruent outcome is expected not to occur, there is hopelessness (Seligman, 1975). One needs some sort of "possibility" in uncertainty in order to inspire hope. In the current case under study, travelers were uncertain about the attainment of their tourism goals and needed "possibility" communicated to assuage the negative emotions of not being able to achieve a positive goal-congruent outcome in terms of their tourism needs.

6.3 The Marketing Communication Campaign

The South African Tourism responded to it various customers in the wake of a pandemic, which prohibited travel and any form of tourism activities. The customers vary from business and leisure tourists, hotels and accommodations, tourist activities and tour guides, tourism authorities and bodies, expos, travel Indaba, and other stakeholders. The problem caused by the ban and lockdown posed socio-economic tragedies, which meant job losses, closing of businesses and long-term sociological effects on the tourism industry. No player in the market had the ability or access to conduct business, leaving many players destitute and in despair. In a phase where South African Tourism could not offer their normal services, they instead facilitated pain relief measures through incentives, loan, grants, empowerment projects and various measures that were not part of their core business or brand model canvas. They cushioned these events with a poignant marketing campaign that reassured customers and encouraged them to corporate in making the industry healthier again, even if it meant staying home.

The South African Tourism was proactive and did not wait for circumstances or other voices to develop a narrative and selling point for travel experiences within the country. They consciously created and led their own proactive response to the dilemma. They remembered that the customer is unyielding when it comes to value and had to be guided to seek the most important value under the current circumstance. Therefore, they needed to engage the required changes in tourism by choosing to contribute effectively through building and nurturing relationships.

What is being recognized is their pre-emptive value-creation strategy in the time of uncertainty and despair. The marketing communication campaign was dubbed "Don't travel now. So, you can travel later". South African Tourism drove value by responding to the relevant customer emotions and concerns brought by the travel ban.

The marketing communication efforts were packaged through video, digital content, and communication collateral on various media platforms. The message was about hope and reassurance, it was a cautionary measure to raise South African spirits regarding the impact of travel ban across the nation. The communication emphasized that staying home will keep us safe, enough to see tomorrow, to travel beyond today, and live to experience those moments with who matters most to us. For South African Tourism, the intention was to create and manage value by engendering comradely and national pride. The South African Tourism sought to reassure each stakeholder, especially travel customers (for business and leisure) that the country will get through this and will be reintroducing themselves to South Africa again—with new hope and new perspective. As indicated by MacInnis and De Mello (2005), hope is a marketable entity that can influence consumer behavior. As a strong brand should do, they stood up to the reality and affirmation that there is panic and there is fear, however, South African Tourism is here and will be there at the end of the tunnel to keep meeting their needs.

"Ithemba lila nyuka—hope is rising" was the core message. This was the South African Tourism's brand promise in the midst of uncertainty when they were incapacitated to activate their core offering as a tourism body. The brand identified and anticipated customer's problems and created a communication campaign, which reflected that "humanity is taking a stand by taking a step back". The brand identified that the country needed to act collectively, instead of seeking capitalistic transactions. The focus was on seeking out and delivering true intangible value of customer wellbeing—a very difficult concept for business centric marketing effort to capture and achieve (McColl-Kennedy et al., 2017). The marketing communication promised that "we will go back to our favourite spots and discover new ones"—a direct functional proposition to their future value as an entity. The communication continued, "but for now, we recede back because to enjoy these benefits tomorrow, we need to stay home and keep each other safe". This substantiates the fact that value is co-created and South African Tourism represented this notion successfully and empathetically (Chen et al., 2020). Sharma et al. (2017) indicate that customers could be vulnerable and that responsible brands through co-creation roles are able to deliver relevant value that protects these vulnerable customers.

The customer value proposition and the perception driven under this campaign highlighted the peculiar nature of the environment that the customers found themselves in. This can also be understood as a unique selling point. They refrained from selling transactions but promoted a clear statement that elevated the benefit of keeping safe and being responsible by not traveling during the pandemic, to which clear benefits were articulated. In the midst of unfathomable conditions, the brand made efforts to point the focus on what customers can control, their movement and contribution to making the industry healthier, that is how they managed to make the value position measurable.

Their differentiated approach reimagined marketing frameworks in a way that involved the customer journey and decisions as the process of value creation. For instance, it became more about redefining the principles of movement and place (staying home is better for you and me—stay home so you can travel tomorrow). The brand was able to co-create value with the customers by explaining the responsibilities and the consequences of customer actions. It repositioned the significance and onus of traveling in a pandemic on the notion of trust. The brand trusted that "you would make the right choice as a customer". The campaign can be likened to the Ikea effect, an ideology that involves the customer in the process of creating something, this way they value it more. The South African Tourism intentional marketing communication crowned the "spirit of Ubuntu"—"Thuma Mina" (a value proposition posed by President Cyril Ramaphosa), Proudly South African, and other quintessential South African unifying beliefs in order to engender the behavioral change. This emphasizes the critical nature of the use of indigenous knowledge in shaping behavior and engendering positive market response (Chisenga, 2002).

The customer problem was either latent or apparent, only rearing its heads as time went on and the industry experienced exponential problems as the pandemic became more stringent. A key component of an effective value proposition is that of sustainability. South African Tourism delivered on the notion that if a brand is able to maintain their customers today, it will be able to gain sales tomorrow. They successfully sustained their brand promise and partnered with their customers in experiencing the new normal amidst the reconfiguration of the job to be done. The customers needed a different value channel beside travel and tourism, which identified new barriers to the entity's barriers and parameters for value creation.

6.4 Managing the Customer Value Through Communication

In this section, we look into the South African Tourism value management during the pandemic by analyzing the functional, experiential, symbolic, and cost of value to the customers within that time. Starting with the functional or instrumental value, South African Tourism was restricted from delivering on the functional benefits they usually offer. This forced the marketing efforts to innovate toward responding to the new pain points which customers may be experiencing. The experiential or hedonic value in the "don't travel now". Travel later marketing efforts created solidarity and empathy through reflecting shared experiences and the acknowledgement of shared feelings, creating appropriate emotional experiences for the customer. The symbolic or expressive value was clearly communicated across the chosen digital media (as that was the only point of contact for both the brand and customers). A digital community was brought together by immersing the brand message on platforms that encouraged people to share their opinions and feelings about this global ordeal, sharing comforting messages across the country while keeping safe at home. The real cost for customers was foregoing their cherished experiences and had to be compensated. The compensation was the value South African Tourism had to deliver through the communications. Through their communications, they created psychological meaning and value for the customers. South African Tourism bared to be the voice of reason and hope in a period of despair.

The attribute of value that was missing from South African Tourism was the delivery of functional value—the performance of the regular experiences through visitation of tourist destinations. There were no product or service components to associate or engage with during the lockdown. The pivotal value to be delivered was through relationship, engagement, and emotional value co-creation through communication. These were delivered through the creation and delivery of emotional empowerment and aspirational consumption experiences. The communication delivered hope—bringing possibility into an uncertain situation where there was despair and slump. The hope was shared and accentuated by the customers to capture the entire nation. The improvement in the national mood was through value co-creation—the customers generated content and influence others which made the campaign sustainable.

The "Don't travel now, travel later" marketing effort was customer centric—focusing on the safety of the customer, society and the entire nation. The marketing communication efforts were driven by context—socio-cultural, socio-economic, and need for collective thinking and action. They looked at their environment and how it affected various customer dynamics in complex and diverse ways. The brand focused on customer leadership by providing a vision, inspiration and motivation for change in behavior and delegating or empowering customers to be self-disciplined and cautious in this immeasurable time. Customer leadership established South African Tourism as a brand that recognizes the need to guide and provide an anchor in the midst of chaos and uncertainty. In terms of the cultural alignment around customer needs, the organizational culture already embraces the nuances and characteristics of a divisive South African landscape. This assists in coordinating marketing efforts well enough to feel the pulse of the nation, and the fear and concerns of the diverse customers. This allows for organizational support, which is critical in managing new value through marketing communication campaign.

South African Tourism told the story that reflects all stakeholders. The marketing efforts were used as a way to educate during a crisis, to teach people about their values and promises of the brand. The marketing efforts for the campaign focused on being inclusive in their approach to create a brand community as it takes a village to realize sustainable change. The brand reimagined the customer journey, developed an innovative and passionate marketing response that focused on building engagement, fostering relationship and deepening cohesion within the brand community. The brand acknowledged and took advantage of talking about the everyday life as a brand and as a people in order to connect authentically to the heart of the customers. That way, their context remained empathetic and accessible.

6.5 Customer Response to the New Value on Offer

The customers saw themselves in the marketing communication materials and identified with what was on offer. The don't travel now; travel later drive proved purpose-centered communication in the absence of tangible services offering. The digital platforms were contested with user-generated content and responses to the campaign material and videos. This demonstrates that brands can create emotional connections with stakeholders, successfully leading to brand affinity. The customers in this instance were South African patrons who were affected by the pandemic and lockdown in different degrees. However, their sentiments were recognized and managed by the meaning and value of the marketing message. They took up the onus and accountability to stay home and do more by staying safe because that was what the industry and the nation needed from them.

The campaign message resonated even with those who were not direct South African Tourism customers. The value was so personal that most South African posted the "don't travel now, travel later" videos on their social media platforms, becoming an extended mouthpiece for the marketing drive. The innovations were adopted and owned by stakeholders who are outside of the direct value chain of the entity. This changed the design and delivery of the customer experience. It released control over the marketing story, although guided, into the hands of those who shared the same sentiments.

In a normal marketing campaign, we would use churn rate, net promoter score or even the customer lifetime value as a measurement of the impact of customer-centric marketing efforts. However, this marketing campaign was not set on sales but creation of meaning connection and customer engagement. Under normal circumstances, we would be observing metrics such as customer value maximization under the pretax of profit or advancement of the company. The aim with don't travel now, travel later drive was to encourage customers- and stakeholder engagement and involvement and not to focus on increasing transactions. It was about encouraging stakeholders to remain as active and responsible customers. The brand was not selling, it was rather doing the opposite. The call to action was to refrain from what the brand would usually encourage them to do. This was for a greater good—for the sake of the industry, the nation and most importantly the customer.

South African Tourism significantly shifted the needle regarding marketing efforts and response, and customer engagement and management. Through the campaign, they generated a diversified pool of audiences despite reaching their customers, extending the targeted community. They created a digital community that was in unison reading the call to action of staying home. Citizens who are key customers wanted to protect South Africa and make sure they do enough to be able to travel in the future. South Africa Tourism was the driver for such social engineering through its marketing communication. The customers valued the leadership and motivation provided by the state entity, which came in the form of the marketing collateral. The communication advocated for customers to keep hope even in a time of despair. The accessibility of the brand and business was reconfigured to generate a collective buy in from customers which was anchored on new values and meeting these new needs, which was to stay safe. The company set aside its strive toward the bottom line. The campaign embodied customer centricity and brought awareness to the impact of working together to come out on the other side, for the sake of the industry, and the nation. This exemplifies customer collaborations to achieve societal goals, national cohesion, public safety, and well-being. Amongst the diverse pool of competing behaviors and stakeholders, South African Tourism managed to call upon everyone to play their part, to cooperate and empathize with what the world is going through.

6.6 Conclusions

There are key lessons to be learnt from how South African Tourism managed the effect of the pandemic on its customers. First being the value of marketing that reflects human centricity and customer centricity. It is vital to design and implement marketing efforts with the context in mind as customers are different and will require different value/solutions as the environment changes. It is, therefore, important to be able to apply design thinking systems around communication and marketing to respond systemically and empathically to the needs of the market. It is also evident that achieving business and brand growth while navigating changing markets landscapes is more effectively maximized by human-centric design and communication approaches that innovate the offering and align it closer to the needs of the diverse pool of customers at the moment.

The case is also a good challenge that teaches about ways in which brands can drive growth when you are unable to deliver on the core offering. It forces the business to reimagine the subsequent offering. This requires the business and brand to refrain from working in silos and collaborate to find valuable solutions to customer problems. The current business climate is forcing collaboration across the business and brand value chain. These collaborations are leading to offerings that deliver on holistic value propositions and customer solutions. The offerings also meet the customer dynamics on physical, digital and service levels.

Customers do not compare brands and core offerings with the direct competitors but with all other offerings capable of meeting their needs and that of the society. Customers are now driving the conversation on what is valuable and not what a particular brand says. This can be attributed to the changing market landscape, customer expectation, and brand contribution to society. Therefore, it has become increasingly important to navigate, reassure, and engage stakeholders more by focusing on the quality of interaction and not just transaction. It is important for customers to know that their voices are heard and that they are at the center of the decision-making processes. Hence, brands are admonished to interact, and not just transact; they are to build relationships through effective marketing communications.

Brands must recognize that they need a conscious approach to building connections and linkages with customers even in harsh market and economic conditions. There are missed opportunities when a brand does not control the storyline and allows competitors or other players to offer value to their customers. Taking ownership of learning how to engage and navigate uncomfortable truths is key to building trust and relationships through the marketing material that the brand disseminates.

Beginning the communication process with the intention of delivering customer value will always win the hearts and commitment of customers as they are guided by substance and structure. Customer value-driven brand positioning and effective marketing communication efforts are the golden threads that secure stakeholder engagements, giving confidence and reassurance to stockholder, and more importantly building a bond with the customer. The marketing campaign by South Africa Tourism was especially experienced by the customers as it drove a brand promise so quintessential to their value proposition that they met the moment with an emotionally connected response.

References

Al Nahyan, M. T., Sohal, A., Hawas, Y., & Fildes, B. (2019). Communication, coordination, decision-making and knowledge-sharing: A case study in construction management. *Journal of Knowledge Management, 23*(9), 1764–1781.

Ball, D., Coelho, P. S., & Machas, A. (2004). The role of communication and trust in explaining customer loyalty: An extension to the ECSI model. *European Journal of Marketing, 38*(9/10), 1272.

Bruhn, M., & Schnebelen, S. (2017). Integrated Marketing Communication–from an instrumental to a customer-centric perspective. *European Journal of Marketing, 51*(3), 464–489.

Chen, T., Dodds, S., Finsterwalder, J., Witell, L., Cheung, L., Falter, M., Garry, T., Snyder, H., & McColl-Kennedy, J. R. (2020). Dynamics of well-being co-creation: A psychological ownership perspective. *Journal of Service Management*. https://doi.org/10.1108/JOSM-09-2019-0297.

Chisenga, J. (2002). Indigenous knowledge: Africa's opportunity to contribute to global information content. *South African Journal of Libraries and Information Science, 68*(1), 16–20.

Eger, L., & Mičík, M. (2017). Customer-oriented communication in retail and Net Promoter Score. *Journal of Retailing and Consumer Services, 35*, 142–149.

Finne, Å., & Grönroos, C. (2017). Communication-in-use: Customer-integrated marketing communication. *European Journal of Marketing, 51*(3), 445–463.

Heino, O., & Anttiroiko, A. V. (2016). Utility-Customer communication: The case of water utilities. *Public Works Management & Policy, 21*(3), 220–230.

Hennig-Thurau, T. (2000). Relationship quality and customer retention through strategic communication of customer skills. *Journal of Marketing Management, 16*(1–3), 55–79.

Koponen, J., Julkunen, S., & Asai, A. (2019). Sales communication competence in international B2B solution selling. *Industrial Marketing Management, 82*, 238–252.

Lee, Y. C. (2017). Corporate sustainable development and marketing communications on social media: Fortune 500 enterprises. *Business Strategy and the Environment, 26*(5), 569–583.

MacInnis, D. J., & De Mello, G. E. (2005). The concept of hope and its relevance to product evaluation and choice. *Journal of Marketing, 69*(1), 1–14.

McColl-Kennedy, J. R., Hogan, S. J., Witell, L., & Snyder, H. (2017). Cocreative customer practices: Effects of health care customer value cocreation practices on well-being. *Journal of Business Research, 70*, 55–66.

OECD. (2020). *OECD tourism trends and policies 2020*. https://www.oecd-ilibrary.org/sites/01ad4412-en/index.html?itemId=/content/component/01ad4412-en.

Othman, B. A., Harun, A., De Almeida, N. M., & Sadq, Z. M. (2021). The effects on customer satisfaction and customer loyalty by integrating marketing communication and after sale service into the traditional marketing mix model of Umrah travel services in Malaysia. *Journal of Islamic Marketing*, 12(2), 363-388.

Porcu, L., del Barrio-Garcia, S., Alcántara-Pilar, J. M., & Crespo-Almendros, E. (2019). Analyzing the influence of firm-wide integrated marketing communication on market performance in the hospitality industry. *International Journal of Hospitality Management, 80*, 13–24.

Reynolds, B., & Quinn, S. C. (2008). Effective communication during an influenza pandemic: The value of using a crisis and emergency risk communication framework. *Health Promotion Practice*, 9(4_suppl), 13S–17S.

Richardson, H. (2020). *Africa's fast-growing tourism industry could lose up to $120 billion and millions of jobs.* https://qz.com/africa/1888306/africa-tourism-market-to-lose-up-to-120-billion-with-covid/. Accessed on October 26, 2020.

Rossiter, J. R., & Percy, L. (1991). Emotions and Motivations in Advertising. *Advances in Consumer Research, 18*(1), 100–110.

Seligman, M. E. P. (1975). *Helplessness: On depression, development, and death*. Freeman.

Sharma, S., Conduit, J., & Hill, S. R. (2017). Hedonic and eudaimonic wellbeing outcomes from co-creation roles: A study of vulnerable customers. *Journal of Services Marketing., 31*(4/5), 397–411.

Zephaniah, C. O., Ogba, I. E., & Izogo, E. E. (2020). Examining the effect of customers' perception of bank marketing communication on customer loyalty. *Scientific African, 8*, e00383, https://doi.org/10.1016/j.sciaf.2020.e00383.

7

Perception of Marketing Communication Practice: Evidence from Rural and Community Banks

Isaac Tandoh, Nicholas Oppong Mensah, and Albert Anani-Bossman

7.1 Introduction

Marketing communications (MCs) remain very essential to the success of every business. People can start a business, but it is not everyone that can nature and see the business survive over time especially in the presence of fierce competition. The most vital aspect of any business to survive the competition is marketing their brand(s) to sustain the business, Uppal (2010). As the economic domain and especially the banking sector in Ghana, an emerging economy is rapidly changing and

---

I. Tandoh (✉) · A. Anani-Bossman
Ghana Institute of Journalism, Accra, Ghana

A. Anani-Bossman
e-mail: albert.anani-bossman@gij.edu.gh

N. O. Mensah
University of Energy and Natural Resources, Sunyani, Ghana
e-mail: nicholas.mensah@uner.edu.gh

© The Author(s), under exclusive license to Springer Nature Switzerland AG 2022
T. Anning-Dorson et al. (eds.), *Marketing Communications in Emerging Economies, Volume II*, Palgrave Studies of Marketing in Emerging Economies, https://doi.org/10.1007/978-3-030-81337-6_7

customers are becoming more enlightened, demanding, and sophisticated, it has become important for financial institutions to determine the factors, which are relatable to the customers' selection process and influence their choice of offers from financial institutions (Woo et al., 2015).

Ghana continues to be touted as one of the world's leading emerging economies with a GDP estimated to be worth about 66.98 billion US dollars in 2019 and a population of about 31.4 million people. This means Ghana's economy contributes about 0.06% to the world economy. Some three decades ago, Ghana's economy was nothing to talk about and the nation was in crisis; impoverished and suffering famine, it was on the verge of economic collapse. Fast-forward to the present day, the West African nation has staged a remarkable comeback and is predicted to be the world's fastest-growing economy in 2019 (IMF data, 2019).

The challenge for the Ghanaian banking sector is a critical contributor to Ghana's economy and more has been how to create sustainable competitive advantage in the areas of customer attraction and retention, corporate image, and brand awareness (Bawumia et al., 2008). Over the years, and more recently, the advancement of technology has influenced customer perception regarding how most banks communicate their offering. This development has made marketing managers in the banking sector, adopt the use of tactical messages using marketing communication mix elements in promoting their brands and forming good and profitable relationships with their customers (Abdul-Qadir & Kwanbo, 2012). Moreover, clients are confronted with a variety of products and services, from various banking and non-banking institutions. Hence, communicating the value prepositions to clients has become very necessary (Tandoh, 2015). The main objective of this chapter is to:

> To explore the orientations and perceptions of the marketing communications mix of the selected Rural and Community Banks (RCBs) in Ghana.

This chapter covers the following themes under the literature review section. The Concept and Perceptions of Marketing Communications, Marketing Communications Objectives, Marketing Communication

Tools, Marketing Communication Strategies. This would be followed by a methodology section that will spell out how the research was conducted and the methodological approached adopted for the study. The last section of this chapter will present the results and discussion for the study.

It is expected that this chapter will provide a deeper understanding of how marketing communications mix is perceived and practiced in the Rural and Community Banks (RCBs) in an emerging economy like Ghana. Additionally, this chapter seeks to provide a framework for knowledge sharing and improve marketing communication strategy and practice in the banking industries in Ghana, and Rural and Community Banks (RCBs) in particular.

Firms do communicate with their customers to achieve a certain purpose. Stafford & Grimes (2012) posits that there are three main goals of marketing communications. According to him, the firms must first communicate to attain brand awareness. He further added that the firm secondary objective is to communicate to make customers express the need for the product and what particular solution the product provides. Finally, to direct the customer's behavior toward the company's goals and desires. The efforts must be made in the communication process to incite a behavioral change favorable to the company that is communicating.

7.2 Theoretical Review

7.2.1 The Concept and Perceptions of Marketing Communications

With the current competitive environment in the business world, the demands of marketing are much more complex and complicated than they used to be 20 years ago. Now marketing is not just about developing better and advanced products with competitive pricing (Tandoh, 2015). Should organizations still rely on trust and experience to sell their services and products? Organizations must communicate their promises on offer to consumers as it is a crucial part of a company's marketing strategy aimed at achieving sustainable competitive advantage. Information about offerings, brand prices, where their products and services can be found has become the major headache of businesses in today's marketing of their offerings and brand activations and positioning (Lee & Jain, 2009). In Ghana, with the development in the financial sector, a lot of pressure is on the managers to adopt effective marketing management strategies for survival. One of the strategies currently being utilized is effective in marketing communications strategies (Aliata et al., 2012; Meidan, 1996).

Marketing communications can be looked at as the voice of the organization. Kotler and Keller (2012) characterize marketing communications as the strategy and a procedure by which institutions tell their stories, impact, and remind customers—specifically or by implication about the brands they showcase. They further reiterated that a study of the marketing mix points to the fact that marketing communication probably is the very last course of action in the institutions' marketing mix when it comes to systems used to make, impart and convey quality to the client. Egan (2007) also stretches the debate a bit further and argues that marketing communications are a means by which a supplier of goods, services, values, and/or ideas showcase themselves and communicate to their target market audience to stimulate dialogue leading and creating profitable mutually beneficial relationships. On his part, Sivesan (2013), marketing communication is simply an information set of connections programmed to meet market needs. He added that marketing communication mix elements aim to inform, persuade, and impress customers in a market place, to raise brand values among others.

Based on these definitions, this author also sees marketing communication as a combination of voice, imaging, pictures, ways of thinking, impressions, and relationships consciously built by a firm over time to create a bond with customers and gain a good public image.

In this regard, marketing communications play an important role in creating brand awareness and a positive image for the company and its offerings in customers' minds. Marketing communications will not be effective without the efficient usage of marketing communication tools.

The most commonly used tools or elements in the marketing communication mix comprise advertisement, public relations, personal selling, and sales promotion, sponsorship, direct marketing, and recently social media and digital marketing.

Largely, many observers and writers in the past have attributed marketing communication to advertising because it is the most visible of all the other elements (Evtikhevich, 2014). However, this author thinks this assertion is flawed as the market place is becoming more digitized and consumers are shifting their communications preference to a more interactive one. Social media and online marketing seem to be a new buzzword in marketing communications. In the social media space, customers inform one another about their organization and brands and thus inform each other (Mangold & Faulds, 2009). According to Petek (2015) in the determination of the promotion mix, the product life cycle plays a huge role. He contends that when it comes to informing customers thereby promoting and creating awareness for brands with new products, advertisement and public relations efforts are emphasized. Comparing to the other elements in the mix, he says while personal selling is very impactful on distributing channels and supply chain, promotions, however, boast customer's desire to trying the product. At the development stage, continuing advertisement and public relations efforts aim to sustain brand loyalty. Based on the product life cycle, personal selling continues its major impact on the distribution channel and supply chain. Promotion activities diminish, during the maturing period, advertisements go on to call attention to the product in customers' memory and promotions are applied enthusiastically to attract new customers to the brand. Personal selling will, however, sustain its dominance on the distribution channel and supply chain.

During the maturing period, advertisements go on to emphasize the product in customers' memory and promotions are applied vigorously to attract new customers to the brand. Personal selling sustains its dominance on the distribution channel and supply chain. During the decline period, the business decreases its advertisement and public relations efforts rapidly while personal selling and promotions are decreased to such a level that it will be sufficient to support the product (Ferrell & Hartline, 2011). The understanding of marketing communications methods and their usage has not properly been understood in the practical world. It seems only academia has done some explanations on the methods and concepts but whether the methods and procedures are thoroughly understood in practice as a potent strategy has been in context (Sarpong & Tandoh, 2015). This is why this study seeks to deepen the understanding of marketing communications and solicit the opinion of customers and staff alike in emerging marketing like Ghana whose economy depends so much on the contribution of small and medium enterprises like the Rural and Communities banks.

7.3 Marketing Communications Objectives

Firms do communicate with their customers to achieve a certain purpose. Stafford & Grimes (2012) posits that there are three main goals of marketing communications. He says the firms must first communicate to attain brand awareness. He explained further that the second objective is to communicate to make customers express the need for the product and what particular solution the product provides. The third he says is to direct the customer's behavior toward your company's goals and desires. Kotler and Armstrong (2011) also contend that efforts must be made in the communication process to incite a behavioral change favorable to the company that is communicating.

Suffice it to say, marketing communication objectives are for the long term, where different kinds of marketing strategies and tactics are aimed at increasing the worth of a company with time. Thus, communication objectives become meaningful and profitable to an institution only when customers are motivated with deliberate and calculated messages that tell them that the company and its offerings are well positioned to solve the problems they are seeking solutions for (Stafford & Grimes, 2012). In another dimension, Fill (2013) argues that with technology and modernity, marketing communication is being now driven by a desire to constantly find new and outstanding ways of effectively communicating with their customers and positioning their brands and offerings on the front pages of their minds. He emphasized that customers have become sophisticated and thereby becoming more demanding in their request for results in the communication being given them and hence the objective of the communication is to meet their demands.

7.4 Marketing Communication Tools

Many renowned researchers, including Kelly (2012), Fill (2013), Egan (2007), and Kotler & Keller (2012), have done the cataloging of marketing communication tools. According to Kotler & Keller (2012, p. 374), marketing communication tools have consisted of advertising, sales promotion, personal selling, public relations, and direct marketing.

These communication tools traditionally as classified traditionally are:

Advertising is any paid form of non-personal presentation and promotion of ideas, goods, or services by an identified sponsor.

Sales promotion is short-term incentives that aim at stimulating sales and encourage purchasing or selling of goods or services particularly for a short period.

Personal selling a marketing communication tool is a personal presentation by the firm's representatives or sales force to identify and make sales and build relationships with customers.

Public relations is a process of creating and establishing a mutually beneficial relationship between an organization and its publics. It builds good mutual relationships with an organization's publics and builds a good company's image, reputation. Public relations also works toward brand building and brand protection.

Direct marketing connects directly with selected customers to obtain an immediate response and build long-term consumer relationships. For example, direct mail, the telephone, the Internet can be used to communicate directly with customers.

Govoni (2004) revealed that marketing managers of intuitions like banks and others should psyche themselves and come to terms that there is no one best channel for all products. Such things as the best communication channel exist only in illusion. What managers of these banks should focus on is looking for the best ways to reach customers of each product separately according to the need and expectations of the customers. He stressed that the best procedure is an analysis of the market in which the firm operates, the kind and type of customers targeted, the features of the product, and the business itself should be of prime concern to deduce the ultimate and prime marketing channel strategy that will bring results and achieve competitive advantage. Keller (2008) and Kotler et al. (2008) concur determinedly that there is in no way like the best marketing communications channel for all items.

7.5 Marketing Communication Strategies

7.5.1 Promotion and Advertising Strategy

The promotion and advertising strategy is aimed at ways by which firms send information, messages about their brands and their offerings to niche markets through a channel. According to Doole and Lowe (2004), inadequate information on current conditions and benefits of a product or service is a characteristic weakness. This, according to him, comes about largely from poor communication systems, low levels of education, and increases in the number of small firms. The author argues that half the information or wrong messages sent by RCBs to their customers will result in customers switching from their brands.

When formulating a promotional and advertising campaign, the main purpose of the campaign should be echoed in addition to what the advertising strategy seeks to attain. The communication should appeal to the sensibilities and emotions of the customers and also messages should be evaluated to see if it meets the expectations of its targets, Govoni (2004).

Smallwood (2018) reiterated that it does not come with ease when selecting or choosing between the categories of a media outlet to use for an advertising campaign. Advertising like television, magazines, newspapers, and direct mails with its huge advantages and demerits always comes with great difficulty in selecting which is which. At best, knowing the nature of the media, its reach, frequency, and the target audience are critical to deciding between which one to select. Second, the type and nature of the product and what the marketer seeks to achieve with the advertising will determine the use of a particular media.

Keller (2008) posited that to assess whether an advertising campaign has been effective, firms should set benchmarks such as the objective of the advertising campaign, and the managers' effectiveness in deploying messages to be used for the advert. These benchmarks may also include such measures as the size of the audience, program ratings, the number of inquiries received, all of which pertain almost exclusively to campaign objectives alone. There is a growing argument by many writers that advertising must be tailored to performance. If an advertisement aims at generating a positive brand image and reputation for a company, the success of the campaign should be measured by a top-of-mind awareness survey from the targeted audience.

7.5.2 Product Strategy

Doole and Lowe (2004) point out that the product is a feature or value, which is presented to a marketplace for attention and patronage (Doole & Lowe, 2004). Product strategy is considered to be the mother of all marketing communication strategies since is the value or feature that is offered to the market for sale. Institutions like banks should get the product strategy right. Keller (2008), in agreement with this view, stated that an organization's entire planning efforts start with the selection of products to offer its intended market. He argues that product planning or strategy must work to make the other elements like pricing structures, selection of marketing channels, promotional plans which are all dependent on the product strategy works successfully to gain a competitive edge for a company.

RCBs are to be very certain of the product's features and the demands of the market to be able to strategically come out with a good product strategy that will take the product to the target market. Consumers of a target market always have certain needs and want that a product is expected to satisfy, and a marketer in formulating a marketing communication strategy should identify these needs and wants to meet these expectations. According to Kotler et al. (2008), the product strategy becomes a function and adequate when the need and expectations of consumers are identified and met.

By this, Keller (2008) observed that a conceptual framework will be made available and that this structure is potentially helpful in evaluating rival offerings, identifying the needs and wants that are not met but it is required of a target market, and craftily developing or designing new products or services. To buttress his point, Doole and Lowe (2008) say the product strategy should not be a standalone plan but rather it should accommodate and feature prominently with other elements like promotion, price, and place.

7.5.3 Channel Strategy

How customers of these banks could be reached is very essential to the success of the marketing communication efforts. The channel strategy aims to reach the customers easily and freely and this calls for the development of an effective channel strategy. The channel strategy that is very essential in the marketing communication strategy should at all costs be planned with the customer in the picture. All focus must be on the customer, his availability and location, and ultimately his satisfaction. It is there and then that the institutions can say they have been able to develop an effective channel strategy (Govoni, 2004).

According to Ejombonteh & Vovobu (2012), a distribution channel dependably incorporates the producer, consumer, and agents; such as wholesalers, retailers, operators, and vendors. He recognized the imperative parts played by the middle people or agents in encouraging the exchange function.

It is important to motivate the intermediaries and in this regard, the sales force is known in banking as mobile bankers or field tellers and relationship officers to perform the services required of them, thus convincing the client to patronize the products and services on offer by the bank.

Govoni (2004) revealed that marketing managers of intuitions like banks and others should psyche themselves and come to terms that there is no one best channel for all products. Such things as the best communication channel exist only in illusion. What managers of these banks should focus on is looking for the best ways to reach customers of each product separately according to the need and expectations of the customers. He stressed the best procedure is an analysis of the market in which the firm operates, the kind and type of customers targeted, the features of the product, and the business itself should be of prime concern to deduce the ultimate and prime marketing channel strategy that will bring results and achieve competitive advantage. Keller (2008) and Kotler et al. (2008) concur determinedly that there is in no way like the best marketing communications channel for all items.

7.6 An Empirical Study of Perceptions of Marketing Communications

Many observers hold different viewpoints about marketing communications and their importance. Some have said some organizations can do without marketing communications while many studies have also proved the efficacy of marketing communications on a firm's performance.

In a study done by Abubakar in 2014, in Nigeria, using regression analysis and T-test, in assessing the impact of marketing communications on the performance of banks, using data from both primary and secondary sources, and selecting two of the components of marketing communications tool for the investigations found that marketing communication was crucial for banks since it has a positive relationship with bank performance. The study again recorded that bank customers perceive marketing communications as very helpful in sending communications about their brands.

On their part, Ghouri et al. (2010) in their study that assessed the determinants of customer-switching behavior in the private banking sector of Pakistan, collecting data from 302 respondents, found that effective marketing communication methods like promotions and advertising contributes enormously in achieving excellence in business activities and enhances the competitiveness of their marketing share.

Nwankwo (2013) using a proxy of return on profits in assessing the effects of advertising on Nigerian banks found that the usage of marketing communications (mc) and for his case advertising is of great importance. The study revealed that banks have acknowledged that the level of competition among the banks has increased as a result of advertising.

Acheampong (2014) explored the effects of marketing communications on church growth in Ghana using the mixed method approach and solicited responses from 400 respondents. SPSS was used to analyze the data collected. She found that there was no significant relationship between public relations and advertising on church growth. However, the study revealed that there was a much significant impact of MC tools like personal selling, direct marketing, sales promotions on church growth.

It can be argued from available studies that the central role of the marketing mix variables that offer an effective use of personnel can act as the linchpin, effectively forging together the elements of product, price, place, and promotion. More efficient and effective usage of the various marketing mix elements can help the business develop a competitive advantage. Kotler (2005) suggest marketing mix comprises the product, price, place, and promotion. However, they also suggest a very important addition or element, 'people', serves to connect the other elements of product, price, place, and promotion.

7.7 Methodology

7.7.1 The Philosophical Position of This Research

Admittedly, as explained by Benbasat et al. (1987) and Kaplan and Duchon (1988) as cited by Mensah (2015), no single research methodology or philosophy can be said to be intrinsically better than the other. A combination of research methods will go a long way to improve the quality of the research. To this end, the study is positioned between the two strands, the truth of marketing communications methods, as practiced by the RCBs in Ghana, and the realities associated with the RCBs' marketing strategy in Ghana. The implementation of marketing communications methods has been contextualized to reflect the picture in the Ghanaian rural banking industry. As a result, this study is set to approach the reality of marketing communications methods and its impact on creating a sustainable competition, as much as an advantage for the RCBs in Ghana, as much as possible, with a combination of the methods of natural science and the tools for interpretive approach. In this regard, the researcher isolated himself from any personal or social biases, which would affect the substantive reality. This position flows from the consistent ontological position taken in the preceding section.

7.7.2 Study Population

The population for the study was all registered Rural and Community Banks in Ghana which according to the Bank of Ghana (2020) stood at 140 as of April 2016. Within the selected RCBs, Managers in charge of marketing communication and other stakeholders including employees and customers was the unit of analysis.

A multi-stage sampling technique was used in selecting the final 561 samples for the study. The quota sampling technique was used in the first stage to select a representative sample of RCB based on the number of registered RCBs in each region. The simple random sampling technique was used in the second stage to select the representative RCBs from each of the ten regions.

Finally, the purposive sampling and the simple random sampling techniques were used to select the managers of marketing communications as well as employees and clients from each of the selected RCBs from the 10 regions, respectively, in the third stage.

7.7.3 The Design Adopted for This Research

As much as the study admits to a large volume of theories in the area of marketing communications (with some of them discussed in the literature under the theories and concepts of marketing communications discussed earlier in the literature review section), the study also seeks to test these theories in the context of Ghana and perhaps generally contextually fitted sets of theories that can appropriately be used locally.

7.7.4 Cross-Sectional Survey Design

A cross-sectional survey of various identifiable stakeholders, which included, management staff of the rural and community banks, officers, and customers of the selected RCBs was carried out basically to solicit opinions and responses from the various stakeholders to evaluate the opinions and perceptions of marketing communications methods as practiced by the RCBs in Ghana. Additionally, it was also to allow the researcher to conduct some form of triangulation for the data collected.

Based on the philosophical orientation of this study, coupled with the nature of questions that the study intended to find answers to, a mixture of exploratory, survey, and cross-sectional designs was deemed most appropriate for the study. This flows from and is in line with the mixed-method approach of concurrent transformative design.

7.7.5 Simple Random Sampling Technique

The simple random sampling technique was used to select the required RCBs from each of the 10 selected regions as estimated using the quota representative. It was again used to select the stakeholders (employees and clients) from each of the selected RCBs from the ten regions of Ghana (Table 7.1).

7.8 Results and Discussions

7.8.1 Socio-Economic Characteristics of Respondents

This section presents the socio-economic characteristics of the respondents employed in the study (both clients and staff of RCBs). Primarily, it presents items such as gender, age, marital status, educational background, type of business of clients, number of years of engaging in such business by clients. Also, the rank of staff and their respective number of years they have been working with their respective RCBs are presented under this section.

Table 7.1 Regional sample size for RCBs

Region	Number of RCBs	% (to the nearest whole number)	Actual sample for the study	Code
Ashanti	25	18	9	AR1-AR9
Upper East	5	4	2	UER1-UER2
Central	20	14	7	CR1-CR7
Northern	7	5	3	NR1-NR3
Eastern	23	16	8	ER1-ER8
Greater Accra	7	5	3	GAR1-GAR3
Brong Ahafo	22	16	8	BAR1-BAR8
Western	14	10	5	WR1-WR5
Upper West	4	3	1	UWR1
Volta	13	9	5	VR1-VR5
Total	140	100	51	

Source Author's construct 2019

7.8.2 Socio-Economic Characteristics of Clients of RCBs in Ghana

The Table 7.2 depicts the socio-economic characteristics of the clients of various RCBs across Ghana that were sampled for the study. The majority (about 57%) of the clients of RCBs were males with their female counterparts recording about 43%. It can, therefore, be concluded that males predominantly conduct services with RCBs in Ghana compared with females. Also, the majority of the clients employed in the study fall within the age category of 20–40 years followed by 41–60 years (about 25%). Only just a few about 2 and 1% of the clients fall within the age categories of below 20 years and above 60 years, respectively. It, therefore, is inferred that the clientele based on RCBs in Ghana are between 41 and 60 years of age making them all eligible to have an account and also making buying decisions on their own since they are adults and of reasonable minds.

Again, the majority, which is about 56% of the clients, are married with about 37% of them being single. Only just about 6 and 1% of the clients employed in the study are either divorced or separated and

Table 7.2 Socio-economic characteristics of clients of RCBs in Ghana

Variable	Category	Frequency ($n = 255$)	Percentage
Gender	Male	146	57.3
	Female	109	42.7
Age (in years)	Below 20	5	2.0
	20–40	183	71.8
	41–60	64	25.0
	Above 60	3	1.2
Marital status	Single	93	36.5
	Married	143	56.0
	Divorced/separated	16	6.3
	Widowed	3	1.2
Educational background	None	13	5.0
	JHS	45	17.6
	SHS	60	23.5
	Diploma/HND	62	24.5
	Bachelor's degree	64	25.1
	Master's degree	11	4.3
Type of business	Trading/commerce	104	40.8
	Agriculture	41	16.0
	Transportation	16	6.3
	Cottage industry	19	7.5
	Civil/public service	57	22.4
	Others	18	7.0
Number of years in business	Below 5	79	31.0
	5–10	124	48.5
	11–15	40	15.7
	16–20	6	2.4
	Above 20	6	2.4

Source Field survey (2019)

widowed, respectively. Thus it can be concluded that married people normally conduct business with RCBs across Ghana. Concerning educational background, it can be seen from the Table 7.3 that there is a somewhat even distribution of educational achievement among the clients of RCBs. Specifically, about 25 and 24% of each of the clients had attained formal education up to the bachelor's, diploma/HND, and SHS, respectively. A few (5%) had no form of formal education, with only 4% attaining formal education, up to the master's level. The result is not surprising that the percentage of clients that have no form of

Table 7.3 Perceived performance rating of RCBs by clients per communication received by them

Rating	Frequency	Percentage
Poor	4	1.6
Fairly poor	57	22.4
Fair-good	17	6.7
Good	108	42.4
Very Good	69	27.1
Total	255	100

Source Field survey (2019)

formal education is quite low due to the nature of conducting business with the formal banking sector. Those with little or no formal education normally prefer and feel comfortable conducting bank-related business with informal financial services.

Most of the clients of RCBs employed in the study are engaged in trading and commerce-related business (about 41%) with about 22 and 16% of them engaged in civil/public service and agriculture, respectively. Also, about 8 and 6% are involved in the cottage industry and transportation business while others (about 7%) are engaged in businesses such as hospitality, publishing, and banking business. Most of the clients (about 49%) have been in their business between 5 and 10 years followed by 31% and about 16% being in business for below 5 years and between 11 and 15 years, respectively. However, the clients employed in the study averagely have been with their respective businesses for about 8 years which is a true reflection of the modal years in business. Additionally, 41% of them have been traders is a true reflection of the clients that asses RCB products, which are designed mostly to suit customers in that category.

However, the number of years the clients have been conducting business with their respective RCBs may influence their perceived performance rating. Clients who have been conducting business with their RCBs are more credible in terms of rating the performance of their RCBs because of the long-term relationship they have with them. The study, therefore, sought to find out if there exists some kind of relationship

Table 7.4 Relationship between years of business with RCB and perceived performance rating

Years with RCB	Performance rating				
	Poor	Fairly poor	Fairly good	Good	Very good
Below 5	2	1	14	70	37
5–10	2	35	3	37	31
11–15	0	11	0	1	1
16–20	0	6	0	1	0
Above 20	0	4	0	0	0
$Chi^2 = 108.92$					
Asymp.Sig = 0.000					

Source Field survey (2019)

between the number of years the clients have been in a working relationship with their respective RCBs and their performance rating. It can be seen from Table 7.4 that, those who have just been in business with their respective RCBs (below 5 years and between 5 and 10 years) rated their performance to be fairly good, good, or very good whiles only a few who have been conducting business with their respective RCBs between 11 and 15 years rated the performance of their RCBs good and very good with the rest rating the performance of their RCBs to be fairly poor. The Chi-square value of 108.92 that is significant at 1% indicates the existence of a relationship between the working years of clients with their RCBs and the perceived performance. It can thus be inferred that those who have a long-term relationship with RCBs perceived them not to be performing to their expectation based on their long relationships with them. It is, therefore, recommended that the RCBs conduct a customer satisfaction survey to ascertain what their clients require of them to be able to achieve a sustainable relationship with them as echoed by Hooley (2008) in their work titled, marketing strategy and competitive positioning, which also affirms that to position a product effectively, customer concerns and aspirations should be factored.

7.8.3 Perception of RCBs on Marketing Communication Mix in Ghana

An individual or firm will only expend resources on an activity if and only if he/she or the firm has a positive perception of the relevance and expected returns on that activity. Thus, RCBs in Ghana will only engage in marketing communication based on the perceived or experienced benefits that can be derived from it. The study, therefore, sought to ascertain the perception of staff of RCBs across Ghana on marketing communication mix using 12 perception statements ranked on a five-point Likert scale ranging from 1 to -1 (where 1 = strongly agree and -1 = strongly disagree). The staff of RCBs sampled for the study across the country strongly agree that the diversity in and the growing population has made the communication of products and services a necessity, competition in the banking industry has made marketing communication imperative in the policy framework of the bank, relationship with customers is of great importance to the bank, marketing communication increases the quality and quantity of products and services offered by the bank, marketing communication can promote the public image of the bank within its operational areas, marketing communication is very important to the bank in sustaining competitive advantage and it forms an integral part of the policies of the bank. These assertions go to affirms an earlier work done by Aliata et al. (2012), which also concluded that one of the main strategies currently used to face competition in the marketing of products and service is effective marketing communications. On the other hand, they disagree that unlike other universal banks, RCBs do not need to spend on marketing communications to be competitive with a mean score of -0.48, meaning the return to the investment made in marketing communication does not pay off, RCBs can continue its business without communicating its products and services to customers and the public and the bank can still retain its customers and attract other potential customers with or without marketing communication. However, they agree that marketing communication is very costly to implement by RCBs with a mean score of 0.15 although the agreement was weak. It can, therefore, be implied that RCBs in Ghana generally have a positive perception of the relevance and need for embarking on marketing communications programs. The overall perception index of 0.37 is also a true reflection of the findings. Although the level of agreement is quite low among the staff sampled for the study, it can be inferred that they have a positive perception as per the overall perception index (Table 7.5).

7.8.4 Marketing Communication Mix Used by RCBS in Ghana

This section discusses the most current marketing communication mix used by RCBs in Ghana. For the correctness and useful information for analysis such as the current marketing mix strategy used, the amount spent on the marketing mix strategy yearly, and the performance of the marketing mix strategy adopted by the RCBs it became imperative that the correct people who have this information be interviewed. As such, the marketing manager, the branch manager, or the accountant/finance officers of the various RCBs selected were asked to provide this information. It may be difficult to ascertain the exact figures given preferably the cost incurred on the various marketing mix strategy selected as most of these are not published in documents of the RCBs and also most of the RCBs do not keep proper records of marketing communications budget and initiatives. Hence, the conclusion made in this section may be inconclusive and subject to further validation. Nonetheless, the conclusion is based on the data gathered directly from the field survey.

7.8.5 Perception of Marketing Communication Mix Tools Currently Used by RCBs

From the Table 7.6, the most widely used marketing strategy is advertising (about 88%) followed by personal selling (about 71%) and public relation (about 49%). Other marketing strategies used by RCBs in Ghana include sales promotion and branding each recording about 45% with social media being the least marketing strategy used also recording about 29%. It can thus be concluded, advertising, personal selling, and public relation are the most current marketing mix tools utilized by the

Table 7.5 Perception of RCBs on marketing communications activities

Statements	1	0.5	0	−0.5	−1	Mean score
The diversity in and the growing population has made the communication of products and services a necessity	191	104	9	1	1	0.95
Competition in the banking industry has made marketing communication imperative in the policy framework of the bank	170	109	4	20	3	0.83
Relationship with customers is of great importance to the bank	212	90	4	0	0	1.01
Marketing communication increases the quality and quantity of products and services offered by the bank	171	109	19	7	0	0.87
Unlike other universal banks, RCBs do not need to spend on marketing communication to be competitive	31	46	11	84	134	−0.48
Marketing communication is very costly to implement by RCBs	49	93	71	69	24	0.15
The return to the investment made in marketing communication does not pay off	34	35	15	123	99	−0.43
Marketing communication can promote the public image of the bank within its operational areas	156	123	16	11	0	0.83

(continued)

Table 7.5 (continued)

Statements	1	0.5	0	−0.5	−1	Mean score
With or without marketing communication, the bank can still retain its customers and attract other potential customers	33	60	33	79	101	−0.30
Marketing communication is very important to the bank in sustaining competitive advantage	163	122	13	5	3	0.86
Marketing communication forms an integral part of the policies of the bank	101	151	48	5	1	0.68
The bank can continue its business without communicating its products and services to customers and the public	19	56	23	79	129	−0.48
Perception Index					0.37	

1 = Strongly agree 0.5 = Agree 0 = Indifferent −0.5 = Disagree and −1 = Strongly Disagree
Source Field survey

Table 7.6 Marketing mix strategy currently used by RCBs in Ghana by staff perspective

Marketing strategy	Frequency ($n = 51$)	Percentage
Advertising	45	88.2
Personal selling	36	70.6
Sales promotion	23	45.1
Public relation	25	49.0
Branding	23	45.1
Social media	15	29.4

Source Field survey (2019)

RCBs although others such as sales promotion, branding, and social media are seldom in use. These findings go a long way, however, to affirm largely (Erdoğan, 2014) observation that many observers and writers attribute marketing communications to advertising because it is the most visible of all the other elements.

7.8.6 Perception of RCBs on Marketing Communication Mix in Ghana

An individual or firm will only expend resources on an activity if and only if he/she or the firm has a positive perception of the relevance and expected returns on that activity. Thus, RCBs in Ghana will only engage in marketing communication based on the perceived or experienced benefits that can be derived from it. The study, therefore, sought to ascertain the perception of staff of RCBs across Ghana on marketing communication mix using 12 perception statements ranked on a five-point Likert scale ranging from 1 to −1 (where 1 = strongly agree and −1 = strongly disagree). The staff of RCBs sampled for the study across the country strongly agree that the diversity in and the growing population has made the communication of products and services a necessity, competition in the banking industry has made marketing communication imperative in the policy framework of the bank, relationship with customers is of great importance to the bank, marketing communication increases the quality and quantity of products and services offered by the bank, marketing communication can promote the public image of the bank within its operational areas, marketing communication is very important to the bank in sustaining competitive advantage and it forms an integral part of the policies of the bank.

These assertions go to affirm an earlier work done by Aliata et al. (2012), which also concluded that one of the main strategies currently used to face competition in the marketing of products and services is effective marketing communications. On the other hand, they disagree that unlike other universal banks, RCBs do not need to spend on marketing communications to be competitive with a mean score of −0.48, meaning the return to the investment made in marketing communication does not pay off. RCBs can continue their business without communicating their products and services to customers and the public and the bank can still retain its customers and attract other potential customers with or without marketing communication. However, they agree that marketing communication is very costly to implement by RCBs with a mean score of 0.15 although the agreement was weak. It can, therefore, be implied that RCBs in Ghana generally have a positive perception of the relevance and need for embarking on marketing communications programs.

The overall perception index of 0.37 is also a true reflection of the findings. Although the level of agreement is quite low among the staff sampled for the study, it can be inferred that they have a positive perception as per the overall perception index.

7.8.7 Perception of Clients on Marketing Communication Mix Used by RCBs in Ghana

According to Fill (2013), a particular mix of marketing communication adopted by a firm, in general, is intended to communicate certain information to a targeted audience. This intended purpose is said to have been achieved or not when the targeted people respond to it positively or negatively. This is no different from RCBs trying to communicate their products and services to existing clients and potential ones. This was measured in many ways based on the intended purposes. Some key indicators may be the number of clients, the number of portfolios patronized, amount of profit gained as well as the amount of loans and deposits. Nonetheless, all of these are dependent upon the clientele based. What clients perceive in the marketing communication mix can be measured by what the client makes of the message being put across by an RCB. As such, the perception of clients on the various marketing communication mix adopted by RCBs in communicating to its clients becomes very imperative as it influences whether or not a particular client would continue to conduct business or not with the RCB.

The study, therefore, sought the perception of clients of RCBs sampled across the country using 20 perception statements ranked on a five-point

Likert scale ranging from 1 to −1 (where 1 = strongly agree and −1 = strongly disagree). The clients strongly agree and have a positive perception of the bank has good and neat banking halls and edifices with a measurement of 0.61 and have trust and confidence in their RCBs with a mean score of 0.66. Again, they agree and have a positive perception that they see themselves conducting business with their respective RCBs in the next 5 years to come with a mean score of 0.56, the RCB having effective and efficient human resources and will recommend their RCBs to other family members and friends with a mean score of 0.55.

Also, the clients agree and have a positive perception that their RCB has a good reputation, the bank advertises their products and services, quality customer service, and a good corporate image in their communities. Other statements such as the procedures for loan application and loan processing are encouraging, RCB has good customer relation, choosing this bank over others because the ways it communicates to customers, the loan product design (variety of loan facility, repayment schedule, and interest rate structure) is excellent, the bank has attractive promotional element such as rewarding clients, special gifts, premiums, etc., banks advertising medium is effective and appropriate, the bank engages the public, interacts, and listens to public opinions about them, RCB has effective communication with its clients among others were agreed by the clients as per their positive mean scores recorded. It is worth noting that although the clients agreed that the bank involves clients in their marketing research activities, the level of agreement was very low (0.27) as indicated by their mean score. The overall perception index of 0.50 further suggests that clients of RCBs across the country have a positive perception about the operation of the RCBs in Ghana and their choice of the marketing communication mix. It is, thus, recommended that RCBs involve their clients in their marketing research as indication shows it is a worry to them based on a mean score of 0.27, which is low (Table 7.7).

More specifically, the perception of clients on the performance of their RCBs determines whether they will continue to conduct business with them or not. Thus, the study further sought the idea of clients on the performance of their various RCBs on a five-point scale ranging from poor to very good. Most (about 42%) rated the performance of their

Table 7.7 Perception of clients on marketing communication mix adopted by RCBs

Statements	1	0.5	0	−0.5	−1	Mean score
The loan product design (variety of loan facilities, repayment schedules, and interest rate structures) is excellent	102	79	44	7	23	0.45
The procedures for loan application and loan processing are encouraging	77	108	56	12	1	0.49
The bank involves clients in their marketing research activities	58	86	63	31	17	0.27
The bank has an attractive promotional element such as rewarding clients, special gifts, premiums, etc	82	91	41	31	10	0.40
The bank advertises its products and services	91	106	44	10	4	0.53
The bank advertising medium is effective and appropriate	91	80	44	35	5	0.43
The bank engages the public, interacts, and listens to public opinions about them	90	84	38	33	10	0.41
The bank has good and neat banking halls and edifices	118	92	33	7	5	0.61
This RCB has good corporate image in this community	105	97	30	7	16	0.53
I have trust in this RCB	134	80	33	7	1	0.66
This RCB has good customer relation	86	112	46	4	7	0.52
I have confidence in this RCB	106	102	40	7	0	0.60

(continued)

Table 7.7 (continued)

Statements	1	0.5	0	−0.5	−1	Mean score
This RCB has quality customer services	81	121	46	6	1	0.54
This RCB has attractive products and services	77	109	45	13	11	0.45
This RCB has effective and efficient human resource	92	109	44	9	1	0.55
I see myself still conducting business with this RCB in the 5 years	105	97	41	2	10	0.56
I will recommend this RCB to other family members and friends	94	109	40	8	4	0.55
I will choose this bank over others because of the ways it communicates to customers	80	111	44	14	6	0.48
This RCB has a good reputation in this community	112	92	25	9	17	0.54
This RCB has an effective communication with its clients	69	110	51	11	14	0.41
Perception Index					0.50	

1 = Strongly agree 0.5 = Agree 0 = Indifferent −0.5 = Disagree and −1 = Strongly Disagree
Source Field survey

RCBs to be well followed by about 27% rating the performance of their RCBs to be very good. About 22% rated the performance of their RCBs to be fairly poor. Only about 7 and 2% rated the performance of their RCBs to be fairly good and poor, respectively. It can, thus, be argued by this author that in the minds of the customers of the RCBs, RCBs are generally doing their level best based on the perceived rating by their clients although there is more room for improvement if you compare with the overall banking trend and ratings in Ghana.

7.9 Conclusion and Recommendations

7.9.1 Orientations and Perceptions of the Marketing Communications Mix

The objective of this study was to dig into the orientations and perceptions of the marketing communications mix of the selected RCBs in Ghana. From the findings, it was implied that RCBs operating in an emerging economy like Ghana generally have a positive perception of the relevance and need for embarking on marketing communications programs/activities. The overall perception index of 0.37 is also a true reflection of the findings. Although the level of agreement is quite low among the staff sampled for the study, it can be inferred that they have a positive perception as per the overall perception index.

It is, therefore, recommended that the RCBs periodically conduct a customer satisfaction survey to ascertain what their clients require of them to be able to achieve a sustainable relationship with them.

It can thus be argued by this author that in the minds of the customers of the RCBs, RCBs are generally doing their level best based on the perceived rating by their clients although there is more room for improvement if you compare with the overall banking trend and ratings in Ghana. This is a positive attribute for an emerging economy like Ghana which needs its microenvironment to be active and strong to support its growth.

In practice, managers of these banks should reflect on the results from this study and improve on their marketing communication strategies to improve the overall opinion on the products and services offer to their customers if they are to make significant gains from their marketing communication campaigns in merging marketing like Ghana. It is, therefore, recommended that the RCBs conduct a customer satisfaction survey to ascertain what their clients require of them to be able to achieve a sustainable relationship with them.

The result from this study has added to the position of many scholars who have argued that for firms especially in growing economies like Ghana to be competitive, a robust appreciation of a promotional strategy was always needed. No firm can get its product and service out there by osmosis. The result has affirmed the innovation diffusion theory.

The clients strongly perceive their banks have good and neat banking halls and edifices and have trust and confidence in their RCBs; clients have a positive perception that they see themselves conducting business with their respective RCBs in the next 5 years to come; the RCBs have a good reputation, effective and efficient human resource and will recommend their RCBs to other family members and friends; the bank advertises its products and services and quality customer service and good corporate image in their communities. Other statements such as the procedures for loan application and loan processing are encouraging, RCB has good customer relations, choosing this bank over others because of the ways it communicates to customers, the loan product design (variety of loan facility, repayment schedule, and interest rate structure) were adjudged excellent. The overall perception index of 0.50 suggested that clients of RCBs across the country have a positive perception of the operations of the RCBs and their choice of the marketing communication mix.

7.9.2 Contributions to the Body of Knowledge

This study has carefully highlighted several findings and recommendations that should address the gaps in the literature as correctly pinpointed in the literature review section and also captured in the research objectives of this current study. This study would improve and add to the existing literature on marketing communication practice in emerging markets. This study also tested and affirmed the innovation diffusion theory and the resource-based view theories.

7.9.3 Management Implications

Additionally, the findings will also help the practice of marketing communications in the banking industry of Ghana and smaller firms in an emerging economy as the empirical results could be adopted by several banking institutions in Africa to improve their choices and amend their marketing communication practices to impact clients' selection of their products and services.

Firms in emerging economies embarking on marketing communications can achieve strategic objectives through positive implementation of marketing communications activities and programs, which will increase the trust and confidence levels of their clients and staff alike thus contributing to profitability and sustainability. When smaller firms become profitable and sustainable the economy grows as GDP is influenced positively. The perception of clients on the various marketing communication mix adopted by RCBs in communicating to its clients becomes very imperative as it influences whether or not a particular client would continue to conduct business or not with a Rural and Community Bank.

7.9.4 Proposed MC Model (Conceptual Framework)

This current study proposed this model as a vital framework for marketing communications for RCBs in creating competitive advantage. The framework depicts the various marketing communication methods used by the RCBs in gaining a competitive advantage.

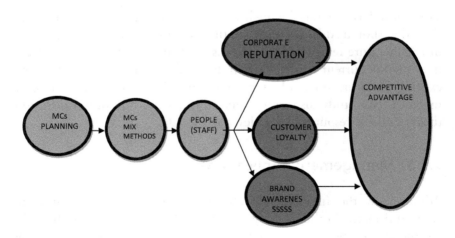

Source Author own contracts (2019)

The above model illustrates the relationship existing between marketing communications and competitive advantages gained by firms. The focus of this model is to provide a road map for the full maximation of marketing communication strategies in gaining a competitive advantage. It expands the AIDA model and other theories by highlighting the crucial role of 'people' in the execution of marketing communication geared toward competitive advantage.

It states that marketing communications when properly planned and controlled will bring into prominence three key ingredients for organizations to achieve competitive advantage. The three key ingredients are corporate image/reputation, customer loyalty, and brand positioning.

7.9.5 Limitations

The major limitation of this study was that it only focused on RCBs in Ghana but did not cover the entire banking sector of Ghana making the findings more focused on marketing communications among RCBs in Ghana.

Additionally, the research intended to include focused group discussions and other designs but this could not happen due to the heavy schedules of staff and clients alike.

References

Abdul-Qadir, A. B., & Kwanbo, M. L. (2012). Corporate governance and financial performance of banks in the post-consolidation era in Nigeria. *International Journal of Social Science and Humanity Studies, 4*(2).

Acheampong, V. (2014). *The effects of marketing communication on church growth in Ghana.* Doctoral dissertation, University of Ghana.

Aliata, V. L., Odondo, A. J., Aila, F. O., Ojera, P. B., Abong'o, B. E., & Odera, O. (2012). Influence of promotional strategies on banks performance. *International Journal of Business, Humanities and Technology, 2*(5), 169–178.

Bank of Ghana. (2020). *Other financial institutions supervision.* https://www.bog.gov.gh/supervision-regulation/ofisd/list-of-ofis/rural-and-community-banks/. Accessed on November 2, 2020.

Bawumia, M., Owusu-Danso, T., & McIntyre, A. (2008). Ghana's reforms transform its financial sector. *IMF Survey Magazine: Countries and Region,* pp. 1–4.

Benbasat, I., Goldstein, D. K., & Mead, M. (1987). The case research strategy in studies of information systems. *MIS quarterly,* 369–386.

Doole, I., & Lowe, R. (2004). *International marketing strategy.* Thomson Publishing.

Doole, I., & Lowe, R. (2008). International marketing strategy: Analysis, development and implementation (5th ed.). *Cengage Learning, Hampshire.*

Egan, J. (2007). *Marketing communications.* Cengage Learning EMEA.

Ejombonteh, E., & Vovobu, P. (2012). Developing a marketing communication strategy: A case study of Taj Mehal Afro, an African and Asian grocery in Finland. *Laurea University of Applied Sciences.*

Evtikhevich, E. (2014). Efficient marketing communications towards Russian customers. Case: Grande Orchidée Fashion Center.

Ferrell, O. C., & Hartline, M. D. (2011). *Marketing management strategies.* South-Western Cengage Learning.

Fill, C. (2013). *Marketing communications: Brands, experience, and participation.* Pearson Education Ltd. 820 s. ISBN 0–273–77054–1 GRAU Stacy Landreth. Marketing for Nonprofit Organizations: Insights and Innovation. 1st ed. Lyceum Books Publishing, 2012, 215 s. ISBN: 978–1935871439.

Ghouri, A. M., Khan, N. U. R., Siddqui, U. A., Shaikh, A., & Alam, I. (2010). Determinants analysis of customer switching behavior in private banking sector of Pakistan.

Govoni, N. A. (2004). *Dictionary of marketing communications.* Sage.

Hooley, D. (2008). *Roman satire.* John Wiley & Sons.

IMF data. (2019). https://www.imf.org/en/Publications/WEO/Issues/2019/03/28/world-economic-outlook-april-2019.

Kaplan, B., & Duchon, D. (1988). Combining qualitative and quantitative methods in information systems research: A case study. *MIS quarterly,* 571–586.

Keller, K. (2008). *Strategic brand management.* Pearson International Limited.

Kotler, P. (2005). The role played by the broadening of marketing movement in the history of marketing thought. *Journal of Public Policy & Marketing, 24*(1), 114–116.

Kotler, P., & Armstrong, G. (2011). *Principles of marketing* (13th Global ed.). Englewood Cliffs: PrenticeHall.

Kotler, P., Armstrong, G., Wong, V., & Saunders, J. (2008). *Principles of marketing*. Pearson International Limited.

Kotler, P., & Keller, K. L. (2012). *Marketing management* (13th Pearson International ed.). Englewood Cliffs: Prentice Hall.

Lee, H., & Jain, D. (2009). Dubai's brand assessment success and failure in brand management–Part 1. *Place Branding and Public Diplomacy, 5*(3), 234–246.

Mangold, W. G., & Faulds, D. J. (2009). Social media: The new hybrid element of the promotion mix. *Business horizons, 52*(4), 357–365.

Meidan, A. (1996). *Marketing financial services*. Hampshire and London: Macmillan Press Ltd.

Nwankwo, S. (2013). *Cross cultural marketing*. London: Thomson Learning Company.

Petek, N. (2015). *Impact of new marketing communication tools on brand equity*.

Sarpong, L., & Tandoh, I. (2015). The role of strategy in a competitive business environment: A case study of Ecobank Ghana limited. *European Journal of Management and Business Economics, 7*(11), 176–196.

Sivesan, S. (2013). Impact of celebrity endorsement on brand equity in cosmetic product. *International Journal of Advanced Research in Management and Social Sciences, 2*(4), 1–11.

Smallwood, E. E. (2018). *Advertising impression measurement: An evaluation of cross-platform advertising delivery* (Doctoral dissertation, Regent University).

Stafford, T., & Grimes, A. (2012). Memory enhances the mere exposure effect. *Psychology & Marketing, 29*(12), 995–1003.

Tandoh, I. (2015). The impact of brand awareness on customer loyalty: A case study of Sinapi Aba savings and loans Ghana limited.

Uppal, R. K. (2010, November). Marketing of bank products: Emerging challenges and new strategies. *JM International Journal of Management Research*, 35–42. Retrieved December 5, 2014, from http://www.jmijitm.com/papers/130082034035_42.pdf.

Woo, J., Ahn, J., Lee, J., & Koo, Y. (2015). Media channels and consumer purchasing decisions. *Industrial Management and Data Systems*.

8

Exploring Drivers of Performance in Advertising Firms in Ghana: A Perspective of Attribution Theory

Henry Boateng, Ibn Kailan Abdul-Hamid, John Paul B. Kosiba, and Robert E. Hinson

8.1 Introduction

Organisational performance has been studied different using a different theoretical approach. For example, some studies have used and have tried to understand organisational performance using theories such as the dynamic capability theory (Teece et al., 1997), resource-based theory (Helfat & Peteraf, 2003). In this study, we explore the factors

H. Boateng (✉)
D'Youville College, Institutional Research and Assessment Support, Buffalo, NY, USA
e-mail: boatengh@dyc.edu

I. K. Abdul-Hamid · J. P. B. Kosiba
University of Professional Studies, Accra, Ghana

R. E. Hinson
University of Ghana, University of Ghana Business School, Accra, Ghana
e-mail: rhinson@ug.edu.gh

© The Author(s), under exclusive license to Springer Nature Switzerland AG 2022
T. Anning-Dorson et al. (eds.), *Marketing Communications in Emerging Economies, Volume II*, Palgrave Studies of Marketing in Emerging Economies, https://doi.org/10.1007/978-3-030-81337-6_8

contributing to the performance of advertising agencies in emerging economies like Ghana. Advertising is of particular interest compared with other forms of marketing communications and has attracted huge expenditure by firms (Buil et al., 2013). The advertising industry in emerging markets is of increasing importance (Zarantonello et al., 2013). Global advertising spending after the world financial crisis has seen an increase in the Asia Pacific, the Middle East/Africa, and Latin America. It is fascinating to see advertising budgets in the Middle East/Africa grow by 3.9% (Nielsen, 2013). Truong et al. (2010) also posit that, notwithstanding the effect of the global economic downturn on advertising budget, there is the likelihood advertising expenditure will continue to increase.

In Ghana, the advertising industry has seen tremendous growth in the last two decades with the arrival of several new multinational agencies like Innova DDB and TBWA to name a few. This growth in the industry got the attention of the International Advertising Association (IAA) to organise a 2-day Advertising conference, from 27 to 28 April 2015 at the Movenpick Ambassador Hotel Ghana and had the theme "Africa Rising—the New Consumer Generation" (International Advertising Association, 2015). Many industry watchers described this Africa Rising conference as the coming of age of the advertising industry in Ghana since it was the first time the International Advertising Association (IAA) had brought any of their international conferences to Ghana. Using the attribution theory, we seek to ascertain the factors that drive performance in advertising agencies in Ghana.

8.2 Developments in the Advertising Sector in Ghana

Advertising practice in Ghana has come a long way going through significant transformations and now has been recognised as one of the most vibrant on the African continent. Currently, the membership of the advertising agencies in Ghana of the International Advertising Association (IAA) has been lauded (International Advertising Association, 2015). There are now several local and international advertising agencies operating in Ghana. Notably, local advertising agencies include Adlines Consult, Telemedia Communications, Yetron, Lando Services, Digicast, Said Publicity, Display Design Publicity, Scanart, and Tropicana Advertising Limited. International advertising agencies on the other hand, which has gained prominence in the Ghanaian advertising industry, are Loewe Lintas, Adams JWT, Ogilvy Ghana, INNOVA DDB Ghana, TBWA Markcom, Dentsu, just to mention a few. Alliance Media and DDP Outdoor are probably the country's premier outdoor advertising agencies, owing to several sites across the country. The advertising industry has also seen many partnerships among advertising agencies in Ghana. Scangroup and Ogilvy announced the launch of two advertising firms, Scanad Ghana Limited and Ogilvy Ghana Limited. In 2012, there was a merger of two advertising companies in Ghana—Adspace and Origin8 (Commonwealth Network, 2016).

These agencies could be said to have varying levels of creative sophistication, account management skills and industry specialisations. Apart from traditional advertising solutions, advertising agencies in Ghana are providing a range of marketing services. A well-established advertising agency, for instance, has the following services: brand and marketing consulting, strategic planning, PR services, event organisation, market research, advertising and sales promotion, print and broadcast productions, media consulting and buying, and digital marketing solution. Concerning marketing communication services advertising agencies have a raft of services including insight development and creative strategy, full through-the-line creative conceptualisation and implementation (TV, radio, outdoor, print, below-the-line, retail, B2B and promotions), field marketing and market research, media strategy, planning and buying, event management, PR; services that typify a global ad agency (TBWA in Africa, 2016).

The Advertising Association of Ghana (AAG) is the industry and professional body for Ghana's booming advertising and marketing communication business (Commonwealth Network, 2016). The AAG is a non-profit making organisation and is funded by subscriptions of members. Over the years, AAG has developed into a formidable professional organisation, which has become the primary engagement platform for advertising agencies in Ghana. AAG is the body responsible for liaising with a multiplicity of public and private sector agencies to ensure sanity in Ghana's advertising sector. Notable institutions the AAG works with include: Ghana Advertisers Board that helps to understand advertising client issues and the International Advertising Association (IAA) to understand international best practices and strives to make this information available to agencies operating in Ghana. The AAG has categorised advertising agencies under the following: creative advertising agencies, outdoor advertising agencies, and media buying agency.

The regulation of the advertising industry, however, had been a significant issue the industry has been facing. The lack of regulation has led to unprofessional advertising practices. Currently, the AAG is negotiating for the passage of Advertising Authority Bill in Ghana (look for reference). At the International Advertising Association Leadership Conference in Accra, April 2015, the President of Ghana—John Dramani Mahama assured advertisers that the Advertising Standards Authority Bill would soon be passed to ensure better regulation of the industry (Myjoyonline.com, 2015). The passage of the Advertising Authority Bill will lead to the establishment of an Advertising Standard Authority that will regulate the advertising sector by law and flush out unprofessional advertising practitioners. The only available regulation in controlling the level of professionalism in the advertising industry is the AAG's code of ethics, which addresses the use of fear appeals, media buying, and conditions regarding alcohol advertising, cigarette advertising, and advertising to children (www.aag.com.gh). Also, the AAG discourages the use of superstition, depiction of violence, adverts that promote sexual virility, placement of adverts for competing products side by side, and request that all adverts are having the AAG approve sexual sensitivities.

The advertising industry also suffers from challenges relating to reform policies of location restraints and government control of outdoor structures (Appiah-Gyimah et al., 2011). The result of these regulatory challenges has led to disagreements between the AAG and Metropolitan,

Municipal, and Districts Assemblies. The primary issue of contention is centred on the fee apportionment issues and sometimes the quality of the outdoor structures. The citing of advertising billboards has always been criticised as advertisers are blamed for violating the law. Many revenue streams in the advertising industry have developed due to the increasing demand for advertising services by business entities. The advertising industry in Ghana recorded a growth in revenue of about 25% in 2013, bringing the value of the advertising sector in Ghana to about 50 million dollars (Commonwealth Network, 2016). This increase in revenue for advertising firms could probably be attributed to economic and media liberalisation (Oxford Business Group, 2012). Advertising spending alone in 2011 amounted to 177.4 million dollars with the communications industry accounting for about 17% of advertising expenditure (Oxford Business Group, 2012). Other high spending industries accounting for the increase in advertising spending are corporate and multi-brand advertising (12%), food and beverage (12%), entertainment (11%), pharmaceutical (10%), and household goods (9%) (Oxford Business Group, 2012).

8.3 Theoretical Background: Attribution Theory

The central theme of the attribution theory is to understand the antecedence and implications of occurrences. The theory was developed to understand the causes of individuals' success and failures. The attribution theory has been studied from three perspectives; causal judgement, social inferences, and prediction and outcome of behaviour (Ross, 1977). This study is aligned with the causal judgement, which seeks to understand the possible causes of events (Heider, 1958). According to Miles (2012), there are three elements of causal judgements; locus, stability, and controllability. Locus refers to the source of the behaviour, whether it is internal or external. Stability concerns with whether the outcome or behaviour is static or dynamic. Controllability refers to the degree of control an individual has over his or her behaviour. Individuals consciously or unconsciously ask "why" when they identify changes in behaviour (Wong & Weiner, 1981). Heider (1958) notes that answers to the "why" emerge from two sources; internal and external. Internal attributions of an individual's success or failure, for example, include ability, personality, attitude. In comparison, external attribution indicates external elements that contribute to the success or failure of an individual. The attribution theory has been used to study topics such as individuals' performance, organisational performance (Jeong, 2009), corporate reputation (Sjovall & Talk, 2004). Following these, we propose that the performance of advertising agencies may be as a result of some internal and external factors. Specifically, we suggest that the performance of advertising agencies in emerging economies like Ghana is result of factors that are related to technological advancement, managerial process and human resource practices of the firms.

8.4 Conceptual Framework and Research Propositions

In line with the attribution theory, we conceptualise attribution from three perspectives; people, process, and technology. That is, we propose that the drivers of performance of advertising agencies in emerging economies can be understood from the viewpoint of technological advancement, managerial process and human resource practices of the firms since some studies have shown people, process, and technology have a positive impact on business operations (see, for example, Cockburn & Highsmith, 2001). Although these elements can individually account for the performance of the advertising agencies, their integration is likely to provide a better outcome.

8.5 Technological Advancement

The use of technology in advertising has led to an increase in digital advertising (Truong et al., 2010). Studies conducted on the impact of technology on advertising had alluded to the fact that technology has helped improve on advertising (Cheng et al., 2009; Kaplan & Haenlein, 2010; Truong et al., 2010). The emergence of the internet has probably led to the takeover of mainstream media due to its high level of accountability, entertainingly interactive, and a targeted medium (Shij & Piron, 2002). Advertising is now undertaking in the form of website advertising, emailing advertising, mobile-phone-based, and short message services advertising (Cheng et al., 2009). Cauberghe and De Pelsmacker (2011) argue that the initiation of new digital technologies has presented advertisers opportunities and threats. Despite television and newspaper leading the global adverting spend of about 21 and 14%, respectively, digital advertising in the form of social media, internet display advertisement, and mobile advertisements is also gaining a considerable share of the global advertising spend (Nielsen, 2015). Truong et al. (2010) posit that the growth in digital advertising correlates with an increase in digital advertising consumption. Kaplan and Haenlein (2010) explain that social media, for instance, has made possible media content to be made publicly available and also helps end-users to create content. A review of studies on the use of social media in advertising revealed that social media is a valuable advertising instrument.

Technology has, therefore, enabled new media to explode, thus augmenting traditional media with non-traditional approaches such as product placement, viral marketing, direct marketing, and virtual community marketing on the web (Drumwright & Murphy, 2009). Tucker (2014) observed that people are more likely to view personal ads leading to a more targeted means of communication. Based on these discussions, it is proposed that:

The growth in digital advertising expenditure is likely to continue despite the pressure on firms to reduce advertising budgets.

Preposition 1 *Technological advancements could be a key driver of advertising firm performance.*

8.6 Managerial Processes

Corporate governance has conventionally been associated with larger companies owing mainly to the separation between ownership and control of the firm (Abor & Adjasi, 2007). Governance and managerial issues in the advertising industry are worth studying considering the ownership mainly multinational advertising firms. The increasing advocacy on the adoption of appropriate governance structure in institutions is that it enables firms to achieve higher performance (Abor, 2007; Bhagat & Bolton, 2008; Erkens et al., 2012). Corporate governance issues have been around corporate charter provisions, management and board compensations, and board characteristics (Bhagat & Bolton, 2008). The composition of a board is very crucial in ensuring that board members can impact organisational outcomes (Johnson et al., 2012). Board independence had become one of the essential requirements of listing on major stock exchange market in the world (Bhagat & Bolton, 2008). Studies on the impact of the board on organisational performance had looked mostly at board size and independence. Still, demography, human capital, and social capital of board members are also crucial in improving organisational performance (Johnson et al., 2012). It is not surprising to see firms in developing countries such as Ghana now embracing the concept of corporate governance, because of its ability to impact positively on sustainable growth (Abor, 2007).

The adoption and use of acceptable corporate governance practices are necessary as it helps eliminate agency problems resulting from misaligned interest between shareholders and managers (Chen et al., 2012). Advertising agencies have traditional departments such as accounting, human resources, and media creative (de Gregorio et al., 2012). Also, Moeran (2013) describes typical functional units of an advertising agency to include: a Presidential/CEO office that oversees all operations and business embarked on by the agency and prepares market forecast of annual turnover and profits; general affairs office is in charge of personnel issues; finance office performs activities relating to media busying and keeping financial records, account service; and marketing office ensures that the agency attracts new accounts using advertising, personnel selling, promotions and other marketing activities to improve the revenue generation of the agency; and finally a creative office that handles planning, designing, and finalising the advertising campaign. This, therefore, requires that the various skills and functions must be aligned to the achievement of overall agency objective. The management of the advertising agency is crucial since there can be an intra-organisational conflict, which are incompatibilities or disagreements among functional units of advertising agencies (de Gregorio et al., 2012). The complexity of the management of an advertising agency makes it necessary for the institution of sound management practices.

Preposition 2 *Managerial process affects the performance of advertising firms.*

8.7 Human Resource Practices

There is evidence from strategic management theories that, internal activities and resources or capabilities such as human resources, are potential means of achieving competitive advantage (Buller & McEvoy, 2012). The availability of skilled and creative staff is a common characteristic of successful advertising agencies. Windels et al. (2013) posit that skill is needed to strategise on meeting the expectations of clients and also developing creative ideas. The advertising industry probably has one of the most reported cases of employee's turnover. Hermelin (2009) posit that advertising agencies are faced with a frequent situation where there is poaching of talented personnel from one advertising agency to other, leading to rivalry.

The curriculum development of advertising is a significant issue of discussion in ensuring quality human resources for advertising agencies (Hachtmann, 2012; Windels et al., 2013). This has resulted in a situation where learning on the job and moving between advertising employers become the opportunity for training and career development (Hermelin, 2009). It could be said that the development of an employee in the advertising industry does not depend on a well-structured academic curriculum.

This situation is, however, minimal in multinational companies who have a long period of advertising experience and can bring onboard personnel from other geographical areas where there are advanced curriculum and practical development. The career development of an employee in the advertising industry is also not clear. Management of agencies is not able to determine the positions employees will occupy or what plans the agency has for them in the future. A rise in the status of an employee is, therefore, determined by the ability of an individual or group establishing their advertising agency (Hermelin, 2009).

Preposition 3 *Human resource practices affect the performance of advertising firms.*

8.8 Methodology

The research propositions formulated in this paper focus on deepening our understanding of the current state of advertising practice in Ghana. The propositions were addressed using qualitative research techniques. The use of a qualitative research technique is justified because the study follows a realism paradigm, which is a relevant paradigm for qualitative research in marketing (Healy & Perry, 2000). This approach enabled the researcher to study a phenomenon within its real-life context, especially when the boundaries between a phenomenon and context are not clear and the researcher has little control over the phenomenon and context (Yin, 2009).

The research methodology consisted of personal interviews and panel discussions of 13 adverting agencies operating in Ghana. The respondents selected are senior advertising executives in multinational and local advertising firms in Ghana who have experience and are experts in the advertising industry in Ghana. A purposive sampling technique was adopted considering the positions the respondents occupy in their respective companies. Table 8.1 represents the positions of each partic-

Table 8.1 Respondent characteristics

	Position	Role
Interviews		
Interviewee 1	Chief Executive Officer	All management functions
Interviewee 2	Chief Marketing Officer	All marketing functions
Interviewee 3	Senior Account Director	Client relationship management
Interviewee 4	An Executive of AAG	Administration/legal functions
Panel discussion		
Panel member 1	Chief Executive Officer/An executive of AAG	Operations and Management
Panel member 2	CEO of Multinational Agency	Brand development
Panel member 3	Senior Account Director	Client relationship management
Panel member 4	Communications Director	Brand communication and public relations
Panel member 5	Communications and Media Director	Brand Development
Panel member 6	Executive of AAG	Administration/Legal
Panel member 7	Managing Director	Operations and Management
Panel member 8	Advertising Consultant	Marketing Professor
Panel member 9	Advertising Consultant	Marketing Lecturer

ipant in their respective advertising agencies. Postal letters and emails were sent to participants to be part of a round-table panel discussion on the advertising sector.

In-depth interviews were conducted before panel discussions to obtain convergence of opinions about the management issues of the advertising industry as advocated by Miles and Huberman (1994). The use of this approach also enables the researcher to draw from multiple sources of data (Matanda & Ewing, 2012), ensuring the reliability and validity of the study (Golafshani, 2003).

The final phase of data collection was done through a panel discussion. The panel discussion provided experts in the advertising industry the opportunity to present information and views to deepen further the positions of those interviewed before the study. This was also done to maximise the validity offered by the two methods (Yin, 2009). The panel discussion lasted for about two hours with each panel member given 5 minutes to comment on each management issue discussed in this paper. The meetings were audio tape-recorded and transcribed for analysis.

The proceedings were recorded and later transcribed. The transcribed data were read several times to ensure the accuracy of the transcription, as suggested by Braun and Clarke (2006). Following the advice of Long and Johnson (2000) to ensure rigour and validity of qualitative study's findings, the participants from whom primary data were collected from were invited to comment on the interview transcription and determine whether the final themes and concepts developed adequately reflect the phenomenon being investigated. Also, the multiple sources of evidence served to strengthen the validity of the study. We analysed the data using the thematic analysis technique. We first read through the transcripts and coded them. Some codes were merged to form the major themes presented in this study.

8.9 Presentation of Findings

The findings of this study show that the factors contributing to the performance of the advertising agencies in Ghana are associated with technological advancement, managerial process and the human practices of the firms.

8.10 Technological Advancement

The participants alluded to the fact that advances in technology have changed the advertising industry in Ghana. Three major sub-themes emerged under technological advancement, and these have been discussed as follows:

8.10.1 Content Creation Technologies

Technological advancements have made the practice of advertising efficiently by reducing content production time and improving the quality of advertising at a cheaper cost. Computerised systems have reduced the overreliance on an artist who uses to draw advertising content manually.

*Nowadays when ads are shot in South Africa, for instance, they are sending it to us through a transfer file and not on the DVD anymore. You forward it through the mail to media agency. Technology has improved the level of creativity since now you can do illustrations, so whatever idea that you need to put across, technology within the shortest possible time you can do that, reducing the turnaround time, enhancing the quality of the work and increasing the quantity of work that you can do within the shortest possible time (**Panel member 7**).*

8.10.2 Interactive Technologies

The advent of social media has led to the creation of new advertising platforms available for advertisers to take advantage of. Social media has led to a situation where advertisements can be made available on different platforms such as Facebook, YouTube, What's App, Instagram. There is, therefore, the creation of new opportunities for advertisers to take advantage of such as being able to make advertising campaigns readily available, and the ability of targets to also create unique content. There is no doubt that social media is augmenting traditional media to reach the target audience effectively.

*We know what social media has done, the virtues it taught us; speed to market and all. Advertising agencies today are faced with competition that is real, and there is a need to take advantage of new media. An advertising agency can develop a social media asset to reach out to Ghanaians even in the diaspora (**Panel member 8**).*

Technology has made advertising more creative, interactive, and more targeted audience. The advances in technology have increased the speed of advertising campaigns, improved the communication advertising agencies have with their clients, improved ways of managing administrative duties.

*Technology is critical to every business operation....... I will give you a classic example. Back in the '70s, '80s if you see a billboard advertising a particular product, what you see is a drawing of people, You will see people being drawn what it means is that to produce such outdoor signage, an artist will have to draw the images to depict what communication the advertiser wants to put out there. We are now able to put a billboard within a matter of 24 hours (**Panel member 1**).*

8.10.3 Improved and Increased Media Outlets

The proliferation of television, radio, online, and newspaper communication channels in Ghana has to some extent resolved the burden of advertisers who had to wait for an extended period to get approval from media houses to run adverts. The availability of media channels to run adverts reduces waiting time and has resulted in non-vetting of adverts to meets the professional standard.

*Back in the day, we had one TV station and we had the good fortune for being able to vet adverts. That channel could say stop press if you had an advert that could not pass an absolute rigour or specific ethical standards. Today there is a multiplicity of TV and Radio Stations so before a media house decides to vet and to convene his team to vet the advert, the advert has aired on another station five or six times already (**Panel member 1**).*

8.11 Managerial Process

Managerial process factors that were found in contributing to the growth of the adverting industry are the size and capabilities of the board of management and external control.

8.11.1 Size and Capabilities of the Board of Management

One of the dominant issues that were identified by respondents is about how the size and quality of their board affect their performance. It would be fair to argue that the size and quality of boards of advertising firms affect the performance of the same.

*Indeed we have a board, we have a local board, and we have an African board as well. The local board is very much part and parcel of what we do and are actively involved in how we operate the business my chairman is somebody I go to for counselling and advice (**Interviewee 2**).*

The management of most advertising firms in Ghana is very crucial as there is the need to have the right expertise and the people with industry knowledge and experience to lead the team.

*Our board is chaired by a Marketing Professor who has two-decade experience in the advertising industry. We make sure all members of our management team have the requisite managerial capabilities to ensure our business grow (**Panel member 7**).*

8.11.2 External Control of Advertising Agencies

There is also the control of some advertising agencies by their parent brands to ensure they operate to standards. This management practice is essential in ensuring that service delivery is not compromised and also leading to the financial sustainability of their businesses.

*You always have a meeting with international representatives of the advertising agency you represent. Someone can be in Tokyo and checking how much money you are making daily (**Panel member 2**).*

The deliberations on the management of advertising agencies also revealed how some advertising agencies have form partnership to execute key advertising projects. The combination of resources by advertising agencies enables them to provide efficient services to clients.

*Although we compete, a lot of the industry players have a formal and informal relationship among ourselves. Usually, we come together through a contractual agreement to provide services to clients. I think it is better to get help from other agencies which have the capabilities than deciding to do it alone and not satisfying the client (**Panel member 8**).*

8.12 Human Resource Practices

The outcome of the analysis of this study shows that human resource practices such as qualified personnel, career development, and remuneration are associated with the growth of the advertising industry in Ghana. The findings here instead show the current human resource practices in the advertising agencies are hampering the development of the firms.

8.12.1 Qualified Personnel

All participants highlighted the importance of qualified human resource in improving the level of professionalism.

*It is quite challenging for the advertising industry itself doesn't have a training field apart from on-the-job training. There currently no collaboration between industry and academia in training advertising workforce. There must be an atmosphere where the advertising programmes initiated are sustained (**Panel Member 6**).*

Concerning the anticipation of a coming into force of a new advertising bill, participants were of the view that the bill is necessary for resolving the unprofessional conduct of advertising in Ghana.

*What the advertising bill is going to do is to ensure quality and now without an adequately licensed certificate or something like that you cannot operate as an advertising consultant or an advertising agency. This will ensure that we attract quality advertising personnel and also the building of systems to train people. So you come in as a client service associate and you can end up after five to ten years as a client service director which qualifies you as a marketing director in any organisation (**Panel member 3**).*

8.12.2 Career Development

We noted from the analysis that many of the employees in the advertising agencies lack the requisite skills to perform their roles well. Many of the participants shared the view that the advertising agencies hardly offer training to their employees.

*The other issue apart from training is that many Agencies with available funds do not invest in human resource. It's a widespread phenomenon which might seem to be unfair and you realise that middle to top management are the only ones who have the benefit of the value that the Agency gets (**Panel member 2**).*

Respondents also lamented on the need for educational institutions to introduce advertising as a course of specialisation to train graduates to fit into the skills needs of advertising agencies in Ghana.

A panel member made the following observation about the failure of Ghana's educational system in producing qualified employees in the advertising industry:

*Over the years, tertiary institutions in Ghana had failed to introduce advertising as a programme for students. The University of Ghana, for instance, currently does not run an advertising programme. The only time a student will get the opportunity to be taught. Advertising is when there is a lecture on marketing communications, where students had the opportunity to learn about advertising (**Panel member 9**).*

8.12.3 Remuneration

Human resource challenges have led to a situation where advertising agencies operating in Ghana are offering relatively cheap and mediocre advertisements to clients. The compensation and remunerations paid to advertising agency staff is another critical area of concern affecting human resource quality. A panel member commented that:

*It is a problem, I mean to retain experienced staff, your staff cost keeps increasing. Still, of course, once you measure you institutions' key performance indicators and peg salary increases to staff productivity, then you can maintain your experienced staff and build your advertising agency and help you sustain it (**Panel member 2**).*

8.13 Discussion and Conclusions

The paper sought to understand the factors that contribute to the performance of advertising firms in Ghana. The advertising industry in Ghana has made significant strides in the last decade and a half with the development of the reasonably active sector. The issues discussed have been relatively addressed in the literature. However, the researchers paid little attention to how these factors impact advertising in a developing country context. The industry continues to experience the entrance of multinational agencies (like Dentsu which arrived in 2015), which has helped raise the standards in the industry. Aside from the infiltration of foreign advertising agencies, the industry has witnessed an increase in local advertising agencies as well; which has made competition keener. Technology in the form of new channels of communication has created a more efficient means of targeting audiences. Social media is increasingly being used as a tool in the advertising industry and technology is rapidly transforming the adverting sector, contributing to increasing output efficiency and assisting in the delivery of value to clients as argued by Kaplan and Haenlein (2010).

The study also revealed an issue of inadequate remuneration of ad agencies in respect of the service provided to clients is a thorny issue. The competitiveness of the market has brought about financial challenges faced by advertising agencies (Nanjom, 2002). Advertising agency professionals contend that even though there have been increases in client marketing communications budgetary allocations, most clients are not willing to compensate adequately for services rendered by agencies. Another issue that came up was the issue of transparency on agency–client relationships with disclosing information on the success of advertising campaigns (Nichols, 2013). Advertising agency clients are not willing to share information on revenue generated from specific advertising campaigns in an attempt to avoid paying extra commissions for work done. Similarly, the difficulty in ascertaining the proportion that advertising campaigns contribute to clients' overall marketing revenues makes it difficult to determine the success of these advertising campaigns. The study found that marketing activities by advertising agencies do not take the form of mass media advertising. Agencies rely more on personal selling through pitches, referrals. Multinational agencies leverage their international reputation to appeal to the target market (Hermelin, 2009). Concerning human resource, advertising agencies bemoaned the lack of nuanced, and compelling marketing communications course degrees in Ghanaian tertiary institutions leading to a situation where on the job training is the available option for career development (Hermelin, 2009).

8.13.1 Theoretical Implications

The findings of this study imply that organisational performance can be attributed to internal and external factors. These factors may be associated with technologies, human resource process, and human resource practices. These factors can impact organisational performance in both negative and positive ways. Since these factors are varied and are derived from different sources, it follows that managers and researchers can make an attributional error. Therefore, researchers must explore ways of ensuring accuracy in attribution. This study supports the notion that people, process, and technology drive organisational performance.

8.13.2 Practical Implications

This paper closes out by proposing three recommendations for building more robust advertising agencies in Ghana, and we also offer a brief commentary on the future of the advertising industry in Ghana. First, advertising agencies must invest in well-qualified and strategically oriented account managers to justify any premium charge they are administering to clients. There is a reasonably low understanding of the need to administer premium pricing for advertising agency services in Ghana and, therefore, account managers (who tend to be the primary interface between agencies and the external world). There is, therefore, a considerable need for strategic account managers in Ghana's advertising sector. The strategic account manager will understand the contribution of marketing communications to value creation in the firms he/she serves; ad agency account must look for cost-effective and creative ways of solving client communication problems. He/she joins the client in becoming a steward of the brand(s) he/she handles and never conducts himself in any way that is not in the interest of building the brand(s) he/she manages. The AAG pledged they must work with educational institutions to develop industry-led undergraduate degrees in marketing communications, and this proposed collaboration might be explored in the future.

Second, on-the-job training and rotating work assignments are good ways to improve the skill level of advertising agency personnel in Ghana as well as sponsoring educational opportunities to gain expertise in aspects of technology that may improve the skills of an advertising firm's employees. Global employers in the advertising industry are increasingly interested in hiring students with intercultural community skills and cultural experience. We argue that staff knowledge or expertise in advertising firms affects the performance of the same. The findings also present opportunities for educational institutions to offer training and courses in advertising to improve the capabilities of the personnel in advertising firms in Ghana.

8.13.3 Direction for Future Research

On future outlook, the advertising business in Ghana will still be vibrant full of opportunities, but this will also increase the intensity of competition. Local advertising firms must build on their leadership capacity, marketing, and human resource to stay competitive as more and more multinational advertising agencies would like to establish their agencies in Ghana. Finally, more advertising agencies will position themselves by increasingly outsourcing their non-core activities to third-party service providers.

Future research may focus on investigating these management issues in a more detailed manner for each management issue. For instance, future research might try to establish the effect of CSR on advertising performance providing the opportunity to build testable constructs. The replication of this Ghanaian study in other African countries is necessary considering its enviable reputation in advertising on the African continent. The limitation of this research is that the development of the advertising industry in Ghana still lags behind that of countries in Europe, North America, and Asia, and results may not apply to those countries. It can, however, be interesting to conduct a cross-geographical study to understand advertising practices from different perspectives.

References

Abor, J. (2007). Corporate governance and financing decisions of Ghanaian listed firms. *Corporate Governance: The International Journal of Business in Society, 7*(1), 83–92.

Abor, J., & Adjasi, C. K. (2007). Corporate governance and the small and medium enterprises sector: Theory and implications. *Corporate Governance: The International Journal of Business in Society, 7*(2), 111–122.

Appiah-Gyimah, R., Agyapong, G. K., & Boohene, K. A. (2011). Customer satisfaction in the outdoor advertising industry: A case of alliance media Ghana limited. *International Journal of Marketing Studies, 3*(2), 82.

Bhagat, S., & Bolton, B. (2008). Corporate governance and firm performance. *Journal of Corporate Finance, 14*(3), 257–273.

Braun, V., & Clarke, V. (2006). Using thematic analysis in psychology. *Qualitative Research in Psychology, 3*(2), 77–101.

Buil, I., De Chernatony, L., & Martínez, E. (2013). Examining the role of advertising and sales promotions in brand equity creation. *Journal of Business Research, 66*(1), 115–122.

Buller, P. F., & McEvoy, G. M. (2012). Strategy, human resource management and performance: Sharpening line of sight. *Human Resource Management Review, 22*(1), 43–56.

Cauberghe, V., & Pelsmacker, P. D. (2011). Adoption intentions toward interactive digital television among advertising professionals. *Journal of Interactive Advertising, 11*(2), 45–59.

Chen, C. X., Lu, H., & Sougiannis, T. (2012). The agency problem, corporate governance, and the asymmetrical behavior of selling, general, and administrative costs. *Contemporary Accounting Research, 29*(1), 252–282.

Cheng, J. M. S., Blankson, C., Wang, E. S. T., & Chen, L. S. L. (2009). Consumer attitudes and interactive digital advertising. *International Journal of Advertising, 28*(3), 501–525.

Cockburn, A., & Highsmith, J. (2001). Agile software development, the people factor. *Computer, 34*(11), 131–133.

Commonwealth Network. (2016). *Advertising, marketing, and PR.* http://www.commonwealthofnations.org/sectors-ghana/business/advertising_marketing_and_pr/.

de Gregorio, F., Cheong, Y., & Kim, K. (2012). Intraorganizational conflict within advertising agencies. *Journal of Advertising, 41*(3), 19–34.

Drumwright, M. E., & Murphy, P. E. (2009). The current state of advertising ethics: Industry and academic perspectives. *Journal of Advertising, 38*(1), 83–108.

Erkens, D. H., Hung, M., & Matos, P. (2012). Corporate governance in the 2007–2008 financial crisis: Evidence from financial institutions worldwide. *Journal of Corporate Finance, 18*(2), 389–411.

Golafshani, N. (2003). Understanding reliability and validity in qualitative research. *The Qualitative Report, 8*(4), 597–606.

Hachtmann, F. (2012). The effect of advertising-focused, short-term study abroad programs on students' worldviews. *Journal of Advertising Education, 16*(1), 19.

Healy, M., & Perry, C. (2000). Comprehensive criteria to judge validity and reliability of qualitative research within the realism paradigm. *Qualitative Market Research: An International Journal, 3*(3), 118–126.

Heider, F. (1958). *The psychology of interpersonal relations.* New York: John Wiley & Sons.

Helfat, C. E., & Peteraf, M. A. (2003). The dynamic resource-based view: Capability lifecycles. *Strategic Management Journal, 24*(10), 997–1010.

Hermelin, B. (2009). Producer service firms in globalising cities: The example of advertising firms in Stockholm. *The Service Industries Journal, 29*(4), 457–471.

International Advertising Association. (2015, April 27–28). *Ad Industry convenes in Accra.* http://www.iaaglobal.org/files/IAA%20Afica%20Rising%20Conference%20Press%20Release%2020%20April%2015.pdf. Accessed 20 May 2016.

Jeong, S. H. (2009). Public's response to an oil spill accident: A test of the attribution theory and situational crisis communication theory. *Public Relations Review, 35*(3), 307–309.

Johnson, S. G., Schnatterly, K., & Hill, A. D. (2012). Board composition beyond independence social capital, human capital, and demographics. *Journal of Management, 38*(1), 83–108.

Kaplan, A. M., & Haenlein, M. (2010). Users of the world, unite! The challenges and opportunities of social media. *Business Horizons, 53*(1), 59–68.

Long, T., & Johnson, M. (2000). Rigour, reliability and validity in qualitative research. *Clinical Effectiveness in Nursing, 4*(1), 30–37.

Matanda, T., & Ewing, M. T. (2012). The process of global brand strategy development and regional implementation. *International Journal of Research in Marketing, 29*(1), 5–12.

Miles, J. A. (2012). *Management and organization theory: A Jossey-Bass reader* (Vol. 9). Wiley.

Miles, M. B., & Huberman, A. M. (1994). *Qualitative data analysis* (2nd ed.). Sage.

Moeran, B. (2013). *Folk art potters of Japan: Beyond an anthropology of aesthetics.* Routledge.

Myjoyonline.com. (2015). *Advertising law to be passed soon: Brand Ghana to be restructured—Mahama.* http://www.myjoyonline.com/business/2015/april-29th/advertising-law-to-be-passed-soon-brand-ghana-to-be-restructured-mahama.php. Accessed 20 May 2016.

Nanjom, S. M. U. (2002). *Factors and challenges in advertising agencies broadcast media planning: The case of convenience consumer goods in kenya* (Doctoral dissertation, University of Nairobi).

Nichols, W. (2013). Advertising analytics 2.0. *Harvard Business Review, 91*(3), 60–68.

Nielsen. (2013). *Global ad spend: 1H global ad spend increases 2.8%, led by latin America and Asia Pacific.* http://www.nielsen.com/us/en/insights/news/2013/global-ad-spend-1H-global-ad-spend-increases-2-8-led-by-latin-am.html. Accesses 20 May 2016.

Nielsen. (2015). *Advertising spending increases but more marketers are exercising caution.* http://www.nielsen.com/hk/en/pressroom/2015/advertising_spending_increases_but_more_marketers_are_exercising_caution_in_2015.html. Accesses 20 May 2016.

Oxford Business Group. (2012). *Ghana report: Media and advertising.* Retrieved from: http://www.oxfordbusinessgroup.com/ghana-2012/media-advertising. Accessed 20 May 2016.

Ross, L. D. (1977). The intuitive psychologist and his shortcomings: Distortions in the attribution process. In L. Berkowitz (Ed.), *Advances in experimental social psychology* (Vol. 10, pp. 173–220). Academic Press.

Shij, T. D., & Piron, F. (2002). Advertising agencies and advertisers' perceptions of internet advertising. *International Journal of Advertising, 21*(3), 381–397.

Sjovall, A. M., & Talk, A. C. (2004). From actions to impressions: Cognitive attribution theory and the formation of corporate reputation. *Corporate Reputation Review, 7*(3), 269–281.

TBWA in Africa. (2016). Retrieved from http://www.tbwa-africa.com/our-networks/agencies-by-country/ghana-1/. Accessed 20 May 2016.

Teece, D. J., Pisano, G., & Shuen, A. (1997). Dynamic capabilities and strategic management. *Strategic Management Journal, 18*(7), 509–533.

Truong, Y., McColl, R., & Kitchen, P. (2010). Practitioners' perceptions of advertising strategies for digital media. *International Journal of Advertising, 29*(5), 709–725.

Tucker, C. E. (2014). Social networks, personalized advertising, and privacy controls. *Journal of marketing research, 51*(5), 546–562.

Windels, K., Mallia, K. L., & Broyles, S. J. (2013). Soft skills: The difference between leading and leaving the advertising industry? *Journal of Advertising Education, 17*(2), 17–27.

Wong, P. T., & Weiner, B. (1981). When people ask "why" questions, and the heuristics of attributional search. *Journal of Personality and Social Psychology, 40*(4), 650–663.

Yin, R. K. (2009). *Case study research: Design and methods.* Sage.

Zarantonello, L., Jedidi, K., & Schmitt, B. H. (2013). Functional and experiential routes topersuasion: An analysis of advertising in emerging versus developed markets. *International Journal of Research in Marketing, 30*(1), 46–56.

9

Using Social Media Communication to Enact Brand Purpose During a Global Health Pandemic

Charmaine du Plessis

9.1 Introduction

Recently, researchers have shown an increased interest in purpose-driven marketing that since the end of 2017 became more prominent because of viral social media debates, where consumers shared their views on important political issues and topics (Barton et al., 2018; The Social Element, 2020). Despite its acknowledged importance, little information is available in the extant literature on how brands can use social media brand communication to represent their brand purpose.

Currently, consumers live in an era of radical visibility because of new technologies and media which make platforms available for them to stand up for their beliefs and opinions on a scale never seen before. This was witnessed in the global #MeToo movement and the increased

---

C. du Plessis (✉)
Department of Communication Science,
University of South Africa, Pretoria, South Africa
e-mail: dplestc@unisa.ac.za

© The Author(s), under exclusive license to Springer Nature Switzerland AG 2022
T. Anning-Dorson et al. (eds.), *Marketing Communications in Emerging Economies, Volume II*, Palgrave Studies of Marketing in Emerging Economies, https://doi.org/10.1007/978-3-030-81337-6_9

consumer resistance against "fake news" on social and other digital media platforms. Similarly, brands increasingly let their voices be heard because many now stand up for what they believe in by refocusing the "us" instead of the "we" and seeing consumers as part of an extended brand ecosystem (Barton et al., 2018; The Social Element, 2020). On the other hand, consumers want brands to be more transparent, authentic, and operate with strong core values, and as a result, having a purpose has become essential for brands (Fabriksbrands, 2020). Overall consumer expectations of brands have changed as they want their brand experiences to align with their values to which brands strive to adhere (Barton et al., 2018).

A global crisis such as COVID-19 put the strengths and weaknesses of brands under the spotlight. It can be argued that during the pandemic, the veil of the purpose of brands has been lifted by either putting their customers' needs first or highlighting brands' real intentions (Adweek, 2020).

Also, the global outbreak of the coronavirus posed several challenges for brands, spanning from media to non-media brands. While some brands continued to let their voices be heard, others simply disappeared. Many brands are familiar with crisis management, but the global extent and continued ambiguity about COVID-19 created exceptional and continued challenges. Never have brands been more in the spotlight than during the public health pandemic in 2020. Starting in Wuhan, China in late 2019, COVID-19 has reached all continents within a very short time, leaving an immense social and economic impact, including in South Africa (Sekyere & Bohler-Muller, 2020).

The government directives to stay at home, extreme changes in demand for certain product categories, underprovided distribution channels, and supply chain difficulties for some companies have disrupted usual behaviours and required customers to shop in new ways. While many brands' demise was the result of stay-at-home directives, the change in consumer behaviour also had an impact on brands as consumers took protective actions against the virus and changed their spending habits. While consumers became concerned with macro issues, they also still needed fundamental necessities in their lives. As a result, many consumers preferred staying with brands that they trusted. Even though consumers have settled into this new normal, many have indicated that they would maintain their newly learned financial skills to save money and make better provision for the future, which added to the confounding time for brands (Think with Google, 2020).

This chapter attempts to address the gap in the literature by illustrating how brands with brand purpose could demonstrate their core values and continue to develop authentic connections with social media brand communication during times of crisis. In doing so, the chapter focuses on an example of a South African leading brand that enacted its brand purpose with social media brand communication during the global health pandemic in 2020 as a unifying force by being an active participant in consumers' lives as an industry leader.

9.2 Literature Review

9.2.1 The Brand as a Social Construct

A brand does not exist because it is a social construct that we, as a society, invent to help make sense of things. A social construct does not exist in objective reality, but because of human interaction and human agreement that something exists (Lindblom, 1999). The social construct theory puts forward that "humans create constructs to make sense of the objective world". Humans can also change their ideas about the existence of a construct as they continue to interact (VeryWellFamily, 2019). Brands, thus, exist in the minds and hearts of consumers, but it is the responsibility of brand managers to create representations of the brand, such as visual identity and brand messaging. Although a brand does not exist without products and services, which consumers buy to use, consumers select a brand based on what it embodies (Batey, 2012). The concept of a brand is, thus, dependent on interpretations by and perceptions of consumers based on their experiences with the brand (Campbell, 2014). A brand only exists when tangible products or services become augmented with images, symbols, perceptions, and emotions to create distinct ideas and meanings in people's minds (Batey, 2012). Products and services are also augmented with brand messaging such as brand stories with cohesive narratives about why a brand exists and matters (Avery, 2019). At its core, a brand resonates with consumers because of its distinctive identity and image (Batey, 2012).

There are numerous definitions of a brand in the academic literature covering different topics. Also, brand experts define brands with different nuances (Kapferer, 2012). A brand is, thus, not a predetermined concept but rather multidisciplinary with different perspectives across disciplines (Le Roux & du Plessis, 2014).

For this chapter, a brand is defined "as a multidimensional construct that exists in a continuous process of cyclical communication between the actions of the firm and the interpretations and redefinitions of the consumers, through which the brand is imbued with certain values and expectations" (Yenicioglu & Christodoulides, 2014). This definition reinforces the idea that a brand solely exists because of consumers' perceptions and interpretations.

Perceptions and interpretations of a brand are, thus, important because the novel coronavirus at the beginning of the outbreak forced consumers into a digital-only way of life. That being the case, consumers now access and interpret online brand messaging differently than before, which has a significant effect on the way that brands will operate in the future. Especially during challenging times such as we are currently experiencing, a brand's response and messaging shape the brand's ability to preserve loyalty and affinity from customers (Fabriksbrands, 2020).

9.2.2 What Is Brand Purpose?

The 2017 Meaningful Brands Report results, based on an analysis of 1500 brands in 33 countries and surveying 300,000 customers, indicate that respondents would not mind if 74% of the brands in the world ceased to exist. These results demonstrate that consumers do not care about brands that have no interest in societal health, the planet or consumers' quality of life (Annweiler, 2017).

The brand's purpose must not be confused with a brand's promise, where the consumer knows what to expect based on prior expectations shaped by the brand. Rather, a brand purpose goes much deeper and represents the reason for the brand's existence beyond making a profit rooted in its brand mission (Kramer, 2017). For a brand with a purpose, it is no longer about me, but about us, which forms the foundation for every experience the consumer has with the brand (Barton et al., 2018). Finding a noble purpose is the core of brand purpose as well as how to use it to better serve consumers and the community at large. Brands that do not focus solely on product benefits but reflect a higher purpose to serve and address the barriers to consumers' aspirations for a better life imprint their authentic reason for being in consumers' minds (BBMG, 2020). It is for this reason that brand purpose creates value, loyalty, and long-lasting emotional relationships with consumers. Purpose-driven brands communicate excitement and emotion rather than functional benefits, and in doing so, have a greater chance of persuading consumers to purchase their products and/or services (BizCommunity, 2019). Brand purpose differentiates brands and provides the foundation for every brand experience and underlying essence that makes a brand relevant and necessary to consumers because it is aligned with their values (Barton et al., 2018).

Also, a brand that is driven by purpose always reflects on its core mission to solve a consumer's problem or to meet society's needs. It is, therefore, important for brands to know why the organisation's products or services exist and how to build everything else, which the brand has to offer on the brand's purpose as a foundation. Furthermore, a brand with a powerful brand purpose aligns its core values with its products and services that resonate with consumers on a personal level. This means that an organisation whose marketing and branding efforts draw inspiration from its core purpose can build deeper connections with consumers, as evidenced by research findings (Hochman, 2012). Hence, it is important for brands to consider the organisation's role in the country and even the world, and why the brand should matter to society (Reiman & Reiman, 2012). By doing so, the brand must also consider its social, political, ecological and environmental positions.

Since brand purpose cannot be separated from the future success and sustainability of an organisation, brands need to create brand meaning that will not only thrive but also survive in an era of total connectedness and, more recently, in times of crisis and a more digital way of life because of COVID-19 (PRNews Online, 2012). Research indicates that brand strategies must be guided by an overarching purpose to become better adapted to the future. A strongly anchored purpose provides the building block that connects all stakeholders beyond making a profit. A carefully attuned and brand-aligned purpose can enable both large and small organisations not only to act merely as profit-making entities but also to shape the future (Kramer, 2017). The most effective way for a brand to shape the future is through doing good. Advanced technologies and platforms provide strengths and advantages that enable the creation of strong brands that can improve societies around the world. Brands that ask the question why they do what they are doing enhance how they do things in addition to applying acquired knowledge that only benefits them. For brands to thrive in future and during times of crisis, the know-why has become more important than the know-how. Deep thinking and soul-searching are important to find and articulate brand purpose (Kramer, 2017). Consumers resonate with a brand with a purpose and can sense that the brand represents a higher quality. In addition, employees also care more about the brand's success (Annweiler, 2017).

It can, thus, be argued that brands must perform with a purpose to grow the brand with brand loyalty and at the same time act as "ethical and responsible citizens of the world" (Gregory, 2018).

In South Africa, the brand purpose must still make stronger inroads among brands. Especially now, South African consumers are seeking inspiration and want to form new connections to fill their lives with purpose. A purpose-led brand that stands for something can create a lasting bond with consumers and inspire meaningful change in their lives (BizCommunity, 2015).

Brand strategists advocated for African brands to respond to COVID-19 with a purpose-driven response and to stand up for what matters (BizCommunity, 2015). Hence, it is argued that African brands who have exhibited a purpose before this pandemic will naturally support their customers and employees and, in doing so, continue to live their purpose and commitment to society which the case illustrates. These are the brands that will still matter in years to come (Ntsubane, 2020).

9.2.3 Why Brand Purpose Matters During Difficult Times

A global crisis such as COVID-19 put the strengths and weaknesses of brands under the spotlight. In particular, it can be argued that during the pandemic, the veil of the purpose of brands was lifted by either putting their customers' needs first or highlighting their real intentions (Adweek, 2020). Also, because of the locked-down nature of the Government's response to the crisis altering consumers' daily experiences, the coronavirus pandemic is not just any crisis. Humans are craving comfort, connections, and familiar experiences. Consequently, if consumers have not cared about a brand before a pandemic or crisis, they will care even less during tough times and these brands will die a natural death. All relationships, including our relationships with brands, have an emotional component, which becomes more visible during times of crisis (Strategy + business, 2020).

The 2018 purpose study by Cone, a Porter Novelli company, confirms that consumers want brands to communicate with a clear purpose. Results indicate that those brands that lead with purpose build better connections with consumers, attract new consumers, and inspire brand advocates to share the brand's message (ConeComm, 2018).

To stay relevant in a world that has changed completely because of the coronavirus pandemic, brands cannot simply reappear and sell more products and/or services. Now, more than ever, consumers expect brands to improve their lives and to understand their struggles, needs, and aspirations and to address those issues that matter to them in meaningful ways (BBMG, 2020).

Hence, a brand that provides greater value to customers beyond making a profit and has made a deeper emotional connection will retain consumers even during difficult times, as the brand's purpose has a unifying influence (Annweiler, 2017). Brands do not exist in isolation but are part of an integrated ecosystem of brand touchpoints where the consumer meets the brand. Brand purpose provides a consistent experience with the brand at all brand touchpoints and creates a good first impression, which is further deepened with customer engagement (Annweiler, 2017). A brand without a purpose will experience much resistance during difficult times, not only from consumers but also from employees, where fear will take over resulting in resistance to the brand's objectives and goals. On the other hand, employees of an organisation with a strong brand purpose will support management's decision-making and work harder and more effectively during difficult times. Collectively, consumers and employees will carry a brand with purpose during difficult times because purpose acts like a bridge with a safety net (Annweiler, 2017).

This is also true for South African brands which, during COVID-19, have had to adhere to their brand purpose to support, inform, and inspire consumers with relevant brand messaging that emphasises their functional value. While under lockdown rules, it was more difficult for some brands to communicate functional value, those brands that were not able to operate could still enact their brand purpose in different ways by engaging employees and important stakeholders or to repurpose their value chains to provide essential services or products (Financial Mail, 2020). While it is true that many consumers do not care about a brand's purpose, their experiences with brands without purpose will be less satisfying. This is because a brand's purpose is instilled through consumers' experiences with the brand and their belief that the brand provides them with more value than others (Business Live, 2020).

During a pandemic such as COVID-19, it becomes possible for brands with a purpose to show true leadership by living the balance between purposefulness and making a profit. In this regard, brands with purpose can highlight the brand's corporate character by taking real action in the community. In doing so, these brands can make an impact in new and creative ways to strengthen goodwill with consumers and stakeholders who will still benefit the brand in the long term (Forbes, 2020). To a certain extent, COVID-19 has also redefined the meaning of having a brand purpose. Many brands that previously only focused on brand differentiation of their products and/or services are now assisting the government, healthcare professionals, and the public in ways previously unimaginable. This partnership could even continue to grow in the years to come (Adobe Blog, 2020).

Findings of a 2020 survey among South Africans by research company Haveyouheard show that consumers held brands to the highest possible standards during the pandemic and expected brands to assist them with a responsible "humanity first" approach. For example, respondents felt that brands could assist them with a cheaper product and/or service offering or support their efforts to be protected from the virus infection. In addition, the findings also reveal how brands' actions and efforts during lockdown could influence consumer perceptions in future (The Media Online, 2020). Because of the digital way of life during COVID-19, brands have had the opportunity to enact their brand purpose in social media, where many consumers spent more time.

9.2.4 Strengthening Brand Purpose with Social Media Brand Communication

Social media has expanded exponentially since O'Reilly introduced the concept Web 2.0 in 2005 and has become part of consumers' daily lives. Web 2.0 redefined the World Wide Web (WWW) as an interactive social platform where individual users could manage their data and create content known as user-generated content (UGC) (PRNews Online, 2020; Voorveld, 2019). Due to the popularity of social media, brands have recognised the opportunity to connect with consumers on different Web 2.0 platforms and have devised their branding strategies to integrate with social media to convey brand messages. Brands' presence on social media can have different forms, for example, with paid advertising (paid media), by publishing branded content (owned media) or with branded engagement to drive social conversations around a topic (earned media) (Voorveld, 2019). Brands have also created brand pages on social media to keep up with technological changes, gain social word of mouth (widen the reach of the brand message because of the viral nature of social media), compete with competitors, build relationships with consumers, and create brand awareness (PRNews Online, 2020). To convey brand messages on social media, brands have adopted social media brand communication, which can be defined as "any piece of brand-related communication distributed via social media that enables internet users to access, share, engage with, add to, and co-create" (Voorveld, 2019).

Apart from instantly connecting with consumers with brand messages, the global health pandemic has provided brands with another kind of "debate" on social media, namely, to illustrate what they state they are standing for. By meaningfully responding and interacting with their target audiences on social media about important COVID-9 related topics and issues with social media brand communication, consumers could obtain a better sense of brands' reason for existence (PRNews Online, 2020). During this difficult time, social media allowed brands to not only reach but also engage with their audiences in spaces where they were already spending more time while showing them their support (3 ER Public Relations, 2020). Because social media brand communication has been recognised by brands as a powerful medium to build relationships with consumers even before the pandemic, they could bring into play their purpose authentically with content that is engaging, useful, and reflecting their core values (Tsimonis & Dimitriadis, 2014).

Brands' social media brand communication during the pandemic not only influenced the actions of consumers but also served as a defining moment for some brands in terms of how consumers will relate with them in future (Khoros, 2020). While acknowledging many other South African brands' initiatives in social media during the pandemic, this chapter focuses on South Africa's largest mobile operator, with 117 million customers across the continent.

9.3   Research Question

The chapter addresses the following research question:

How did a South African brand represent the reason for its existence with social media brand communication during the 2020 public health pandemic?

9.4 Research Methodology

A general inductive approach was followed to establish how the mobile brand executed its brand purpose on two social media platforms, namely, Facebook and Twitter. The brand was purposively selected as a best practice example because it effortlessly continued with its social media brand communication per its brand purpose during the pandemic (Global Compact Network South Africa, 2020).

The analysis covered the period from 27 March 2020, when the lockdown in South Africa was announced, until 31 July 2020; thus, a period of five months during the highest alert levels' restrictions. At the time of analysis, the brand had almost two million followers on Facebook and more than 465,000 followers on Twitter.

A corpus with a sample size of 117 tweets on Twitter and 209 Facebook posts was analysed. Overall, the raw data consisted of 6689 words for Facebook and 4718 words for Twitter. Using the NVivo qualitative data analysis software by QR International, the raw text data were first condensed into a summary format, after which clear links between the research question and the summary findings were established. Data analysis was, thus, data driven and iterative moving back and forth among the research question, data collection, and data analysis until data saturation was reached and no new ideas became evident. The inductive analysis allowed the development of an underlying structure of how the brand executed its brand purpose with social media brand communication during the period under review (Liu, 2016; Thomas, 2006).

A thorough and methodical reading and coding of the corpus allowed specific ideas to emerge. After grouping similar ideas, three main ideas became evident in the data that are discussed as the most important themes. However, although each associated idea in the corpus is treated as discrete, they are to a large extent also intertwined.

The trustworthiness of the results was enhanced by a coding consistency check, whereby another coder was given text that had not been coded and was asked to allocate sections of the new text to the initial themes (Thomas, 2006).

Table 9.1 depicts the process that was followed for the general inductive data analysis strategy.

Table 9.1 The process followed for the general inductive data analysis strategy

Step	Meaning for the analysis
The initial reading of the text	6689 words for Facebook and 4718 words for Twitter
Segmenting relevant text data	Using NVivo, 69 codes for Facebook and 27 codes for Twitter text emerged
Labelling these text segments into initial overall themes	Several overall broad themes became obvious when the relevant text data for both Facebook and Twitter were considered
Consistency check	Another coder assigned unlabelled Facebook and Twitter data to the initial themes
Reducing overlaps and redundancy among themes	Grouping themes with similar ideas together
Creating a structure with the most important themes	Three most important themes became evident to report in the findings

Sources Liu (2016), Thomas (2006)

9.5 Findings

The three main themes that became evident in the data can be explained as follows:

9.5.1 Theme 1: Aligning Consumer Priorities with Core Brand Values

The underscoring idea of *Theme 1: Aligning Consumer Priorities with Brand Values* encapsulates all brand communication by the brand that was shaped around the priorities of consumers while being cognisant of their core brand values. Especially during the lockdown alert levels 4 and 5, some of the biggest priorities of consumers were, among others, to stay in touch with family and friends and having access to reliable technology to connect to the internet to do their work from home and to organise their lives (Think with Google, 2020).

Data show that during the COVID-19 pandemic under review, the brand aligned consumer priorities with their brand values of trust, simplicity, and speed. These core values acted as guiding principles regarding how the brand conducted business and showcased its perspective on the world. In doing so, the brand communicated with compassion by focusing on consumers' immediate needs rather than merely highlighting the functional benefits of their products and services. Brand messaging was, among others, focused on how the brand could be trusted to unite family and friends who could not be together because of the lockdown. Also, the brand highlighted its value of simplicity by illustrating how Vodacom's technology could improve consumers' lives under lockdown by optimally applying it in their everyday lives. The brand value of speed was emphasised by referring to the convenience of the brand's mobile application, while highlighting how a fast connection would address consumers' questions and problems quickly, without having to leave their homes.

Overall, the brand's purpose of "keeping people connected" was implemented by embedding their core values in compassionate brand messages and grouping them with the hashtags #Stayconnected and #Staytogether.

Table 9.2 shows the different codes, their underlying meaning in the text, and most representative quotes of how the brand aligned their brand values with consumer priorities during the period under review.

9.5.2 Theme 2: Being Future-Focused

The underscoring idea of *Theme 2: Being Future-Focused* encapsulates all brand communication by Vodacom that was focused on highlighting and presenting opportunities to ensure an exciting digital future for the brand and all their stakeholders. Data show that during the period under review, the brand's brand messaging was guided by an overarching purpose to expand and simplify its connectivity and to provide consumers with online opportunities to enhance their lives—not only during but also after the lockdown period—by "connecting to a better future". In doing so, the brand activated its brand purpose by directing consumers to focus on the future by making available home-school education opportunities via its E-School and digital platforms, assisting

Table 9.2 Different codes, their underlying meaning and most representative quotes are evident in Theme 1

Code	Underlying meaning in the text	Representative quote
Reliance	Being reliable and honest while always delivering	"Our network was born to unite. Every day we work to make it more reliable and powerful because even though we can't be close, we can still be together. Our role of keeping people connected has never been more important than right now"
Effortlessness	Making things simpler for consumers with technology	We show you "how life is made better with technology and how it can be put to the best use in everyday life"
Swiftness	Being able to address consumers' problems swiftly and prioritising things that matter the most (being able to stay home)	"Looking to control your account without leaving home? Simply use the App to access all the account details you need. Download the app and put your account in your hands"

teachers and consumers to acquire new skills and making available free data for students from the University of Witwatersrand. The brand has also illustrated how they have been focused on improving its network by forming new partnerships for a better digital future and inclusivity for all, even beyond the pandemic.

Overall, the brand purpose of "keeping people connected" was also embedded in being focused on the future in a quest to assist consumers and for both the brand and consumers to become better equipped and to yield benefits after the pandemic.

Table 9.3 shows the different codes, their underlying meaning in the text, and most representative quotes of how the brand was focused on the future during the period under review.

Table 9.3 Different codes, their underlying meaning, and most representative quotes are evident in Theme 2

Code	Underlying meaning in the text	Representative quote
Partnerships for a better future	Entering into partnerships to expand its network and education opportunities	"To help students stay on track to successfully complete the 2020 academic year despite not being on campus, we partnered with the University of the Witwatersrand (WITS) to keep students connected and on track with the curriculum"
Improving network capabilities	Illustrating solutions on how to deal with increased consumer traffic demand during COVID-19 lockdown	"The future is here!.... This will help us manage the increase in mobile network traffic and fixed traffic experienced during the COVID-19 lockdown"
Educated youth for a sustainable future	Assisting learners during the lockdown to have access to the school curriculum in multiple languages to assist them with their future	"An educated youth has the potential to touch tomorrow. With technological innovation enabling access to a brighter future, let the inspiration come to you and #StayConnected to our Digital Classroom"

(continued)

Table 9.3 (continued)

Code	Underlying meaning in the text	Representative quote
Digital skills training	Providing digital skills training to customers to benefit them even beyond the pandemic	"In our new digital society, we want to help you to grow, learn and #StayConnected. That's why we've partnered with Udemy and Perlego e-learning and online library to offer free, customized access to their online courses and books to our customers. Whether solo or collaboratively, discovering new skills or developing existing knowledge, we are with you ever"

9.5.3 Theme 3: Helpful Information-Sharing for Principle-Driven Solutions and Support

The underscoring idea of *Theme 3: Helpful Information-Sharing for Principle-Driven Solutions and Support* encapsulates all brand communication by the brand that illustrated an understanding of consumers' situation by responding with principle-driven solutions and action-driven support. Data show that during the COVID-19 pandemic period under review, the brand shared brand messages that were not only focused on the brand but also on both the brand and consumers (hence emphasising the idea of *we are in it together*), which served as the foundation for all consumer experiences with the brand during the harder period of the lockdown restrictions. In addition, the brand's information-sharing was rooted in promoting positivity while providing helpful, authentic information to consumers to assist them with their daily struggles and problems. Consequently, the brand only referenced fact-based information sourced from the government, the Department of Health, and other reputable online sources with simple, transparent, and helpful messages. Vodacom-shared information with consumers on safety measures (sanitising) kept them abreast of the latest information about the virus, debunked myths, advised them how to obtain medical access, how to be entertained (performances and news), and focused on the needs of parents with kids at home. In doing so, Vodacom's actions provided support in a meaningful manner.

Overall, the brand's purpose was also enacted with principle-driven solutions that considered its reason for being, namely, to solve consumers' problems during the lockdown.

Table 9.4 shows the different codes, their underlying meaning in the text, and most representative quotes of how the brand provided helpful information-sharing for principle-driven solutions and support during the period under review.

9.6 Discussion

The inductive approach for the qualitative analysis illustrates how the brand delivered on its brand purpose during the higher alert levels of the lockdown period in South Africa by being an active participant in consumers' lives as an industry leader. The brand's social media brand communication acted as a roadmap, assisting consumers during a difficult period in their lives. Furthermore, their brand purpose is rooted in truth because it is at the core of what makes the brand relevant. During the period under review, the brand activated the reason why they exist in social media as a demonstrative signal to the outside world of the values and belief system behind them. Their brand purpose was activated with conviction by executing their core values with skillfully constructed social media brand communication.

The example has shown that the brand aligned their brand purpose *We connect for a better future* with consumer priorities following their values, being focused on the future and with principle-driven solutions to adequately address consumers' problems during the lockdown period.

Table 9.4 Different codes, their underlying meaning, and most representative quotes evident in Theme 3

Code	Underlying meaning in the text	Representative quote
Debunking myths	Debunking myths about the virus, access to health, and expensive online learning	"Some people think that face masks don't help at all. It's a #Mythconception. They help limit the spread of airborne droplets that come out of our mouths when we speak, sneeze or cough. For more myths, #StayConnected"
Communicating safety measures	Information about how to stay safe from the virus, online, and during emergencies	"Information is key, and there are a few tips that will help make sure you stay safe"
Providing entertainment	Highlighting opportunities to be entertained during the lockdown	"If you're looking for a way to enjoy your favourite books while on the go or when you're unable to concentrate on written text, give audiobooks a go. They're functional and extremely immersive as the narrator carries you through the story. Here are some of the best"
Education about the virus and pandemic	Being able to access information about the virus and symptoms by using a mobile phone's Unstructured Supplementary Service Data (USSD) function	"If you're looking for information on COVID-19, Online Doctor Consult offers education and resources relating to the pandemic, and a self-assessment tool if you are concerned that you may have the virus. If needed, you will have the ability to schedule virtual healthcare professional consultations and get advice with #OnlineDoctorConsultations. Find out more here"

(continued)

Table 9.4 (continued)

Code	Underlying meaning in the text	Representative quote
Considering parents' needs	Focusing on parents with kids' needs while having to work at home	"If you're working from home, keeping an eye on your kids is not only possible but quite easy. How? Use your #VHome Safety Starter Kit to monitor areas around the house – and see what everyone is getting up to. You can add extra monitors to your set as you need"

In doing so, the brand acted as a unifying force between consumers' lived experiences of the pandemic and the brand's overarching reason for its existence. This was possible because everything that the brand had to offer was based on the brand's purpose as a foundation (Annweiler, 2017). While brand communication on Facebook was more focused on how the brand's values aligned with consumer priorities and by providing value-driven solutions and support during the lockdown period, Twitter was used to focus on the future by highlighting opportunities, which could benefit consumers and the brand well beyond the pandemic.

Humans wanted comfort, connections, and familiarity during the higher alert levels. The data show that the brand's purpose was attuned to align with consumers' needs, concerns, and problems (Strategy + business, 2020) and acted as a bridge with a safety net to continue being relevant in consumers' lives (BBMG, 2020). Furthermore, the brand's purpose provided a consistent experience for consumers, which was further enhanced with brand communication that put them at the centre of the brand's focus (Annweiler, 2017).

All things considered, and unlike many other brands, the brand was able to use advanced technologies and platforms to do good and to improve consumers' lives during the lockdown period. The pandemic, however, highlighted the brand's strengths in that the brand showed true leadership by achieving a balance between purposefulness and making a profit (Adobe Blog, 2020; Forbes, 2020). The brand meaningfully responded to and interacted with its target audiences on social media in line with why the brand exists (PRNews Online) and could, thus, execute its purpose authentically by providing information and product offerings to its fans and followers who reflect their core values (Tsimonis & Dimitriadis, 2014).

9.6.1 Theoretical Implications

Theoretically, the findings add to the body of knowledge of purpose-driven marketing during an eventuality. Purpose-driven marketing is still an underdeveloped area of investigation in the marketing communication literature, especially when it comes to emerging economies (BizCommunity, 2015). Also, previous work has focused mostly on purposeful brands concerning the relationship and cause-related marketing fields and neglected how social media brand communication can be leveraged to convey and initiate brand purpose to navigate the brand's relevance during contingencies. Scholars in emerging economies can use this study as a point of departure to build more cases of best practices with academic-practitioner collaboration.

9.6.2 Practical Implications

When it comes to practical implications, the findings can serve as a heuristic for brand managers in emerging economies how to use social media brand communication to represent and leverage brand purpose. The case demonstrates that a brand's purpose must be clearly articulated, authentic, and be focused on the long-term and conveyed on social media with relevant brand messages. This current study has also illustrated how COVID-19 has redefined the concept of brand purpose to also extend to partnerships with government and other organisations and that brands must not only focus on brand differentiation. In this regard, brand managers in emerging economies must plan social media brand communication to highlight their brands' reason for existence concerning bigger issues in their countries and be able to continue with these messages during eventualities. Also, brand managers in emerging economies must integrate brand purpose into core business strategies to set them apart from competitors. Consumers today across the globe want their beliefs and values to align with those of brands with which brand purpose can assist.

9.7 Conclusion

The results of this study contribute to a better understanding of how brand purpose can be enacted with social media brand communication during a pandemic or any other crisis, which can benefit scholars and brand managers in emerging economies. The brand purpose must also be extended to other contexts and not focus solely on brand differentiation as was illustrated with the case.

During the coronavirus pandemic, many brands' purpose was put to the test as they had to activate their reason for being. The findings demonstrated how South Africa's largest mobile operator instinctively used its brand purpose as the foundation for all its offerings and social media brand communication. Although the findings cannot be generalised beyond the brand's social media brand communication during the period under review, the insights gained can nonetheless create value for brand managers in emerging economies in terms of how brand purpose can assist brands to stay relevant in consumers' lives during difficult times. On social media, where large audiences are present, brands can aptly respond to and interact with consumers and build community loyalty. By aligning consumer priorities with their values, being focused on the future and providing value-driven solutions, the brand not only enacted its brand purpose but, in doing so, also communicated effectively and was authentic.

However, a purpose-driven brand is not only about promoting core values, creating a social media hashtag, a pledge, or viral content but must inspire by providing comfort, connections and familiar experiences with real actions that improve consumers' lives and contribute to society. Research indicates that consumers expect brands to play a meaningful role in their lives by understanding their struggles, needs, and aspirations and to address those issues that matter most to them. These consumer expectations mattered especially during COVID-19 when consumers had to adjust to a new way of life and a new normal.

Further research on this topic in emerging economies could provide more insight into audiences regarding their consumption of social media brand communications and what role brand purpose plays. The research could also be expanded to focus on the employees of purpose-driven brands. This will further assist scholarship in emerging economies with theory-building of how brands can enact their purpose by living up to their reason for existence.

References

3 ER Public Relations. (2020). https://www.3epr.com/social-media-during-the-pandemic-protests. Last accessed 15 July 2020.

Adobe Blog. (2020). https://cmo.adobe.com/articles/2020/5/through-covid-19--leading-brands-have-found-their-purpose-.html#gs.clzryl. Last accessed 5 Aug 2020.

Adweek. (2020). https://www.adweek.com/brand-marketing/purpose-driven-brands-need-to-change-their-approach-post-covid. Last accessed 15 July 2020.

Annweiler, B. (2017). Purpose is at the core of branding. *Journal of Brand Strategy, 7*(3), 225–232 (2018).

Avery, J. (2019, January). Brand storytelling. *Harvard Business School Technical Note* (Revised March 2019), 519–549.

Barton, R., Ishikawa, M., Quiring, K., & Theofilou, B. (2018). To affinity and beyond. From me to we: The rise of the purpose-driven brand. Accenture Strategy Report: Accenture.

Batey, M. (2012). *Brand meaning* (2nd ed.). Routledge.

BBMG. (2020). http://bbmg.com/brand-purpose-in-divided-times/. Last accessed 10 July 2020 (2017).

BizCommunity. (2015). https://www.bizcommunity.com/Article/196/82/129273.html. Last accessed 10 July 2020.

BizCommunity. (2019). https://www.bizcommunity.com/Article/196/721/185931.htm. Last accessed 10 July 2020.

Business Live. (2020). https://www.businesslive.co.za/redzone/news-insights/2019-08-05-having-a-brand-purpose-is-not-enough. Last accessed 5 Aug 2020.

Campbell, N. (2014). The signs and semiotics of advertising. In E. Bell, S. Warren, & J. Schroeder (Eds.), *The Routledge companion to visual organization* (pp. 130–145). Routledge.

ConeComm. (2018). https://www.conecomm.com/research-blog/2018-purpose-study#download-the-research. Last accessed 5 Aug 2020.

Fabriksbrands. (2020). https://fabrikbrands.com/brand-positioning-and-brand-response-in-a-pandemic. Last accessed 15 Aug 2020.

Financial Mail. (2020). https://www.businesslive.co.za/redzone/news-insights/2020-04-15-brands-can-help-to-inspire-and-support-consumers-during-covid-19. Last accessed 15 July 2020.

Forbes. (2020). https://www.forbes.com/sites/aaronkwittken/2020/04/18/its-time-to-support-truly-purpose-driven-brands-who-exemplify-true-leadership-amidst-this-coronavirus-pandemic-heres-a-starter-list/#190da85d612e. Last accessed 5 Aug 2020.

Global Compact Network South Africa. (2020). https://globalcompactsa.org.za/how-south-african-companies-are-responding-to-covid-19. Last accessed 15 July 2020.

Gregory, G. H. (2018). Performance with purpose: The PepsiCo challenge. *Journal of Brand Strategy, 6*(4), 328–355.

Hochman, K. (2012). Integrating your brand purpose: How Procter and Gamble's Secret deodorant increased market share and profit through its brand purpose. *Journal of Brand Strategy, 1*(4), 327–332.

Kapferer, J. N. (2012). *The new strategic brand management: Advanced insights and strategic thinking* (5th ed.). Kogan Page.

Khoros. (2020). https://khoros.com/blog/social-medias-role-during-covid-19. Last accessed 15 July 2020.

Kramer, M. (2017). Brand purpose: The navigational code for growth. *Journal of Brand Strategy, 6*(1), 46–54.

Le Roux, C., & du Plessis, C. (2014). An exploratory Q study of corporate brand identity elements governing corporate brand image formation. *Southern African Business Review, 18*(3), 119–141.

Lindblom, J. (1999). Brands as structures and social constructs: Network approach to branding. In D. McLoughlin & C. Horan (Eds.), *Proceedings of the 15th Annual IMP Conference* (pp. 1–14). Dublin: University College.

Liu, L. (2016). Using generic inductive approach in qualitative educational research: A case study analysis. *Journal of Education and Learning, 5*(2), 129–135.
PRNews Online. (2012). https://www.prnewsonline.com/social-conversations-coronavirus. Last accessed 15 July 2020.
PRNews Online. (2020). https://www.prnewsonline.com/social-conversations-coronavirus. Last accessed 7 Nov 2020.
Reiman, J., & Reiman, J. (Eds.). (2012). *The story of purpose: The path to creating a brighter brand, a greater company, and a lasting legacy.* Wiley.
Sekyere, E., & Bohler-Muller, N. (2020). *The impact of COVID-19 in South Africa* (Wilson Centre Africa Program Occasional Paper).
Strategy + business. (2020). https://www.strategy-business.com/blog/Redefining-customer-experience-Connecting-in-the-time-of-COVID-19?gko=245c0. Last accessed 5 Aug 2020.
The Media Online. (2020a). https://themediaonline.co.za/2020/05/south-africans-want-brands-to-keep-being-active-in-their-lives-during-lockdown. Last accessed 15 July 2020.
The Media Online. (2020b). https://themediaonline.co.za/2020/06/african-brands-need-to-drive-a-purpose-led-response-to-covid-19. Last accessed 15 July 2020.
The Social Element. (2020). https://thesocialelement.agency/2018-brand-communication-year-of-purposeful-content. Last accessed 10 July 2020.
Think with Google. (2020). https://www.thinkwithgoogle.com/future-of-marketing/digital-transformation/coronavirus-crisis-marketing-examples Last accessed 7 Nov 2020.
Thomas, D. R. (2006). A general inductive approach for analyzing qualitative evaluation data. *American Journal of Evaluation, 27*(2), 237–246.
Tsimonis, G., & Dimitriadis, S. (2014). Brand strategies in social media. *Marketing Intelligence and Planning, 32*(3), 328–344.
VeryWellFamily. (2019). https://www.verywellfamily.com/definition-of-social-construct-1448922. Last accessed 10 July 2020.
Voorveld, H. A. M. (2019). Brand communication in social media: A research agenda. *Journal of Advertising.* https://doi.org/10.1080/00913367.2019.1588808
Yenicioglu, B., & Christodoulides, G. (2014). Branding in the age of digital connectivity. In L. Moutinho, E. Bigné, & A. K. Manrai, *The Routledge companion to the future of marketing* (pp. 268–281). Routledge.

10

Aesthetics Response to Point-of-Purchase Advertising and Purchase Intentions of Groceries

Kojo Kakra Twum, Andrews Agya Yalley, Kwamena Minta Nyarku, Masud Ibrahim, and Godwyn Manful

10.1 Introduction

In emerging countries like Russia, China, India, and South Korea, there is a growing presence of hypermarkets, multiplex malls, mega markets, and have become a common feature of retailing (Sarkar & Adhikary, 2018). The International Finance Corporation (IFC) (2020) reports that retail giants started to expand their operations in several emerging markets in the 1990s. These retail outlets have since provided customers

---

K. K. Twum (✉)
Presbyterian University of College, Abetifi, Ghana
e-mail: twumkojo@presbyuniversity.edu.gh

A. A. Yalley · K. M. Nyarku
University of Cape Coast, Cape Coast, Ghana
e-mail: andrews.yalley@ucc.edu.gh

K. M. Nyarku
e-mail: knyarku@ucc.edu.gh

© The Author(s), under exclusive license to Springer Nature
Switzerland AG 2022
T. Anning-Dorson et al. (eds.), *Marketing Communications in Emerging Economies, Volume II*, Palgrave Studies of Marketing in Emerging Economies,
https://doi.org/10.1007/978-3-030-81337-6_10

with access to food, clothing, household appliances, technology gadgets, etc. Also, these retail outlets are making good use of technology and processes that enable them to achieve greater economies of scale, bringing down cost of goods and services, raising standard of retail, and improving the quality of goods and services (IFC, 2020).

Visual aesthetics is a product attribute that is reflected in many consumer experiences, most obvious in fashion and the arts but also significant in other products like automobiles, appliances, and food packaging (Yamamoto & Lambert, 1994). Schroeder (2006) asserts that the struggles of brands happen within the visual domain and that products are marketed via images. The marketing perspective of concern in the view of Charters (2006) is the link between the consumers' encounter with aesthetics and the evaluation of product preferences. There is an acknowledgement of the efficacy of store aesthetics (Mishra, 2014), and product aesthetics (Toufani et al., 2017) in influencing purchase intentions.

For fast-moving consumer goods, Bues et al. (2017) found that about 50–60% of purchase decisions are made in-store, which may be attributed to in-store marketing stimuli. In emerging markets such as India, impulse buying is considered as a major buying behaviour (Mittal et al., 2016). Consumers are exposed to many messages in an attempt to inform, persuade, or convince them to purchase products (Jansson et al., 2002). Marketers present consumers with stimuli to elicit favourable behaviour such as purchase (Giese et al., 2014). One of the common ways of marketing promotions is the use of POP advertising (Bianca & Simona, 2008). POP advertising is one of the marketing techniques that convey messages to consumers to gain consumers' attention in cluttered markets (Jansson et al., 2002). POP advertising is a promotional material situated in retail stores (Cross, 2009). It is the final opportunity

---

M. Ibrahim
Department of Management, Akenten Appiah-Menka University of Skills Training and Entrepreneurial Development, Kumasi, Ghana

G. Manful
Blueskies Ghana Limited, Accra, Ghana

that marketers can get to consumers before the moment of truth, that is, before they make a purchase decision (Bues et al., 2017). There is their evidence in a study in China by Zhou and Wong (2004) that impulse purchases by shoppers are influenced by the use of POP posters.

Point-of-purchase advertising has some advantages over traditional advertising because, first, it makes it more difficult to ignore the advert. Second, it targets consumers at the place where they buy the product to draw their attention and remind them of previous advertising message or introduce consumers to new advertising messages (Howard et al., 2004). Advertising restrictions have made POP advertising common among marketers of alcohol (Howard et al., 2004) and tobacco (Brown et al., 2012). For food and beverages, Nelson et al. (2020) assert that POP advertising is important because consumption decisions are usually made out of home. The use of in-store marketing material has an effect on unplanned buying at point-of-purchase (see Bell et al., 2011). This is because in-store POP displays are a marketing technique to immediately catch the consumer's eye and increase sales. For instance, Freedman and Connors (2010) and Wang (2013) explain that POP information helps to encourage purchase choices of food brands.

About 60.3% of merchandising executives indicated in 2016 that they allocated their marketing budget on point-of-sale promotional displays in the USA (Statista, 2020). Despite the increasing use of POP materials, their effectiveness in enhancing purchase intentions has not received much research attention. Horstmann (2017) acknowledges that the investments on point-of-sale displays by marketers must lead to corresponding research on the measure of customers' evaluation of this promotion. Jansson et al. (2002) propose that the evaluation of the effectiveness of POP materials must be done to find out its effect on an in-store purchase. Also, Wang et al. (2013) propose that marketers need to understand the effect of aesthetics on consumer psychological and behavioural consequences. To address this, a lot of research studies have been conducted on the effect of POP on purchase behaviour (Freedman & Connors, 2010; Milliron et al., 2012; Sproul et al., 2003).

Also, there is a need for more studies to clarify the relationship between exposure to the POP promotions and marketing outcomes (Paynter & Edwards, 2009). Sigurdsson et al. (2010) assert that POP stimuli have been extensively researched but the findings on their effect on purchase behaviour are mixed. Bell et al. (2011) assert that unplanned buying is very crucial to retailers, but there is sparse academic research in this area. The consensus that POP stimuli lead to purchase response maybe just a creed than an empirical fact (Sigurdsson et al., 2010). Toufani et al. (2017) assert that the effect of aesthetics elements of products on purchase intentions remains unclear. More importantly, the influence of POP material aesthetics on purchase intentions has not received much research attention.

10.1.1 Marketing Using Aesthetics

Vilnai-Yavetz and Koren (2013) assert that, an aesthetic, explains the level of attractive appearance of an object. Aesthetics are not limited to artistic expressions, visual domains, styling, but are limited to the gratification that comes from the sensory perception of an object (Hekkert & Leder, 2008). Aesthetics are seen as a non-instrumental quality, which forms part of product experience and appeal (Hassenzahl, 2008). Wang et al. (2013) explain that aesthetics has been viewed from the objective of beauty perspective and also from the subjective perspective (human sense). This implies that apart from the evaluation of the beauty of an object, the evaluation of the object from an individual's point of view is also important. The subjective standpoint of aesthetics has become popular in recent times leading to researchers relying on individual judgement and aesthetic experience (Wang et al., 2013). A person's positive evaluation of an aesthetic can assist in differentiating products thereby leading to the development of preferences for products (Toufani et al., 2017).

10.1.2 POP Material as a POP Advertising Tool

Bianca and Simona (2008) describe POP communication as any promotional material placed at the POP such as interior displays, printed materials at shop counters or window displays. It also includes in-store broadcasts, video screen demonstrations, shopping-trolley advertising, shelf-talkers, coupon dispensers, wastepaper baskets and interactive kiosks. Also, Jansson et al. (2002) state that POP materials can be described as free-standing display units that are designed to hold and display products and can be regarded as more than just an advert but as products in their own right (Jansson et al., 2002). In describing POP materials, Cross (2009) states that they usually adopt substantially constrained words because too many words will make the headlines too long for consumers to understand. Also, Cross (2009) identified that POP advertising contains writing that are in bullet points and headlines, messages are limited to nine words and focused on communicating just essential parts of the message. The POP information or message must also be at the upper (eye) level or the perception level, which is the level that will get the attention of consumers (Cross, 2009).

POP materials enhance the interaction with customers leading to their response (Sigurdsson et al., 2010). The ability to generate immediate response makes POP displays differ from traditional advertising, or word-of-mouth (Sigurdsson et al., 2010). The communication objective of POP material is similar to that of marketing communication objectives. The use of marketing communications to create attention, remind the customer, and persuade customers to buy can be achieved using POP materials. In creating attention, the positioning of the unit, and the features of the POP materials attract in-store customers. The brand logo and information provide reminders to the customers, and information about pricing and use of products may persuade customers to make a purchase.

10.2 Theoretical Issues

The influence of POS materials and sale promotions on purchase intentions can be explained using marketing theories. In the view of Jacoby (2002), consumer behaviour studies have researched how economic and financial factors (inputs) affect purchase behaviour (output). These studies assume that the consumer is rational and did not pay much attention to the mental state and processes of consumers (Jacoby, 2002). Also, apart from economic and financial factors, there is a need to pay attention to other environmental factors and individual reactions that could affect consumer's responses. One such theory that has attracted attention and application in the field of marketing is the stimulus–organism–response theory. Mehrabian and Russell (1974) developed the theory to explain how individuals respond to external stimuli. The theory assumptions link the exposure to external stimuli (S) and a reaction (O), which is followed by a response (R), hence the name S-O-R model.

In the marketing literature, stimuli are referred to as any marketing input such as advertising, marketing strategy, packaging, etc. Donovan et al. (1994) used the stimulus–response model to explain how the store atmosphere affects purchase behaviour. In the case of this study, the stimuli are the POP materials, which lead to customer's reaction, and response in the form of purchase intention. One of the most important aspects of the theory is the role of perceptions of value, and emotions of individuals serving as a moderator between stimuli and purchase behaviour (Liu & Jang, 2009). The perceptions, attitudes, and knowledge of POP material are therefore crucial in explaining their response (purchase intentions). An aesthetic stimulus has utilitarian (order, simplicity, and organisation) and hedonic (impressiveness, creativeness, and meaningfulness) properties that invoke consumers' cognitive, affective, and behavioural responses (Wang et al., 2013).

From the stimulus–organism–response theory, POP material in this study is regarded as the stimuli, and perceptions of individuals as organisms, leading to purchase intention as a response. Zhou and Wong (2004) refer to POP materials as marketing stimuli that is needed in exposing customers to products and aid retailers in establishing a relationship at the final stage of the distribution channel. POP materials are visual stimuli that are a common feature of retail atmosphere. POP materials serve as an indication to shoppers about the availability of products in shops. They also contain messages that persuade shoppers to make a decision to buy products.

10.3 Measuring How Perception of Point-of-Purchase Elements Influence Purchase Intentions

There is evidence to show that consumers respond to POP communications (e.g. Buscher et al., 2001; Eckman et al., 1990; Jansson et al., 2002). A common reference given to POP material in these studies is that they are regarded as aesthetics. In the case of Eckman et al. (1990), perception of POP material was evaluated using variables such as colour, styling, fabric, uniqueness, appearance, versatility, matching, appropriateness, utility, performance, comfort, care, workmanship, and other extrinsic criteria such as brand, price, and competition. Also, Giese et al. (2014) state that the design properties of marketing aesthetics that influence consumer responses include perceived attractiveness (the valenced evaluative response to the artefact), and perceived strength (the ability of the artefacts to create attention). Another study by Murray et al. (2019) considered aesthetics features such as typicality, novelty, unity, and variety to examine customer response to store atmosphere.

For the present study, the dimensions used in evaluating aesthetics are useful in examining the perception of customers towards the marketing aesthetics (POP material). Kaplan (1972) states that a reliable and compact way of characterising the visual environment should be of interest. The aesthetic response model by Kaplan proposes that human functioning depends on information, which is provided by the immediate environment (Kaplan & Kaplan, 1989). The environment contains signs, both verbal and non-verbal that provide guidance to human behaviour. The environment in the view of Kaplan and Kaplan (1989) does not only relate to only natural settings but also to construct elements that we experience. Therefore, aesthetics created by marketers can be regarded as part of the environment, and consumer's behaviour can be informed when individuals are exposed to them.

This study adopted the conceptualisation of evaluating POP material by Kaplan (1987) and used by Jansson et al. (2002) to assess how consumers perceive the aesthetics features of the POP material. The dimensions include mystery, coherence, complexity, and legibility. These dimensions are discussed in detail and also their link with purchase intention is presented.

10.3.1 Mystery of Point-of-Purchase Material and Purchase Intentions

Mystery dimension looks at the degree to which individuals perceive that the material contains "hidden information", which leads to the possibility that the individual attempts to seek for other information to understand what it says (Jansson et al., 2002). Kaplan (1987) explains that mystery causes people to go deeper to study a scene leading to getting more information. Hill et al. (2016) explain that mystery is a tactic used by marketing practitioners to gain attention. Mystery appeals are usually adopted by retailers by withholding vital information about the product or promotion from customers (Hill et al., 2016). Jansson et al. (2002) found that mystery has a significant effect on aesthetic response of objects. This leads to the following hypothesis:

H1 *Shoppers' perception of mystery of POP material has a significant effect on purchase intentions.*

10.3.2 Coherence/Clarity of Point-Of-Purchase Material and Purchase Intentions

The coherence and clarity of POP advertising lead to the comprehensibility of the advertising. Pieters et al. (2010) state that comprehensibility is the ability of the consumer to identify the advertised brand as well as being able to accurately process the message in the advertisement. This is the degree to which a scene "hangs together" or has organisation leading to the preference of scene (Jansson et al., 2002). Kaplan (1987) states that some drawings on scenes lack the symmetries, repeating elements that lead to a "good gestalt". Coherence is the ability of an individual to predict within the scene (Kaplan, 1987). The organisation of the information in the scene using a smaller number of chunks is key (Kaplan, 1987). A study by Jansson et al. (2002) fused the coherence variable into the mystery variable. Clarity was found to have a significant effect on aesthetic response of subjects (Jansson et al., 2002). It is hypothesised that:

H2 *Shoppers' perception of coherence of POP material has a significant effect on purchase intentions.*

10.3.3 Complexity of Point-of-Purchase Material and Purchase Intentions

Complexity dimension refers to a variety of elements in a scene (Jansson et al., 2002). Kaplan (1987) explains that complexity assesses the immediate availability of information on a scene rather than promised or inferred. Visual complexity refers to a situation where most images contain redundancy and the more complex they are the less redundant they become (Pieters et al., 2010). Complexity of advertising relates to the elaborate designs of an image in terms of shapes, objects, and patterns (Pieters et al., 2010). Jansson et al. (2002) aver that the greater the complexity, the greater the preference to the material (Jansson et al., 2002). This study hypothesises that:

H3 *Shoppers' perception of complexity of POP material has a significant effect on purchase intentions.*

10.3.4 Legibility of Point-of-Purchase Material and Purchase Intentions

Legibility dimension refers to the perception of the individual about the distinctiveness of material that aids in understanding the content (Jansson et al., 2002). Kaplan (1987) explains that legibility enhances inferences and predictions, which encourage understanding of aesthetics. Newman (2007) asserts that, legibility of an object is created when there are distinctive features that lead to point of reference. On the other hand, a poor legibility tends to disorient consumers (Newman, 2007). There is a likelihood therefore that, a POP material with a good legibility will influence consumers to have a preference for the product that is being marketed. This leads to the development of the following hypothesis:

***H4** Shoppers' perception of legibility of POP material has a significant effect on purchase intentions.*

10.4 Research Model

From a theoretical perspective of stimulus–organism–response, this study proposes that a shopper's evaluation of a POP material will influence a response in the form of purchase intentions. Using the dimensions proposed by Kaplan (1987) in evaluating POP materials, this study proposes a relationship between mystery, coherence, complexity, legibility and purchase intentions. The perception of the mystery, coherence, complexity, and legibility of POP material will lead to purchase intentions. The proposed effect of POP material evaluation on purchase intention is presented in Fig. 10.1.

10.5 Methods

The target population were shoppers of fast-moving consumer goods (FMCG) within a grocery store in a major shopping centre in Ghana. Considering the unavailability of a sampling frame of the population, the researcher conveniently selected respondents in a store. The researcher sought permission from management of the grocery retail outlet. After permission was sought, the researcher approached shoppers who visited the grocery store. The aim of the study was explained to them, and for respondents who agreed to be part of the study, a questionnaire

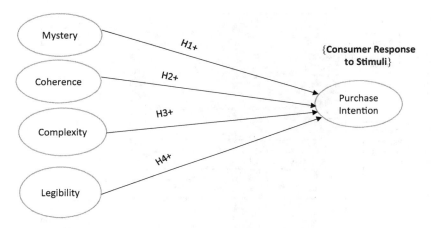

Fig. 10.1 Research model

was presented to them. Following the approach used by Eckman et al. (1990), respondents were told the researcher has nothing to do with the store.

The promotional tool studied is a POP advertising material—Nestle Cerelac Point of Sale Display (see Fig. 10.2) displayed in the grocery store. A copyright was obtained to use the POP material used for the study. This POP advertising material was selected due to its features such as having headline words to be less than 9 words, call to action, and having products at the hand level of consumers. The features of this POP are ideal because it has colourful and attractive features. Also, the advertising message "Choose Big Nutrition" is not too wordy, which instructs buyers to perform an action. Study participants were asked to evaluate this POP advertising material. This approach is parallel with the approach used by Horstmann (2017) where the point-of-sale material that was displayed in the store is evaluated by study participants.

The participants in the store who got attracted to the POP display were approached. After their permission was sought to be part of the study, they were asked whether they are regular visitors at the shop and also whether they have made purchases of the same product from the POP display. Shoppers who indicated they have made purchases from the POP display are excluded from the study. This is to ensure that

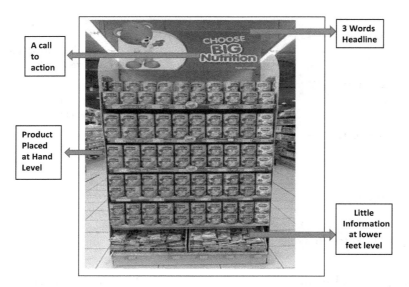

Fig. 10.2 Cerelac point-of-purchase display

the study does not include shoppers who are familiar with the product display and have made or about to make repeat purchase. Shoppers who are first-timers were recruited for the study. After permission has been sought from first-time shoppers of the product in the store, they were asked to view the promotional material for some time. They were then asked to assist the researcher to complete a survey based on their perception of the promotional material. These interactions and explanations were vital in ensuring respondents understand the purpose of the survey. This approach in soliciting responses allows the shopper to take a critical look at the aesthetic. The participants completed a structured study questionnaire designed to measure the study variables. The exercise lasted for about 10 minutes per respondent. It took the researcher a week to collect data from shoppers from September 16–21, 2019. Data were collected from 195 selected shoppers in the grocery store.

The study used structured survey questionnaires. To ensure reliability, the scales for measuring customer evaluation of POP materials and purchase intentions were obtained from the literature. In the case of evaluation of POP material (mystery, complexity, coherence, complexity), measurement items were adapted from Jansson et al. (2002). Purchase intention scales were adapted from Vilnai-Yavetz and Koren (2013). Customer evaluation of the POP material generates consumer response. The dependent variable is the customer response (purchase intention). The variables were measured using a five-point Likert Scale (1—strongly disagree to 5—strongly disagree). The average of the responses to survey items creates a continuous scale to enable the testing of hypotheses. The scale items are presented in Table 10.2. Analysis of the data was done using the Statistical Package for Social Science (SPSS) and SmartPLS. The data were coded using SPSS. The structural equation modelling approach involves the measurement model, which includes the reliability and validity test (Wong, 2013). The structural model was performed to test for significance level. This was done using path coefficients and bootstrapping techniques.

10.6 Results

The study participants include 96 males and 99 females. In Table 10.1, it is indicated that the majority of the shoppers used in the study are

Table 10.1 Demographic profile

Demographic profile	Frequency	Percent
Gender of respondent		
Male	96	49.2
Female	99	50.8
Age of respondent		
18–25	19	9.7
26–33	67	34.4
34–41	79	40.5
42–49	14	7.2
50 and above	16	8.2
Educational level		
No formal education	6	3.1
Primary	8	4.1
Junior high school	51	26.2
Secondary/college	90	46.2
Tertiary	40	20.5

within the age category of 34–41. The least represented shoppers were within age 18–25. The majority of the respondents have junior high, college, and university education and were able to read and understand the survey questionnaire. Only six of the study participants had no formal education.

Table 10.2 indicates the perception of study participants on the various indicator items. The results revealed that study participants generally did not think the POP material contains information not yet

Table 10.2 Descriptive statistics of variables

Indicator	Evaluation of point-of-purchase material	N	Mean	Std
Mystery				
Myst1	I think this POP material contains information not yet disclosed	195	2.097	0.700
Myst2	There is information in this POP material that is suggested but obscured from view	195	2.272	0.595
Myst3	I know there is more to this POP material then meets the eye	195	2.231	0.568
Coherence				
CR1	The different elements of this POP fit together	195	4.541	3.636
CR2	The message on this POP is very clear	195	4.328	0.588
CR3	It is easy to work out the meaning of this POP	195	4.299	0.646
CR4	The POP is designed in an organised manner	195	4.287	0.673
CR5	This is a logical design	195	4.301	0.745
Complexity				
Comp1	There is a lot of information in this POP	195	3.984	0.911
Comp2	Overall, this POP is complicated	195	2.892	1.367
Comp3	This POP is made of many features	195	4.056	0.826
Legibility				
Leg1	The overall design of this POP is plain and simple	195	4.260	0.667
Leg2	I can imagine this POP fitting well in other product categories	195	4.257	0.569
Leg3	I am very attracted to this POP	195	4.150	0.784
Leg4	This POP is distinctive from others I have seen	195	3.887	0.917
Purchase intentions				

(continued)

Table 10.2 (continued)

Indicator	Evaluation of point-of-purchase material	N	Mean	Std
PI	I believe that most people would like to buy this product	195	4.485	0.652
PI	I would be glad to try the product in this POP material	195	4.323	0.668
PI	I would purchase this product	195	4.282	0.702

discovered. They did not perceive there is more to the POP than meets the eye. On the coherence of the POP material, respondents indicated that information on the material fits very well; it is clear, understandable, and organised in a logical manner. On complexity, the responses of the shoppers indicate they do not agree that the POP material is complex. However, they perceived it to be made of many features. They also perceived the POP material to have a lot of information. On legibility of the POP material, the study participants agreed the design of the POP material is plain and simple. The responses also indicate that the survey respondents could imagine the POP material fitting well into the respective product category. The study also found that the study respondents indicated they were attracted to the POP material. This generally indicates a likeness for the POP material. On the distinctiveness of the POP material, study participants perceive that the POP material stands out well. The questions on the intentions of study participants to buy the product used in the study were also presented. The respondents indicated they believed most people would like to buy the product in the POP material. Most of the respondents also indicated they will be glad to try the product and would also purchase the product.

10.7 Measurement Model

The reliability and validity of the study items measuring shopper evaluation of aesthetics (POP material) and purchase intention were examined using partial least squares (PLS) specifically SmartPLS, developed by Ringle et al. (2005). The development of the measurement model led to testing for reliability and validity (see Table 10.3). For the reliability test,

Table 10.3 Reliability and validity

Variable	Indicators	Loadings	Indicator reliability	Composite reliability	AVE
Coherence	CR2	0.767	0.586		
	CR3	0.886	0.784	0.813	0.686
Complexity	COMP1	0.758	0.575		
	COMP3	0.918	0.843	0.829	0.709
Legibility	LEG1	0.772	0.596		
	LEG3	0.827	0.685	0.781	0.640
Mystery	MYST1	0.938	0.879		
	MYST2	0.736	0.541	0.829	0.71
Purchase	PI1	0.846	0.720		
Intentions	PI2	0.877	0.769	0.875	0.700
	PI3	0.783	0.612		

indictor reliability and internal consistency reliability were performed. The study used the composite reliability to test for internal consistency reliability. Hair et al. (2012) claimed that the composite reliability is preferred than the use of Cronbach's Alpha in PLS-SEM. A higher level of internal consistency reliability was achieved since all the composite reliabilities of the variables were above 0.7 as suggested by Bagozzi and Yi (1988). Indicator reliability was also achieved since the indicators of the variables maintained were above the minimum acceptable level of 0.4 and most were closer to or higher than 0.7 as recommended by Hulland (1999). In SEM, outer loadings of 0.7 are retained (Wong, 2016). All other indicators that were below 0.7 were excluded from the analysis (e.g. *CR1, CR4, CR5, COMP2, LEG2, LEG4, MYST3, PI1*).

The average variance extracted (AVE) was used to test for convergent validity. All the AVE for the variables was higher than the acceptable level of 0.5 as recommended by Bagozzi and Yi (1988). The discriminant validity of the variables was examined using the Fornell–Lacker test (see Table 10.4). This was done by manually calculating the square root of the AVE of the variables and checking whether this result is higher than the correlations of the variable with others (Wong, 2013). Discriminant validity was achieved because the square root of all the AVE is higher than the correlations between the variables.

Table 10.4 Correlation and Fornell–Lacker criterion analysis

	Coherence	Complexity	Legibility	Mystery	Purchase intention
Coherence	**0.8281**				
Complexity	0.1809	**0.8418**			
Legibility	0.4081	0.3671	**0.8002**		
Mystery	−0.1774	0.2324	0.1059	**0.8426**	
Purchase intention	0.3836	0.2786	0.3976	−0.2162	**0.8369**

10.8 Structural Model

The proposed relationship between the evaluation of POP material and purchase intentions was analysed. The study formulated four hypotheses, linking four dimensions of aesthetic evaluation (mystery, coherence, complexity, and legibility) and purchase intentions (*H1–H4*). The coefficient of determination, R^2 is 0.294 for purchase intentions. This result means that the dimensions of evaluation of an aesthetic material (mystery, coherence, complexity, and legibility) explain 29.4% of the variance in purchase intentions of grocery product. This is a weak relationship between shopper aesthetic evaluation of POP material and purchase intentions. The results indicate that legibility (distinctiveness, understanding) is the strongest predictor of shopper purchase intention (see Table 10.5). This is followed by mystery (possibility of more information). The study found that all the dimensions of evaluating aesthetics (POP material) have a significant relationship with purchase intentions.

Table 10.5 T-statistics of path coefficients

Hypothesis	Relationship	B-estimate	t-test	Decision
H1	Mystery → Purchase Intentions	−0.262	3.084	Supported
H2	Coherence → Purchase Intentions	0.189	2.559	Supported
H3	Complexity → Purchase Intentions	0.204	2.458	Supported
H4	Legibility → Purchase Intentions	0.273	3.816	Supported

There was a negative relationship between mystery and purchase intentions. However, the mystery was found to be a predictor of purchase intentions.

10.9 Discussion of Findings

The study examines how shoppers in a grocery store perceive a POP material. The evaluation of this promotional material was done by first looking at the four dimensions of evaluating aesthetics. In assessing the mystery of the POP material, the study respondents indicated the material did not have elements the suggested more information, and also, respondents did not perceive that there is more to the POP than meets the eye. The study participants also evaluated the POP material as fitting together and also communicate clear messages. The POP material was also found to have a lot of information. The aesthetic evaluation also found that the POP material is simple and attractive. The study participants also indicated that there is a high possibility of buying the grocery product indicating the existence of purchase intention.

The hypotheses that were tested to explain the relationship between POP material and shopper response (purchase intention) found that all the dimensions of evaluation of POP material have a significant relationship with purchase intentions. In a study by Jansson et al. (2002), mystery and clarity were found to improve the attraction of shoppers to POP materials. In this study, the dimensions (mystery, coherence, complexity, and legibility) of evaluating aesthetics were found to influence shoppers' intentions to purchase a product. The study findings support other studies on the use of different elements of product aesthetics to influence purchase intentions such as packaging aesthetics (Giese et al., 2014; Vilnai-Yavetz & Koren, 2013).

10.10 Conclusions

In the absence of adequate empirical research on POP material on purchase intentions, this study provides both theoretical and practical contributions. The study proves the possibility of examining shoppers' aesthetic response to POP material using Kaplan's model. This contributes to the literature on using this approach to evaluate the perception of shoppers towards the POP material. The findings of this study contribute to the theory on consumer responses to marketing stimuli. The study findings support the stimulus–organism–response theory, since the POP material influences to some extent the purchase intentions of shoppers. Also, a favourable evaluation of POP material using the dimensions of evaluating an aesthetic by Kaplan (1987) is linked to the intentions of shoppers to purchase products. This provides a valuable contribution to literature on measuring the effect of aesthetics relating to marketing and customer responses.

10.11 Implication to Retail Marketing in Emerging Markets

The practical implications of this study involve the approach to designing POP materials, the key elements to consider, and attempts to consider other important factors that may influence purchase intentions. POP material is useful in attracting the customer and also informing the customer about the availability of offerings and about products in shops. This study provides empirical support for the need to introduce and develop and deploy POP materials within the grocery outlets. There seems to be an over-reliance on price reductions as the main form of POP promotion. POP material can gain the attention of shoppers. Shoppers are also informed about promotions and products using POP materials, which creates purchase intentions. Other promotions such as gifts, free samples, competitions are also ways manufacturers could engage shoppers to improve sales at POP. Also, POP material features must be carefully developed to avoid negative reactions. The most important among these features is the attractiveness and distinctiveness of the POP material. In emerging markets, the role of culture in marketing communications can be explored in designing promotional aesthetics. The use of local language, symbols, and expressions that generates favourable responses from customers can be pursued.

10.12 Future Research

Future research could focus on other aesthetic elements in the POP environment. This could be the store environment and product aesthetics. Apart from focusing on product aesthetics, other factors affecting purchase intentions at POP such as POP promotions (e.g. discounts), and the perceived value of the product could be considered. Also, future studies can use other measures of aesthetic responses of POP materials since there exist different ways of evaluating aesthetics from the perspective of the shopper. From the aesthetics literature, factors such as colour, sharp, unity, novelty, typicality, and many more could be used to examine consumer aesthetic response. These could be employed to examine their influence on purchase intentions. The use of actual sales of products relative to others in stores could be measured to indicate the effect of POP materials on sales.

References

Bagozzi, R. P., & Yi, Y. (1988). On the evaluation of structural equation models. *Journal of the Academy of Marketing Science, 16*(1), 74–94.

Bell, D. R., Corsten, D., & Knox, G. (2011). From point of purchase to path to purchase: How preshopping factors drive unplanned buying. *Journal of Marketing, 75*(1), 31–45.

Bianca, C. I., & Simona, T. A. (2008). Some aspects regarding the importance of point of purchase communications in the marketing communications mix. *Ştiinţe Economice Tom XVII, 4*, 809–812.

Brown, A., Boudreau, C., Moodie, C., Fong, G. T., Li, G. Y., McNeill, A., Thompson, M. E., Hassan, L. M., Hyland, A., Thrasher, J. F., Yong, H.-H., Borland, R., Hastings, G., & Hammond, D. (2012). Support for removal of point-of-purchase tobacco advertising and displays: Findings from the International Tobacco Control (ITC) Canada survey. *Tobacco Control, 21*(6), 555–559.

Bues, M., Steiner, M., Stafflage, M., & Krafft, M. (2017). How mobile in-store advertising influences purchase intention: Value drivers and mediating effects from a consumer perspective. *Psychology and Marketing, 34*(2), 157–174.

Buscher, L. A., Martin, K. A., & Crocker, S. (2001). Point-of-purchase messages framed in terms of cost, convenience, taste, and energy improve healthful snack selection in a college foodservice setting. *Journal of the American Dietetic Association, 101*(8), 909–913.

Charters, S. (2006). Aesthetic products and aesthetic consumption: A review. *Consumption, Markets and Culture, 9*(3), 235–255.

Cross, G. A. (2009). Presenting consumer technology with POP: A rhetorical and ethnographic exploration of point-of-purchase advertising. *Journal of Technical Writing and Communication, 39*(2), 141–175.

Donovan, R. J., Rossiter, J. R., Marcoolyn, G., & Nesdale, A. (1994). Store atmosphere and purchasing behavior. *Journal of Retailing, 70*(3), 283–294.

Eckman, M., Damhorst, M. L., & Kadolph, S. J. (1990). Toward a model of the in-store purchase decision process: Consumer use of criteria for evaluating women's apparel. *Clothing and Textiles Research Journal, 8*(2), 13–22.

Freedman, M. R., & Connors, R. (2010). Point-of-purchase nutrition information influences food-purchasing behaviors of college students: A pilot study. *Journal of the American Dietetic Association, 110*(8), 1222–1226.

Giese, J. L., Malkewitz, K., Orth, U. R., & Henderson, P. W. (2014). Advancing the aesthetic middle principle: Trade-offs in design attractiveness and strength. *Journal of Business Research, 67*(6), 1154–1161.

Hair, J. F., Sarstedt, M., Ringle, C. M., & Mena, J. A. (2012). An assessment of the use of partial least squares structural equation modeling in marketing research. *Journal of the Academy of Marketing Science, 40*(3), 414–433.

Hassenzahl, M. (2008, September). User experience (UX) towards an experiential perspective on product quality. In *20th Conference on l'Interaction Homme-Machine* (pp. 11–15). ACM Digital Library,

Hekkert, P., & Leder, H. (2008). Product aesthetics. *Product Experience, 259*– 285. https://doi.org/10.1016/B978-008045089-6.50013-7.

Hill, K. M., Fombelle, P. W., & Sirianni, N. J. (2016). Shopping under the influence of curiosity: How retailers use mystery to drive purchase motivation. *Journal of Business Research, 69*(3), 1028–1034.

Horstmann, F. (2017). Measuring the shopper's attitude toward the point of sale display: Scale development and validation. *Journal of Retailing and Consumer Services, 36,* 112–123.

Howard, K. A., Flora, J. A., Schleicher, N. C., & Gonzalez, E. M. (2004). Alcohol point-of-purchase advertising and promotions: Prevalence, content, and targeting. *Contemporary Drug Problems, 31*(3), 561–583.

Hulland, J. (1999). Use of partial least squares (PLS) in strategic management research: A review of four recent studies. *Strategic Management Journal, 20*(2), 195–204.

International Finance Corporation. (2020). *The power of retail: delivering development impact in emerging markets.* https://www.ifc.org/wps/wcm/connect/news_ext_content/ifc_external_corporate_site/news+and+events/news/the+power+of+retail-eca. Accessed 9 Feb 2021.

Jacoby, J. (2002). Stimulus-organism-response reconsidered: An evolutionary step in modeling (consumer) behavior. *Journal of Consumer Psychology, 12*(1), 51–57.

Jansson, C., Bointon, B., & Marlow, N. (2002). Determinants of consumers' aesthetic responses to Point-of-Purchase materials. *International Journal of Consumer Studies, 26*(2), 145–153.

Kaplan. R. (1972). *The dimensions of the visual environment: Methodological considerations.* https://www.researchgate.net/profile/Rachel_Kaplan/publication/268434960_THE_DIMENSIONS_OF_THE_VISUAL_ENVIRONMENT_METHODOLOGICAL_CONSIDERATIONS_I/links/55d5cb3b08ae9d659488a62b.pdf. Accessed 9 Feb 2021.

Kaplan, S. (1987). Aesthetics, affect, and cognition: Environmental preference from an evolutionary perspective. *Environment and Behavior, 19*(1), 3–32.

Kaplan, R., & Kaplan, S. (1989). *The experience of nature: A psychological perspective.* Cambridge University Press Archive.

Liu, Y., & Jang, S. S. (2009). The effects of dining atmospherics: An extended Mehrabian-Russell model. *International Journal of Hospitality Management, 28*(4), 494–503.

Mehrabian, A., & Russell, J. A. (1974). *An approach to environmental psychology.* Cambridge: M.I.T. Press.

Milliron, B. J., Woolf, K., & Appelhans, B. M. (2012). A point-of-purchase intervention featuring in-person supermarket education affects healthful food purchases. *Journal of Nutrition Education and Behavior, 44*(3), 225–232.

Mishra, P. (2014). Persuading effect of store aesthetics on shoppers' purchase intentions: The gender difference. *Indian Journal of Marketing, 44*(9), 43–53.

Mittal, S., Chawla, D., & Sondhi, N. (2016). Segmentation of impulse buyers in an emerging market–An exploratory study. *Journal of Retailing and Consumer Services, 33*, 53–61.

Murray, J., Teller, C., & Elms, J. (2019). Examining store atmosphere appraisals using parallel approaches from the aesthetics literature. *Journal of Marketing Management, 35*(9–10), 916–939.

Nelson, M. R., Ahn, R. J., Ferguson, G. M., & Anderson, A. (2020). Consumer exposure to food and beverage advertising out of home: An exploratory case study in Jamaica. *International Journal of Consumer Studies, 44*(3), 272–284.

Newman, A. J. (2007). Uncovering dimensionality in the servicescape: Towards legibility. *The Service Industries Journal, 27*(1), 15–28.

Paynter, J., & Edwards, R. (2009). The impact of tobacco promotion at the point of sale: A systematic review. *Nicotine and Tobacco Research, 11*(1), 25–35.

Pieters, R., Wedel, M., & Batra, R. (2010). The stopping power of advertising: Measures and effects of visual complexity. *Journal of Marketing, 74*(5), 48–60.

Ringle, C. M., Wende, S., & Will, A. (2005). *SmartPLS 2.0 M3 Beta.*

Sarkar, D., & Adhikary, M. (2018). Effect of store loyalty on impulse buying behaviour in emerging markets: Observations and propositions. In A. Adhikari (Ed.), *Strategic marketing issues in emerging markets* (pp. 69–81). Springer. https://doi.org/10.1007/978-981-10-6505-7_7.

Schroeder, J. E. (2006). Introduction to the special issue on aesthetics, images and vision. *Marketing Theory, 6*(1), 5–10.

Sigurdsson, V., Engilbertsson, H., & Foxall, G. (2010). The effects of a point-of-purchase display on relative sales: An in-store experimental evaluation. *Journal of Organisational Behaviour Management, 20*(3), 222–233.

Sproul, A. D., Canter, D. D., & Schmidt, J. B. (2003). Does point-of-purchase nutrition labeling influence meal selections? A test in an Army cafeteria. *Military Medicine, 168*(7), 556–560.

Statista. (2020). *Point-of-purchase marketing budget allocation according to CPG merchandising executives in the United States as of June 2016, by type of display.* https://www.statista.com/statistics/733335/us-pop-marketing-budget-allocation-by-display-type/. Accessed 9 Feb 2021.

Toufani, S., Stanton, J. P., & Chikweche, T. (2017). The importance of aesthetics on customers' intentions to purchase smartphones. *Marketing Intelligence and Planning, 35*(3), 316–338.

Vilnai-Yavetz, I., & Koren, R. (2013). Cutting through the clutter: Purchase intentions as a function of packaging instrumentality, aesthetics, and symbolism. *The International Review of Retail, Distribution and Consumer Research, 23*(4), 394–417.

Wang, E. S. (2013). The influence of visual packaging design on perceived food product quality, value, and brand preference. *International Journal of Retail an Distribution Management, 41*(10), 805–816.

Wang, Y. J., Cruthirds, K. W., Axinn, C. N., & Guo, C. (2013). In search of aesthetics in consumer marketing: An examination of aesthetic stimuli from the philosophy of art and the psychology of art. *Academy of Marketing Studies Journal, 17*(2), 37.

Wong, K. K. K. (2013). Partial least squares structural equation modeling (PLS-SEM) techniques using SmartPLS. *Marketing Bulletin, 24*(1), 1–32.

Wong, K. K. K. (2016). Mediation analysis, categorical moderation analysis, and higher-order constructs modeling in Partial Least Squares Structural Equation Modeling (PLS-SEM): A B2B example using SmartPLS. *Marketing Bulletin, 26*, 1–22.

Yamamoto, M., & Lambert, D. R. (1994). The impact of product aesthetics on the evaluation of industrial products. *Journal of Product Innovation Management, 11*(4), 309–324.

Zhou, L., & Wong, A. (2004). Consumer impulse buying and in-store stimuli in Chinese supermarkets. *Journal of International Consumer Marketing, 16*(2), 37–53.

11

Analyzing the Use of Social Media Communication Strategies in Indonesia and Malaysia: Insights and Implications

Fandy Tjiptono, Ghazala Khan, and Ewe Soo Yeong

11.1 Introduction

There is no single universally accepted definition of social media. Defined broadly, social media refers to "any online service through which users can create and share a variety of content" (Bolton et al., 2013, p. 248), while a more specific conceptualization views it as "Internet-based channels that allow users to opportunistically interact and selectively self-present, either in real-time or asynchronously, with both broad and

---

F. Tjiptono (✉)
Victoria University of Wellington, Wellington, New Zealand
e-mail: fandy.tjiptoono@vuw.ac.nz

G. Khan · E. S. Yeong
Monash University Malaysia, Subang Jaya, Malaysia
e-mail: ghazala.khan@monash.edu

E. S. Yeong
e-mail: ewe.sooyeong@monash.edu

narrow audiences who derive value from user-generated content and the perception of the interaction with others" (Carr & Hayes, 2015, p. 50). In general, social media includes user-generated services (e.g., blogs), social networking sites (e.g., Facebook, Google+) professional network sites (e.g., LinkedIn), online review/rating sites, virtual game sites, video sharing sites and online communities, whereby participants design, generate, interact, contribute, post, search for, or edit content (Carr & Hayes, 2015; Krishnamurthy & Dou, 2008; Kusumasondjaja & Tjiptono, 2019).

Traditionally, social media was used for online interaction and social networking (Page, 2010; Sheldon, 2008). Consumers tend to share their experience and stories with their peers, family and friends on social media such as Facebook, Instagram, and WhatsApp. Therefore, the connectedness with others is one of the primary reasons for using social media (Grasmuck et al., 2009). In addition, online social media provides users means to express their personalities and views in a public forum (Goodman, 2007). Social media allows users to engage in self-presentation of identity while communicating with others (Felix et al., 2017). Consumers of mass media may use their experience and interpretations as topics to engage with other users of online social media.

In recent years, the use of social media is much more than social interaction. It provides opportunities for consumers to perform online purchase, engage with companies, access to new career opportunities, and get the updates of global events (The ASEAN Post, 2020). Consumers in ASEAN countries, especially Generation Z, spend more time on social media as compared with few years ago for various reasons, from connecting people to online purchases (The ASEAN Post, 2020). Although Facebook has been the most popular social media worldwide (Clement, 2020), Meltwater's 2019 report on beauty industry found that Instagram becomes more popular channel for influencers, followed by Twitter and YouTube in Indonesia and Malaysia (Meltwater, 2019).

The economic growth and information technology advancement have contributed to the rapid adoption of social media in the Southeast Asian region. Indonesia and Malaysia are no exception, where social media has been part of daily lives of people living the two countries. Not only sharing similar cultural backgrounds, both Indonesia and Malaysia have high penetration of Internet and social media usage. Due to the availability of affordable smartphones and free Wi-Fi connections in public places (e.g., shopping malls, campuses, restaurants, etc.), Indonesians and Malaysians enjoyed spending about one third of their daily time using Internet and committed about 3 hours per day to stay connected on their social media. They are highly engaged and attached to their smartphones for multiple purposes, ranging from communication, socialization and learning to entertainment and commerce. The rapid adoption of social media among consumers around the globe, including in Indonesia and Malaysia, is driven by its promising capabilities in several aspects: (1) satisfying consumer needs for updated, non-commercial, and first-hand information that they can access through sources beyond the boundaries of their physical social communities (Boerman & Kruikemeier, 2016; Kim & Lee, 2017); (2) fulfilling consumer needs for self-actualization by facilitating the processes of self-describing, reconstructing, and sharing consumption experiences (Felix et al., 2017; Xiang & Gretzel, 2010); (3) providing opportunities for consumers to express their love and hate of brands (Dessart et al., 2015; Laroche et al., 2013); and (4) presenting a medium to initiate social relationships with other people with similar interests, hobbies, and activities (Kaplan & Haenlein, 2010; Labrecque, 2014).

It is not surprising that companies have started to respond to the rapid growth of social media adoption by utilizing social media marketing strategies, including advertising, public relations, relationship building, community engagement programs, corporate social responsibility, complaint handing, and electronic word-of-mouth (e-WOM). Social media has been a crucial part of many consumers' shopping habits even before the COVID-19 pandemic (Wold, 2020). Consumers use social media to search for product, brand, and company information before they make online purchases. Consumers discover new products via social media and make purchases from their social media discoveries. They also read other customers' comments and consider them when making comparison between alternative brands, products, retailers, and/or service providers. Furthermore, consumers know better about the brand information and have better engagement with the companies via the brand's social media presence (Wold, 2020).

In view of the importance of social media communication in Indonesia and Malaysia, this chapter focuses on drawing relevant insights into social media consumption in these two countries and proposing important managerial implications on how to build, maintain, and extend effective social media communication strategies, especially in the context of the two countries.

11.2 Social Media Usage in Indonesia and Malaysia

11.2.1 Social Media Usage in Indonesia

There were about 160 million social media users in Indonesia in January 2020 (Kemp, 2020a), which was more than 6 times larger than those in Malaysia for the same period. In 2017, the number of social media users in Indonesia was just 143.12 million (Statista, 2020c). Furthermore, most Indonesia's social media users are active users who spend about 3 hours and 26 minutes on average logged on to social media every day, which is higher than the global average (i.e., 2 hours and 22 minutes) (Greenhouse, 2019). It is predicted that there will be even more social media users in Indonesia by 2025, which is around 256.1 million (Statista, 2020c) (Refer to Table 11.1 for more details).

The top five social media platforms in Indonesia are Youtube, Whatsapp, Facebook, Instagram, and Twitter (WeAreSocial, 2020). It was estimated that 88% of the Indonesian Internet users (about 132 million people) were YouTube users in 2020 (WeAreSocial, 2020). Indonesia is among leading countries based on the number of social media platform users, such as Facebook (top 3 with 140 million users in July 2020, after India and the U.S.), Instagram (top 4 with 78 million users in October 2020, after the USA, India, and Brazil), Whatsapp (top 4 with 59.9 million users in 2019, after India, Brazil, and the USA), and Twitter (top 7 with 13.2 million users in October 2020, after the USA, Japan, India, Brazil, the UK, and Turkey) (Statista, 2020c).

About half of the Indonesians access YouTube to look for product information and understand how to use products (Greenhouse, 2019).

Table 11.1 Brief profiles and social media usage of Indonesia and Malaysia

Aspect	Indonesia	Malaysia
• Total population	• 267 million (July 2020 est.)	• 32.6 million (July 2020 est.)
• Population growth	• 0.79% (2020 est.)	1.29% (2020 est.)
• Median age	• **Male: 30.5 years** • **Female: 31.8 years** • **Total: 31.1 years** • (2020 est.)	• **Male: 28.9 years** • **Female: 29.6 years** • **Total: 29.2 years** • (2020 est.)
• GDP per capita (PPP)	• USD 12,400 (2017 est.)	• USD 29,100 (2017 est.)
• GDP growth	• 5.1% (2017 est.)	• 5.9% (2017 est.)
• Mobile phone connections (% of population)	• 338.2 million (127%)	• 40.69 million (124.8%)
• Internet users (% of population)	• 175.4 million (65.7%)	• 26.69 million (81.88%)
• Active social media users (% of population)	• 160 million (60%)	• 26 million (75.75%)
• Mobile phone ownership	• 96% (94%—smartphone)	• 98% (97%—smartphone)
• Top five most used social media platforms	• YouTube • Whatsapp • Facebook • Instagram • Twitter	• YouTube • Whatsapp • Facebook • Instagram • FB Messenger
• Daily time spent using Internet	• 7 hours, 59 minutes	• 7 hours, 57 minutes
• Daily time spent using social media	• 3 hours, 26 minutes	• 2 hours, 45 minutes
• Average number of social media accounts per Internet user	• 10.1	• 9.7

Sources www.cia.gov, www.wearesocial.com/digital-2020

In addition, Indonesians like to catch up on TV content via YouTube (which is free of charge) instead of TV-on-demand services such as Netflix. Indonesians also actively use Facebook for product information via business pages, and make online purchase based on the information or recommendations on Facebook (Greenhouse, 2019). Besides YouTube and Facebook, Instagram is also an active social marketplace in Indonesia. According to a survey conducted by Ipsos (2018), up to 81% of Instagram users obtain better knowledge about the product and brand on Instagram, and 76% of them reported to have made a purchase after exploring product and brand information on Instagram. In addition, Indonesian small businesses also actively engage their customers via Instagram direct messages.

11.2.2 Social Media Usage in Malaysia

Compared with Indonesia that has a larger population base, the number of social media users in Malaysia is smaller, i.e., 26 million people in January 2020 (Kemp, 2020b). However, active social media users in Malaysia have been increasing substantially for the past few years. According to the survey conducted by Statista (2020a), social media users as a percentage of the total population in Malaysia have been increased from 62% (2016) to 81% (January 2020). Among all social media platforms available, Facebook gained the biggest share in social media usage in Malaysia, followed by Pinterest, Twitter, Youtube, and Instagram (Refer to Table 11.2). Furthermore, considering the continual demand for Facebook among social media users, it is predicted that the total of Facebook users in Malaysia may reach about 24 million in 2023 (Statista, 2020b). According to a survey conducted by Ipsos (2018), most Malaysians felt that social media is crucial to them that brings them

Table 11.2 Comparison of usage of top five social media between Indonesia and Malaysia before and during the COVID-19 pandemic

Social media	Indonesia		Malaysia	
	January 2020 (%)	October 2020 (%)	January 2020 (%)	October 2020 (%)
Facebook	35.75	37.84	74.59	84.47
YouTube	31.76	35.21	2.73	2.92
Pinterest	11.09	12.08	5.71	6.55
Twitter	11.67	8.23	10.61	3.47
Instagram	9.2	6.28	5.75	1.99

Source StatCounter (2020)

happiness. Therefore, social media would be always part of their life (Hirschmann, 2020), where they spend about 2 hours and 45 minutes accessing social media every day (Kemp, 2020b).

11.2.3 Social Media Usage Before and During COVID-19 Pandemic

In 2020, after COVID-19 was discovered and transmitted outside of China, consumers in both Malaysia and Indonesia used social media to find out more about the virus and other related information. In a short period, news and opinions about COVID-19 had been spread wider across social media (Molla, 2020). Fear, worry and anxiety increase on social media (Gao et al., 2020). Malaysian government had warned social media users not to publish fake news or misinformation on social media with strict action against COVID-19 fake news spreaders (Karim & Radhi, 2020). Indonesian government also gave strict sanctions for fake news spreaders related to COVID-19 over social media, following the Law of Electronic Information and Transactions (Bali Picture News, 2020).

During the COVID-19 pandemic, Malaysian government has implemented movement control order (MCO), while Indonesian government has put in effect large-scale social restrictions. As a result, the majority of Malaysians and Indonesians have to maintain social/physical distance and stay at home. Fears of infection and movement restrictions have driven a higher penetration rate on social media. People have spent more time online, including accessing social media, to get the latest COVID-19 updates. This has been the new normal for consumers in both Malaysia and Indonesia since the outbreak of the COVID-19 in the countries. In Malaysia, for instance, about 79% of the respondents surveyed by Ipsos in the end of March 2020 claimed to use social media more often during the MCO (Kong, 2020). Social media provide platforms to communicate the news and reasons for quarantine and social distancing and provide practical advice in order to overcome the threat of this crisis (Depoux et al., 2020). This has reduced the psychological distance among the social media users and has helped in reducing anxiety and mental health problem during the lock-down period. Furthermore, during the COVID-19 pandemic, the ways consumers interact with others on social media have been quite different from the past, as people tend to seek more creative and inspiring entertainment (Snyder, 2020). During this period, more free online resources including reading materials, webinars, online courses, applications and entertainment are available on social media platforms. Consumers in Malaysia and Indonesia also tried to find entertainment such as free online concerts and movies on social media.

During the COVID-19 pandemic, online business and online purchase via social media have also experienced a substantial increase (Statista, 2020d). When spending more time online, consumers have been exploring new platforms and discovering company information, brand and products that they have not noticed previously. For instance, at the beginning of the COVID-19 pandemic, consumers experienced the buying crisis in Malaysia when many people tried to buy the essential products like toilet paper and many dry food items (NST, 2020). Panic buying also hit supermarkets across Jakarta in Indonesia following the government announcement on the country's first two confirmed cases of COVID-19 (The Jakarta Post, 2020a). The consequence of this panic buying was many essential items were out of stock. During that period, social media platforms offered consumers the alternative ways to obtain the items that they wanted. More consumers have been exploring information on fresh products and household products online.

In addition, due to the lockdown instruction, many businesses had been negatively affected, as the movement restriction and physical distancing policy have caused people to stay at home, study from home and interacting with friends via social media. Most businesses have been trying to advertise and promote products online. Consumers also headed to online stores and order essential or non-essential items, causing substantial increase in online purchase. Home delivery has been increasing significantly during that period. Statista (2020e, 2020f) show that about 64% Malaysian and 55% Indonesian respondents reported an increased online purchase.

Table 11.2 shows the comparison between Malaysia and Indonesia in terms of social media usage before and during the COVID-19 pandemic.

According to Table 11.2, social media users in both countries have used more Facebook during the COVID-19 pandemic (9.88% increase in Malaysia; 2.09% increase in Indonesia). This increase may be due to the desire for social interaction and the seeking of product/brand information. Indonesians have been using YouTube more than Malaysians and have increased the usage of YouTube during COVID-19 pandemic as compared to before. Due to the COVID-19 pandemic, many people have lost their jobs. In order to survive, more Indonesians have used online platforms such as YouTube to sell products or to post informative videos to gain enough views for a living as well as to learn new Do-It-Yourself skills (e.g., cooking, playing musical instruments, gardening, carpentering, computing, etc.). Facebook also gained more access during the same period in both Malaysia and Indonesia, as more online advertisements are available on this platform and more consumers access it to get product information and to make purchase.

11.3 Social Media Marketing Strategies

Since the advent of Web 2.0, social media marketing has gained prominence among organizations from various sectors. Social media strategy is defined as "a goal-directed planning process for creating user-generated content, driven by a group of Internet applications, to create a unique and valuable competitive position" (Effing & Spil, 2016, p. 2). The interactive nature of the medium permits firms and brands to share and exchange information with their customers. It also encourages customers to share and exchange information with other customers. In essence, social media has changed the dynamics of customer relationships from "dialogue" to "trialogue" (Tsimonis & Dimitriadis, 2014). This interactive nature further enhances the opportunities to engage with customers and establish relationships with both existing and potential customers. From increasing sales to providing customer support as well as generating leads to creating awareness, social media marketing may be used to accomplish a host of marketing goals (Effing & Spil, 2016). Social media is immediate and involves real-time conversations, which offers vast opportunities for marketers to engage in dialogue with customers.

The abundance of social media with its varied audience offers a gateway to organizations of any size or industry to engage with customers and remain competitive in the marketplace.

Larger firms tend to utilize social media marketing to provide customer services and build brands, but smaller firms may focus on customer services and networking (Tsimonis & Dimitriadis, 2014). Smith (2019) asserts on the importance of social media marketing, particularly for smaller businesses, as investment in social media strategy may provide a better chance for consumer acceptance of messages posted on social media. Not only cost-effective, social media can assist a firm or brand to increase brand recognition, inbound traffic, and search engine ranking. Furthermore, social media may help a firm to reach out to new segments or identify potential leads (Smith, 2019).

Several studies note how and why social media marketing strategies have been adopted by businesses. For instance, Tsimonis and Dimitriadis (2014) assert that the primary motivations for organizations to invest in social media are growth, the presence and competitor activities on social media, growing popularity of social media and pressures to reduce cost. Companies may use a range of activities or approaches to engage with customers and these include competitions, announcements related to new products, providing useful information and handling customer services issues (Tsimonis & Dimitriadis, 2014). In a study of the types of creative message appeals and social media channels used by top brands, Ashley and Tuten (2015) found that the most common creative message appeals used by marketers were functional and resonance, followed by experiential and emotional appeals. The researchers also found that the most popular media channels were Microblogging and Social Networking and Microsites. Echoing findings by Tsimonis and Dimitriadis (2014), Ashley and Tuten (2015) report that sales contests were among the most popular sales promotion techniques used to engage with customers followed by discounts. A recent study by Drummond et al. (2020) proposes several strategies and social media tactics built upon four main themes: collaboration, engagement, communication, connection, and coordination. For instance, social media posts that solicit ratings, reviews or recommendations are ways in which firms may engage with their customers and social media strategies that encourage post sharing are ways to connect with customers. A framework of social media marketing strategies and actions by Ananda et al. (2016) proposes three main social media actions that are popular and commonly used by marketing firms (i.e., representation, engagement, and listening-in). They argue that these actions are driven by firm's internal or external motivations and enable firms to achieve both transactional and relational goal. Thus, a brand or company can actively engage with the customers through promoting via influencers or solicit actions such as participation in contests or sweepstakes. Alternatively, a firm's social media marketing strategy may just emphasize communicating their products and promotions online. Finally, a firm may collect market intelligence through social listening.

An exploration of the social media marketing strategies and practices in Malaysia and Indonesia for the business-to-consumer (B2C) sector resulted in our proposed typology of social media marketing strategy (see Fig. 11.1). The typology is based on two key dimensions: engagement and commerce. Customer engagement marketing refers to "the firm's deliberate effort to motivate, empower, and measure a customer's voluntary contribution to its marketing functions, beyond a core, economic transaction" (Harmeling et al., 2017, p. 312). Essentially, engagement is all about creating, maintaining, and extending connections, interactions, involvement, contributions, and two-way flow of information with the customers (Brodie et al., 2011; Pansari & Kumar, 2017; Smith & Wallace, 2010).

		Commerce	
		Hard Selling	**Soft Selling**
Engagement	Active	**Social Media Optimization Strategy** • Influencer Marketing • Content seeding • Interactive (real-time) advertising	**Social Media Engagement-Focused Strategy** • CSR • Customer marketing/management • Video advertising
	Passive	**Social Media Commercial-Focused Strategy** • Sales promotions • Advertising	**Social Media Early Extension Strategy** • Messaging (WhatsApp) • FB Messenger • FB advertisements • Instagram

Fig. 11.1 A typology of social media marketing strategy

Meanwhile, social media has become an important resource in business activities, such as sales (Bocconcelli et al., 2017). The second dimension, commerce, refers to marketing tactics that portray a firm or brand on the social media channels with a strong emphasis on push elements of marketing strategies (i.e., sales or business/economic transactions). The interaction between the two dimensions (active versus passive customer engagement and hard selling vs soft selling) results in four social media marketing strategies: social media optimization strategy, social media engagement-focused strategy, social media commercial-focused strategy, and social media early extension strategy.

11.3.1 Social Media Optimization Strategy

In Social Media Optimization Strategy (Active Engagement and Hard Selling), firms attempt to actively engage with their customers and also encourage economic or sales transactions. There is an equal emphasis on the push and pull elements of the marketing strategy. This strategy is more popular among large established firms and may involve strategies such as Influencer Marketing, Content Seeding, and Interactive Advertising. Brands are likely to connect and create two-way dialogues with customers using a variety of social media platforms, such as Facebook, Twitter, Instagram, and engage with influencers to endorse their brands and encourage word-of-mouth. This strategy may also involve interactive advertising and calls for participatory actions in typical transactional-related activities, such as sweepstakes, contests or general responses to discounts or limited offers.

Influencer marketing as a strategy is popular in both Malaysia and Indonesia. Using algorithms, influencers can be selected based on their level of engagement. Influencers are used to give product reviews and brand mentions, act as an ambassador and participate in company marketing events. A strategy that is often seen is that companies employ multiple influencers to promote the same brand. Influencers generally curate their own caption and content, whilst adhering to the requirements of the sponsored company. Regional virtual shopping malls like Shopee and Lazada employ influencer marketing on a regular basis to interact with their customers and establish long-term relationships, while creating awareness of new products and encourage repeat purchases. In 2019, Shopee featured international celebrity footballer Cristiano Ronaldo, where he was featured dancing and promoting Shopee (https://shopee.com.my/m/99). As a result of the campaign, Shopee's negative sentiments dropped from 3.5 to 1.9% and 80% of the share of voice was about the ad campaign (Chen, 2019). Lazada focuses more on local or regional influencers. For instance, in Indonesia, Lazada used 1000 influencers to promote its 11.11 sale, a regional mega-sale. With a thousand plus influencers, the campaign reached 255 million social media users and more than 2.5 million engagements (Hamdani, 2017). Using multiple influencers allows companies to reach a wider audience and create awareness of the campaign.

Influencer marketing is also employed by firms to reposition or refresh its brand image. Lazada Malaysia collaborated with six local influencers to personify its new image, that of playful, bold, limitless and insatiable (Marketing, 2019). Each influencer was selected based on their Instagram personalities that corresponded with Lazada's refreshed image. The company was able to garner over 5580 likes within 24 hours of the launch of the campaign.

Due to the sheer size of Indonesia, both geographically and demographically, there is a shift in the Indonesian market, and a preference for employing hyperlocal influencers is on the rise (Utomo & Noormega, 2019). Hyperlocal influencers are city-based with strong following in their respective cities. As such, an influencer in Jakarta may not be as popular in Medan or Balikpapan, making it challenging to relate to the locals in cities other than Jakarta. The execution of such a strategy is appropriate in large and diverse countries, as it allows the firms to engage with the target audience through creation of relevant content and is also cost-effective.

Another new social media optimization (active engagement and hard selling) strategy is live streaming, which is often employed by e-commerce platforms. The global pandemic has seen an upward trend in live streaming for many e-commerce platforms. Combined with influencers on Instagram and Facebook, live streaming of promotions by shopping platforms like Tokopedia in Indonesia and Lazada in Malaysia creates an interactive environment for shoppers to engage with the sellers, learn about new products or services and new promotions, and be entertained. For the sellers, it provides an opportunity for two-way interactions between vendors and the shoppers, increases audience, enhances brand credibility and authenticity, collects customer feedback, drives website traffic, and boosts sales (Digital Intelligence, 2020; Innity, 2020).

In some instances, micro-campaigns may take the form of a social media optimization strategy, for instance, McDonald's Malaysia officially collaborated with TikTok via the #BigMac TikTok Challenge and promoted a contest to dance and win prizes up to RM 20,000 (approximately USD 4800). The super successful campaign that rated high in both engagement and commerce resulted in many online influencers promoting the challenge, an example of content seeding. The campaign also saw an increase in sales and approximately 5.9 million counts were spotted (SM Editor, 2018).

Real-time advertising is yet another strategy that is utilized through employing a combination of active engagement and hard selling (social media optimization) strategy. For instance, capitalizing on a social media spat that went viral, many retailers used a very tongue-in-cheek appeal to encourage sales of their products (Dayangku, 2020). For instance, on its Instagram account, Bata Malaysia promoted its sneakers by stating "You don't need to spend RM460 on a burger to impress someone", followed by the actual price of the sneakers (https://www.instagram.com/p/CGCD-DQjCLq/). Joining the bandwagon, Kyochon, a Korean fried chicken outlet, employed a very interactive and rewarding contest, challenging its customers to suggest meals from their own menu "What would you get for RM460?" (https://www.instagram.com/p/CGCN2PfjPZU/). The lucky winner was promised dining vouchers worth RM460.

11.3.2 Social Media Engagement-Focused Strategy

Firms that employ social media engagement-focused (active engagement and soft selling) strategy aim at establishing active engagement with stakeholders, while communicating or promoting low levels of sales purposes. This strategy involves the usage of a wide variety of social media, but with a higher emphasis on building a positive brand image, creating opportunities for a two-way dialogue with the customers and building long-term community relationships. In other words, the primary aim of this strategy is to disseminate information, build brand image, create an interactive virtual environment to establish a dialogue with their customers and strengthen relationships with various stakeholders. Using this approach, large businesses in Malaysia such as local and international banks promote their Corporate Social Responsibility programs through social media such as Facebook and Instagram. For instance, a local Malaysian bank CIMB, engages with the stakeholders via its corporate Instagram account. The corporate Instagram account is used to promote their CSR outreach programs (https://www.instagram.com/p/CFQypGkpFAh/). The bank uses Instagram to update the public on their activities, attracting volunteers and forging strategic alliances with other not-for-profit organizations. Posting behind-the-scenes photos of employees engaging in community work showcases the bank's commitment and efforts to and for the betterment of the local communities.

HSBC in Malaysia also engages extensively with both its end-users and corporate customers on its Facebook page (https://www.facebook.com/HSBCMalaysia). HSBC uses video advertising as a means of engaging with its customers. For instance, it uses Facebook for its corporate social responsibility campaign in raising awareness of breast cancer in October 2020. Videos and regular informative posts are published targeting small business owners. The primary purpose of such posts is to educate corporate clients about financial literacy and indirectly influence companies to make HSBC their primary financial partner. The corporate social media account is also a platform to share with the public the bank's commitment to the underprivileged. Social listening is yet another function that both CIMB and HSBC employ, whereby, both banks attempt at answering queries and complaints promptly.

Active engagement with the various stakeholders is seen as imperative for a firm to be successful, particularly for non-profit organizations. Such organizations or institutions rely heavily on public support to survive. FurryKids Safehaven (https://www.facebook.com/furrykidssafehaven/), a shelter for abandoned, abused and homeless dogs, regularly engages with volunteers, donors and potential adoptees through video advertising/marketing. Bleak and gloomy videos of rescued dogs appeal the altruistic nature of the public in general and animal lovers. The shelter also posts appeals to the public for regular donations to cover monthly and medical expenses.

Five-star hotels like Four Seasons in Jakarta employ a social media engagement-focused (active engagement and soft selling) strategy through video marketing. The hotel posts videos mirroring the hotel ambience, the facilities, local attractions and occasional reminders to hotel guests to rejuvenate themselves (https://www.facebook.com/FourSeasonsHotelJakarta). During the global pandemic, Four Seasons Jakarta posted highly engaging videos of their executive chefs' recipes, whilst encouraging guests to stay at home and learn new skills (https://www.facebook.com/FourSeasonsHotelJakarta/videos/248746749757489). Guests were also reminded to share online and hashtag the hotel if they recreated the recipes at home. These videos not only encouraged guests to stay at home but also enhanced the brand image of the hotel and brand recall, especially since customers would remember the hotel every time they used the recipes.

During the COVID-19 outbreak, firms have taken to social media to display their commitment to society. Employing a social media engagement-focused strategy, in October 2020, a popular Malaysian fashion retailer, FashionValet, utilized its Instagram (https://www.instagram.com/fashionvaletcom/) and Facebook pages to advertise their fundraising campaigns for the worst-hit areas in Malaysia, managed to collect RM 128,000 (USD 31,219) in less than 24 hours. In an earlier campaign in April 2020, the company successfully raised RM 1.4 million (approximately USD 341 thousand) to assist with shortages of medical supplies and equipment facing the front liners (Ihsan, 2020).

The global pandemic saw new patterns of behavior during Large-Scale Social Restrictions in Indonesia and Movement Control Order (MCO) in Malaysia, generally known as lockdown. During these trying times, Indonesians and Malaysians were reportedly turning to online entertainment, learning, socialization, and shopping. Trending hashtags were used by companies to encourage Indonesians and Malaysians to stay at home. This challenge was seen as a way to remind people to stay at home, engage with their customers and demonstrate social responsibility. For instance, Bernama, a local newspaper in Malaysia, shared infographics on its Twitter account aimed at promoting general mental health and included emergency hotline numbers (Malek, 2020). In Indonesia, several artists and musicians performed and shared their knowledge online in an event called #bahagiadirumah (happy at home) during 30–31 March 2020 (The Jakarta Post, 2020b).

11.3.3 Social Media Commercial-Focused Strategy

Firms and brands that implement a social media commercial-focused (passive engagement and hard selling) strategy are likely to call attention a heavier push rather than pull tactics. Through dissemination of pre-dominantly one-way information to create awareness of new products or new promotions, the brands emphasize on encouraging sales and repeat purchases. This strategy is popular among brands whose primary objective may be survival and are sales-oriented. For instance, in 2019, Frisian Flag, a popular dairy brand, increased online sales through collaboration in Indonesia. By using Facebook Collaborative Ads, Frisian Flag partnered with Lazada for its Single's day and 12.12 important regional mega-sales days. Using video and photo ads, the brand created awareness of the upcoming promotions, and on the main mega sales days, Frisian Flag ran Collaborative Ads, displaying products that customers were more likely to purchase or have an interest in based on their preferences. This low engagement and hard-selling campaign reached 9 million people and saw a 6.3 times return on ad spent (https://www.facebook.com/business/success/frisian-flag-indonesia).

Budget hotels in Indonesia such as Red Planet employ the social media commercial-focused strategy to attract customers and encourage sales. Red Planet regularly posts its special offers or limited promotions on its Facebook page (https://www.facebook.com/redplanetindonesia/photos/a.1445612579089478/2672511986399525/), with occasional sharing of important information or travelers' pictures found on other platforms such as Tripadvisor. Furthermore, J.Co a popular franchise donut brand from Indonesia, utilizes both Facebook and Instagram to promote their donuts, new flavors, special celebrations and availability or announcements of new outlets, with little efforts to engage with the customers (https://www.facebook.com/iamjcolovers/photos/pcb.10159344596852792/10159344596672792/).

In Malaysia, local but established pharmacy chains like Caring Pharmacy put emphasis on a push rather than a pull strategy and implement a social media commercial-focused strategy via platforms such as WhatsApp and Facebook pages (https://www.facebook.com/caring2u/). The primary purpose of WhatsApp messaging is to retain customers through creating awareness of limited promotion offers and reminders to loyal members of any new rewards such as e-vouchers or redemption of loyalty points before expiry dates. Senheng, an established electronics retail chain, uses its Facebook and Instagram pages to create product and sales promotion awareness. Senheng also uses Link Advertisements on Facebook to capture leads to their websites and drive sales (https://www.facebook.com/SenhengMY/photos/pcb.10158627013138548/10158627011173548/). Furthermore, many banks, such as HSBC, have used social media to promote cash backs or sweepstakes and encourage customers to use their credit or debit cards (https://www.facebook.com/HSBCMalaysia/photos/a.1745148675599148/3383764498404216/).

11.3.4 Social Media Early Extension Strategy

The last strategy is the social media early extension (low engagement and soft selling) strategy. This strategy is used by firms and brands that are still in the early adoption stage of social media as an extension of their marketing strategies. It appears to be more popular with small business operators, where Whatsapp, FB Messenger, and Instagram accounts were created and used for basic marketing communication purposes. It is also likely that businesses may be experimenting with the whole idea of social media marketing strategy, where they use the social media accounts as points of contact to handle product enquiries, provide product information, respond to customer complaints, and so forth. For instance, in Indonesia and Malaysia, small grocery stores utilize WhatsApp to communicate their availability of products or services, such as mineral water and gas delivery. Several small business retailers have taken to Facebook through Link Ads to increase traffic to their online stores and encourage customers to make purchases via their websites. For instance, Berkat Madinah Malaysia, advertises on Facebook via a Link ad to encourage customers to visit the website and make purchases and create awareness of their brand (https://www.facebook.com/TYKfarmdirect/). Another example is that of Farm Direct, an organic farm advertises on social media through Link ads to inform the availability of their produce and increase traffic to their farm both physically and virtually (https://www.facebook.com/BerkatMadinahRestaurant/). Small caterers or suppliers of home-cooked food use Link or Carousel advertisements on Facebook, to broaden their reach, build brand awareness, increase traffic to their online stores and drive sales. Once satisfied with this strategy, the managers or owners may increase their engagement and/or commerce by moving towards any of the other strategies: social media commercial-focused strategy, social media engagement-focused strategy or social media optimization strategy.

11.4 Concluding Remarks: The Roads Ahead

Due to the accessibility and affordability of information technology (e.g., the hardware, software, and infrastructure), social media has played an important role in daily lives of the majority of people living in Indonesia and Malaysia. People use multiple social media platforms (e.g., Instagram, YouTube, Facebook, Twitter, and Tik Tok) for many purposes, including accessing the most up-to-date information, sharing knowledge and skills (e.g., recipes, practical tips and tricks, songs, videos, tutorials, and so forth), showing off new experiences, shopping for products and services, learning, socializing with family and friends, and looking for entertainment. From business perspectives, social media marketing has been growing in the two countries. It has been adopted in a wide range of fields, such as public relations, corporate social responsibility, community engagement, customer service, relationship building, electronic word-of-mouth (e-WOM), complaint handling, and many others. This chapter provides several important insights and implications.

The first key insight is the typology of social media marketing strategy based on two key dimensions (engagement and commerce). Social media optimization strategy (active engagement and hard-selling approach) reflects the firm's strategic efforts to utilize the potential capacity of social media platforms to both engage customers actively and to promote the brands, products, and the company in such a way to create and increase sales. New media, such as interactive (real-time) advertising, could be utilized for this purpose. Another way is to identify and hire popular influencers (e.g., YouTubers, Instagrammers, and TikTokers) to help create high engagement among the target market as well as do some hard-selling activities.

In contrast, social media early extension strategy (passive engagement and soft-selling approach) is adopted by firms exploring the potential, advantages, and suitability of social media marketing for their current marketing strategies. Small- and medium-sized firms may explore some new media (e.g., WhatsApp, Facebook, Instagram, Telegram, and LINE) for this purpose.

As the name indicates, social media engagement-focused strategy coordinates efforts to actively motivate, empower, and involve customers in marketing functions without heavy emphasis on driving sales. Larger firms or NGOs (non-government organizations) may pursue this strategy by involving the volunteers and community as well as communicating their Corporate Social Responsibility (CSR) initiatives via social media. Videos of their activities may also be posted on their Facebook accounts to inform and attract more awareness and support from the public.

The last strategy, social media's commercial-focused strategy, uses social media as a means to drive sales and repeat purchases. This strategy reflects a traditional push (rather than pull) element of marketing strategy highlighting on sales, such as by using Facebook Link Advertisements to create awareness of new products/brands or provide a sales promotion program (e.g., sweepstakes). Firms that adhere to a traditional marketing approach may well benefit from employing this strategy.

The selection of the most appropriate strategy depends on several factors, including company's strategic marketing objectives, available resources (budget, human resources, technology, networks, customer bases), specific brand positioning, target market's behavior, competitive actions, and relevant macro-environmental (e.g., economic, legal, technological, and socio-cultural) conditions. It is important to note that a company may choose different social media marketing strategies for different brands, products, business units, and geographical markets.

The second insight relates to one of the most powerful impacts of social media, i.e., word-of-mouth marketing. Many businesses prefer to hire macro-influencers (those with 100,001 to 1 million followers) and mega influencers (more than 1 million followers) than micro (10,001–100,000 followers) and nano influencers (3000–10,000 followers). However, the same choice might not be feasible for small businesses due to budget constraints and market coverage factors. As an alternative, hyperlocal influencers can be a better option to generate higher engagement rates for local small businesses. Hyperlocal influencers consist of local (micro and nano) influencers like Instagrammers and Youtubers who have a strong audience in a city, state, province, or region and can affect buying decisions among consumers in their area (Tokotown, 2020; Utomo & Noormega, 2019).

Third, firms need to consider using multiple platforms, including new ones, to build visibility and credibility among relevant stakeholders. Social media marketing strategy needs to be consistent with other elements of integrated marketing communications to create a consistent image and positioning. Future trends of technology may also need to be explored and incorporated in the social media communication design and delivery, such as Artificial Intelligence, Virtual Reality, robotics, voice and visual recognition, and so forth.

Fourth, while the focus of this chapter is social media marketing strategies in the business-to-consumer (B2C) sector, the lessons learned from the applications can be extended to the context of business-to-business (B2B), especially on how interactive online technologies can be used for information sharing, relationship building, and market sensing (Chae et al., 2020). However, the emphasis is different in the B2B area, where social media plays an important role as an enabler for interacting with partners in the company's upstream supply chain and sharing important information with partners to increase operational efficiency (Chae et al., 2020; Chan et al., 2017; Siamagka et al., 2015).

Fifth, the rapid and wide adoption of social media in the Southeast Asian region has also brought some specific challenges. Consumers in Indonesia and Malaysia tend to be susceptible to the dissemination of fake news (hoaxes) about almost all types of information: gossips, entertainment, business, politics, health, product and brand information, and so forth. Many of them tend to like, forward and/or share news, photos, or videos without proper verification. Other issues that need a special attention include "the dark side of social media", such as privacy abuse, trolling, cyberbullying, online witch-hunts, and online firestorms (Baccarella et al., 2018), and "freedom to hate" (Lim, 2017). All these negative practices may pose significant challenges for companies in designing, delivering, and evaluating social media marketing strategies effectively.

These five insights provide relevant practical implications for organizations doing business in an emerging economy in different regions, such as Asia (e.g., Indonesia, Malaysia, Thailand, the Philippines, Bangladesh, and Sri Lanka), Afrika (e.g., South Africa, Nigeria, and Ghana), and South America (e.g., Brazil, Colombia, and Argentina). Companies need to choose the most appropriate social media marketing strategy (social media optimization strategy, social media engagement-focused strategy, social media commercial-focused strategy, and social media early extension strategy) and plan, coordinate, execute, and control it strategically. Multiple social media platforms (especially those with high numbers of users, e.g., YouTube, WhatsApp, Facebook, and Instagram) and social media influencers (including Youtubers and Instagrammers) can be included in the strategy. Furthermore, continuous innovation is crucial for successful social media marketing. For instance, Lazada introduces the "shoppertainment" concept, where they integrate social media, livestream shows, shopping vouchers and discounts, and in-app games to create exciting and innovative customer engagement, entertainment, and shopping experiences (Lazada Group, 2019; The Edge Markets, 2020).

This concept has been successful in increasing the number of users and sales for Lazada, one of the biggest e-commerce players in the Southeast Asian region (Li, 2020; The Edge Markets, 2020).

References

Ananda, A. S., Hernandez-Garcia, A., & Lamberti, L. (2016). N-REL: A comprehensive framework of social media marketing strategic actions for marketing organizations. *Journal of Innovation and Knowledge, 1,* 170–180.

Ashley, C., & Tuten, T. (2015). Creative strategies in social media marketing: An exploratory study of branded social content and consumer engagement. *Psychology and Marketing, 32*(1), 15–27.

Baccarella, C. V., Wagner, T. F., Kietzmann, J. H., & McCarthy, I. P. (2018). Social media? It's serious! Understanding the dark side of social media. *European Management Journal, 36,* 431–438.

Bali Picture News. (2020). *COVID-19 fake news spreaders to face imprisonment and 1 billion penalty.* https://balipicturenews.com/imprisonment-for-covid-19-fake-news-spreaders/. Accessed 15 Oct 2020.

Bocconcelli, R., Cioppi, M., & Pagano, A. (2017). Social media as a resource in SMEs' sales process. *Journal of Business and Industrial Marketing, 32*(5), 693–709.

Boerman, S. C., & Kruikemeier, S. (2016). Consumer responses to promoted tweets sent by brands and political parties. *Computers in Human Behavior, 65,* 285–294.

Bolton, R. N., Parasuraman, A., Hoefnagels, A., Migchels, N., Kabadayi, S., Gruber, T., Loureiro, Y. K., & Solnet, D. (2013). Understanding generation Y and their use of social media: A review and research agenda. *Journal of Service Management, 24*(3), 245–267.

Brodie, R. J., Hollebeek, L. D., & Jurić, B., & Ilic, A. (2011). Customer engagement: Conceptual domain, fundamental propositions, and implications for research. *Journal of Service Research, 14*(3), 252–271.

Carr, C. T., & Hayes, R. A. (2015). Social media: Defining, developing, and divining. *Atlantic Journal of Communication, 23*(1), 46–65.

Chae, B. K., McHaney, R., & Sheu, C. (2020). Exploring social media use in B2B supply chain operations. *Business Horizons, 63,* 73–84.

Chan, H. K., Lacka, E., Yee, R. W. Y., & Lim, M. K. (2017). The role of social media data in operations and production management. *International Journal of Production Research, 55*(17), 5027–5036.

Chen, J. (2019, August 22). *Social media campaign report on the Cristiano Ronaldo Shopee campaign*. https://www.synthesio.com/blog/social-media-campaign-report-cristiano-ronaldo-shopee-campaign/.

Clement, J. (2020). *Number of monthly active Facebook users worldwide as of 2nd quarter 2020*. https://www.statista.com/statistics/264810/number-of-monthly-active-facebook-users-worldwide/.

Dayangku, S. (2020). *14 popular companies who used the viral RM460 burger drama in their own marketing schtick*. https://vulcanpost.com/716991/rm460-burger-viral-meme-malaysia-brand-marketing/.

Depoux, A., Martin, S., Karafillakis, E., Preet, R., Wilder-Smith, A., & Larson, H. (2020). The pandemic of social media panic travels faster than the COVID-19 outbreak. *Journal of Travel Medicine, 27*(3), 1–2.

Dessart, L., Veloutsou, C., & Morgan-Thomas, A. (2015). Consumer engagement in online brand communities: A social media perspective. *Journal of Product and Brand Management, 24*(1), 28–42.

Digital Intelligence. (2020, May 3). *Case study: Indonesian online retailer doubles sales with Instagram Live social media ads*. https://www.digitalstrategyconsulting.com/online-advertising/online-advertising-research-tips-and-news-for-marketers/case-study-indonesian-online-retailer-doubles-sales-with-instagram-live-social-media-ads/48701/.

Drummond, C., O'Toole, T., & McGrath, H. (2020). Digital engagement strategies and tactics in social media marketing. *European Journal of Marketing, 54*(6), 1247–1280.

Effing, R., & Spil, T. A. M. (2016). The social strategy sone: Towards a framework for evaluating social media strategies. *International Journal of Information Management, 36*, 1–8.

Felix, R., Rauschnabel, P. A., & Hinsch, C. (2017). Elements of strategic social media marketing: A holistic framework. *Journal of Business Research, 70*, 118–126.

Gao, J., Zheng, P., Jia, Y., Chen, H., Mao, Y., Chen, S, Wang, Y., Fu, H., & Hashimoto, K. (2020). Mental health problems and social media exposure during COVID-19 outbreak. *PLoS One, 15*(4), e0231924.

Goodman, J. (2007). Click first, ask questions later: Understanding teen online behaviour. *Aplis, 20*, 84–86.

Grasmuck, S., Martin, J., & Zhao, S. (2009). Ethno-racial identity displays on Facebook. *Journal of Computer-Mediated Communication, 15*, 158–188.

Greenhouse. (2019, May 16). *Indonesia's social media landscape: An overview.* https://greenhouse.co/blog/indonesias-social-media-landscape-an-overview/.

Hamdani, T. A. (2017, November 28). *Lazada had 1,000 Influencers during 11.11 promo.* https://translate.google.com/translate?hl=en&sl=id&u=https://www.tek.id/insight/lazada-punya-1-000-pasukan-influencer-saat-pesta-belanja-11-1-b1RTn9z2&prev=search&pto=aue.

Harmeling, C. M., Moffett, J. W., Arnold, M. J., & Carlson, B. D. (2017). Toward a theory of customer engagement marketing. *Journal of the Academy of Marketing Science, 45*, 312–335.

Hirschmann, R. (2020, July 13). *Malaysia likelihood using social media less.* https://www.statista.com/statistics/1090784/malaysia-likelihood-using-social-media-less/.

https://www.facebook.com/BerkatMadinahRestaurant/.

https://www.facebook.com/business/success/frisian-flag-indonesia.

https://www.facebook.com/caring2u/photos/a.242333019125350/495099693 1592245/.

https://www.facebook.com/FourSeasonsHotelJakarta.

https://www.facebook.com/FourSeasonsHotelJakarta/videos/248746749 757489.

https://www.facebook.com/HSBCMalaysia.

https://www.facebook.com/HSBCMalaysia/photos/a.1745148675599148/340 0139550100044/.

https://www.facebook.com/HSBCMalaysia/photos/a.1745148675599148/340 2814966499169.

https://www.facebook.com/HSBCMalaysia/photos/a.1745148675599148/338 3764498404216/.

https://www.facebook.com/HSBCMalaysia/videos/345214703384995.

https://www.facebook.com/redplanetindonesia/photos/a.1445612579089478/ 2672511986399525/.

https://www.facebook.com/SenhengMY/photos/pcb.10158627013138548/ 10158627011173548/.

https://www.instagram.com/p/CFQypGkpFAh/.

https://www.instagram.com/p/CGCD-DQjCLq/.

https://www.instagram.com/p/CGCN2PfjPZU/.

https://www.facebook.com/TYKfarmdirect/.

Ihsan, S. L. A. (2020, October 14). Covid-19: FashionValet launches fundraising for hard-hit areas. *New Straits Times.* https://www.msn.com/en-my/lifestyle/lifestyle-buzz/covid-19-fashionvalet-launches-fundraising-for-hard-hit-areas/ar-BB19ZZJv?ocid=ems.msn.dl.CaracolBelize.

Innity BLOG. (2020, April 27). *How brands can use live streaming as their brand voice in times of crisis.* https://blog.innity.com/2020/04/how-brands-can-use-live-streaming-as-their-brand-voice-in-times-of-crisis/.

Ipsos. (2018). *Instagram's impact on Indonesian businesses.* https://www.ipsos.com/sites/default/files/ct/publication/documents/2018-11/instagram_report_english_version.pdf.

Kaplan, A. M., & Haenlein, M. (2010). Users of the world, unite! The challenges and opportunities of social media. *Business Horizons, 53*(1), 59–68.

Karim, K. N., & Radhi, N. A. M. (2020, April 24). Govt warns of strict action against Covid-19 fake news spreaders. *New Straits Times.* https://www.nst.com.my/news/nation/2020/04/587202/govt-warns-strict-action-against-covid-19-fake-news-spreaders.

Kemp, S. (2020a, February 18). *Digital 2020: Indonesia.* DATAREPORTAL. https://datareportal.com/reports/digital-2020-indonesia.

Kemp, S. (2020b, February 18). *Digital 2020: Malaysia.* DATAREPORTAL. https://datareportal.com/reports/digital-2020-Malaysia.

Kim, M., & Lee, M. (2017). Brand-related user-generated content on social media: The roles of source and sponsorship. *Internet Research, 27*(5), 1085–1103.

Kong, S. (2020, April 26). *Covid-19 changes consumer buying behaviours.* Borneo Post Online. https://www.theborneopost.com/2020/04/26/covid-19-changes-consumer-buying-behaviours/.

Krishnamurthy, S., & Dou, W. (2008). Advertising with user-generated content: A framework and research agenda. *Journal of Interactive Marketing, 8*(2), 1–7.

Kusumasondjaja, S., & Tjiptono, F. (2019). Endorsement and visual complexity in food advertising on Instagram. *Internet Research, 29*(4), 659–687.

Labrecque, L. I. (2014). Fostering consumer-brand relationships in social media environments: The role of parasocial interaction. *Journal of Interactive Marketing, 28*(2), 134–148.

Laroche, M., Habibi, M. R., & Richard, M. O. (2013). To be or not to be in social media: How brand loyalty is affected by social media? *International Journal of Information Management, 33*(1), 76–82.

Lazada Group. (2019, March 29). *Shoppertainment sets new record for Lazada 7th birthday celebrations.* PRNewswire. https://en.prnasia.com/releases/apac/shoppertainment-sets-new-record-for-lazada-7th-birthday-celebrations-241390.shtml.

Li, C. (2020, July 21). *Lazlive shapes the future of shopping in Southeast Asia*. ALiZila. https://www.alizila.com/lazlive-shapes-the-future-of-shopping-in-southeast-asia/.

Lim, M. (2017). Freedom to hate: Social media, algorithmic enclaves, and the rise of tribal nationalism in Indonesia. *Critical Asian Studies, 49*(3), 411–427.

Malek, N. H. A. (2020, April 6). *Malaysians turn to social media, streaming services to fill time during MCO*. The Malaysian Reserve. https://themalaysianreserve.com/2020/04/06/malaysians-turn-to-social-media-streaming-services-to-fill-time-during-mco/.

Marketing. (2019, July 11). *Lazada engages 6 influencers to manifest different dimensions of its brand identify*. https://www.marketing-interactive.com/lazada-engages-6-influencers-to-manifest-different-dimensions-of-its-brand-identity.

Meltwater. (2019, July 30). *Beyond skin deep: Understanding the shopping journey of the Southeast Asian beauty buyers*. https://learn.meltwater.com/2019-07-30BeautyReport_01.Registration-NewsRelease.html.

Molla, R. (2020). *How coronavirus took over social media*. https://tinyurl.com/ycwtmx3u. Accessed 30 Oct 2020.

NST. (2020, March 17). *Covid-19: Panic buying at supermarkets nationwide*. https://www.nst.com.my/news/nation/2020/03/575302/covid-19-panic-buying-supermarkets-nationwide-nsttv.

Page, R. (2010). Re-examining narrativity: Small stories in status updates. *Text Talk, 30*, 423–444.

Pansari, A., & Kumar, V. (2017). Customer engagement: The construct, antecedents, and consequences. *Journal of the Academy of Marketing Science, 45*, 294–311.

Sheldon, P. (2008). Student favorite: Facebook and motives for its use. *Southwestern Mass Communication Journal, 23*(2), 39–53.

Siamagka, N. T., Christodoulides, G., Michaelidou, N., & Valvi, A. (2015). Determinants of social media adoption by B2B organizations. *Industrial Marketing Management, 51*, 89–99.

SM Editor. (2018, October 30). *A closer look at McDonald's Tik Tok campaign #BigMac TikTok*. Silvermouse. https://blog.silvermouse.com.my/2018/10/a-closer-look-at-mcdonalds-bigmac-tiktok-campaign.html.

Smith, K. (2019, August 12). *15 reasons why marketing through social media is a must for every small business*. LYFE. https://drive.google.com/drive/u/0/folders/1f6PBcA-VcqkJYgap-SSRsoHJcTwHDkoB.

Smith, S. E. & Wallace, O. (2010, September 10). *What is customer engagement?* http://www.wisegeek.com/what-is-customer-engagement.htm.

Snyder, V. (2020, August 11). *What marketers need to know about people's social media patterns during the pandemic.* business.com https://www.business.com/articles/social-media-patterns-during-the-pandemic/.

StatCounter. (2020). *Social media stats.* https://gs.statcounter.com/social-media-stats/.

Statista. (2020a, July 13). *Active social media users as percentage of the total population in Malaysia from 2016 to 2020.* https://www.statista.com/statistics/883712/malaysia-social-media-penetration/.

Statista. (2020b, July 28). *Number of Facebook users in Malaysia from 2017 to 2025 (in millions).* https://www.statista.com/statistics/490484/number-of-malaysia-facebook-users/.

Statista. (2020c, August 13). *Number of social network users in Indonesia from 2017 to 2025 (in millions).* https://www.statista.com/statistics/247938/number-of-social-network-users-in-indonesia/.

Statista. (2020d, June 30). *Frequency of online purchases during COVID-19 pandemic Malaysia 2020 by age group.* https://www.statista.com/statistics/1128946/malaysia-frequency-of-online-purchase-covid-19-by-age-group/.

Statista. (2020e, June 29). *Impacts of COVID-19 pandemic on the online purchase behavior among consumers in Malaysia as of May 2020.* https://www.statista.com/statistics/1128401/malaysia-impact-on-online-purchase-behavior-covid-19/.n-online-purchase-behavior-covid-19/.

Statista. (2020f, June 23). *Impacts of COVID-19 pandemic on the online purchase behavior among consumers in Indonesia as of May 2020.* https://www.statista.com/statistics/1127876/indonesia-impact-on-online-purchase-behavior-covid-19/.

The ASEAN Post. (2020, May 3). *The new generation of social media.* https://theaseanpost.com/article/new-generation-social-media.

The Edge Markets. (2020, September 28). *Lazada's enhanced customer experience and engagement a boon for brands and sellers.* https://www.theedgemarkets.com/content/advertise/lazadas-enhanced-customer-experience-and-engagement-boon-brands-and-sellers.

The Jakarta Post. (2020a, March 3). *Panic buying hits Jakarta supermarkets as govt announces first COVID-19 cases.* https://www.thejakartapost.com/news/2020/03/03/panic-buying-hits-jakarta-supermarkets-as-govt-announces-first-covid-19-cases.html.

The Jakarta Post. (2020b, March 28). *Artists to perform, share knowledge online for stay-at-home audience.* https://www.thejakartapost.com/life/2020/03/28/artists-to-perform-share-knowledge-online-for-stay-at-home-audience.html.

Tokotown. (2020). *Hyperlocal influencer marketing: A winning influencer marketing strategy.* https://tokotown.com/hyperlocal-influencer-marketing-a-winning-influencer-marketing-strategy/.

Tsimonis, G., & Dimitriadis, S. (2014). Brand strategies in social media. *Marketing Intelligence and Planning, 47*(2), 384–344.

Utomo, W., & Noormega, R. (2019, December 26). *Why the future of influencer marketing will be hyperlocal influencers.* Lifestyle Digital Commerce 360. https://www.thejakartapost.com/life/2019/12/26/why-the-future-of-influencer-marketing-will-be-hyperlocal-influencers.html.

WeAreSocial. (2020). https://wearesocial.com/blog/2020/01/digital-2020/.

Wold, S. (2020, September 16). *COVID-19 is changing how, why and how much we're using social media.* https://www.digitalcommerce360.com/2020/09/16/covid-19-is-changing-how-why-and-how-much-were-using-social-media/.

Xiang, Z., & Gretzel, U. (2010). Role of social media in online travel information search. *Tourism Management, 31*(2), 179–188.

12

Marketing Communications in Emerging Economies: Conclusions and Recommendations

Stanley Coffie, Thomas Anning-Dorson, Robert E. Hinson, Genevieve Bosah, and Albert Anani-Bossman

12.1 Introduction

This book offers a number of important lessons for firms, practitioners, and scholars interested in the emerging market context. Through the insightful chapters, great insights into how effective marketing communication can be achieved in the EE context have been highlighted. The final chapter offers some reflections and useful lessons for both practice and research. We highlight some key issues that emerging economies

S. Coffie (✉)
Ghana Institute of Management and Public Administration, Accra, Ghana
e-mail: scoffie@gimpa.edu.gh

T. Anning-Dorson
University of the Witwatersrand, Johannesburg, South Africa

R. E. Hinson
University of Ghana, University of Ghana Business School, Accra, Ghana
e-mail: rhinson@ug.edu.gh

(EEs) managers should focus on to achieve business success. We also offer some directions for researchers interested in EEs.

Marketing communication is one of the most important aspects of the business. The importance of communication cut across the different aspects of business; both within and outside the firm. Developing a communication strategy especially in marketing communications has a huge impact on the success of the business, the various strategic business units within the firm and the brands it sells. The marketing communication function is critical to both private and public enterprises, profit and not-for-profit organizations, private corporate and public sectors. Irrespective of motive, we strongly admonish all entities to develop an integrated marketing communication strategy to ensure message coherence and to create positive appeals, which prompt favorable positioning in the minds of its audiences. All firms, large and small, are admonished to consciously develop and implement marketing communication strategies in order to enjoy the benefits thereof.

The context of emerging markets, is critical and highlights the peculiarities that impact the effectiveness of strategy development and implementation. Marketing communication is no different and even demands a more careful look at the context if success is to be achieved. The current book pays a particular attention to this context through both conceptual and empirical lenses to offer both practitioners and researchers key insights into marketing communications in EEs.

There are several other benefits, which result from adopting and implementing an integrated approach to marketing communication. According to Shimp and Andrews (2013), one key benefit that accrues to firms is synergy. The synergistic advantages through the integration of the various marketing communication tools and channels allow firms to achieve a higher level of performance compared with when the various

---

G. Bosah
University of Hertfordshire, Hatfield, UK
e-mail: g.bosah@herts.ac.uk

A. Anani-Bossman
Ghana Institute of Journalism, Accra, Ghana

elements are implemented individually and in an uncoordinated fashion. An integrated communication approach also ensures that messages communicated by entities to their target audience are well planned, consistent and unified; hence, firms can create an enhanced image and positioning in the minds of customers. This further creates sustainable competitive advantages over other competitors in the industry.

The need for this book is rooted in the contextual uniqueness of emerging markets, which demands the sharing of distinctive and important pathways and evidence of marketing communications in emerging economies. The sheer size of emerging economies and their nature of being home to a number of multinational corporations and local firms tell of its importance. Additionally, EEs contribute immensely to global productivity, employment and growth. EEs constitute the largest market for consumer goods and drive a chunk of global trade volumes.

The glaring and significant differences between developed economies and that of their emerging counterparts make it necessary to have a dedicated focus on them. To highlight pathways and marketing communication activities, this book has provided important lessons going forward. In the next section, we highlight some reflections and provide lessons to guide the marketing communication discourse in EEs.

12.2 Reflections and Lessons

As the concept of marketing has gone through some transformation from the traditional to the 'modern' so has the notion of the 4 Ps been transformed and expanded into the 7 Ps. The process has also seen a drive away from emphasis on transactional to the development and building long-term relationship with the customer and other stakeholders (Jabbar et al., 2020). The focus of marketing has shifted from emphasis on attracting customers to the product to attracting the customer to the brand and in building long-term relationship. Marketing communication has become an important strategic tool for firms that want to attract customers, build long-term relationships with them and remain competitive. However, a lot more firms and practitioners are paying less attention to the changing trends in marketing communications. The customer has become an important source in transmitting the extent to which brands are able to communicate their relevance to the society.

Social and technological changes have contributed to the recognizable changes in the way marketing and marketing communication are pursued in the contemporary time. Contemporary marketing places emphasis on relationship marketing, industrial marketing and business marketing to the extent that traditional marketing did not. The focus of contemporary marketing is on society and consumers. In particular, the advent and the effect of the Internet have been significant in the use of e-marketing in what is often described as the digital age/marketing. The unlimited availability of space and the comparatively inexpensive nature to the organization allow for greater reach to existing or intended customers with information amidst high-level interactivity (Grönroos, 2004). The effect has been the opportunity for organizations to respond with speed to customer feedback and demands.

While the changes have called for a shift in strategies and tools, in EEs, a blend of the traditional and contemporary forms of marketing communication is highly recommended. The nature of our society and the rate of infrastructure development in these contexts call for a blend of contemporary and the traditional strategies. The traditional marketing communication strategies placed emphasis on media such as print, radio and television, film, bill boards, face to face as a means of reaching out to many. These forms and tools of marketing communication have their advantages by enabling the business to reach out to its audience via visual appeal and frequency that appeared to have its own appeal. The physical existence of the print form, for example, encouraged and supported recycling of communication materials, and consequently influenced the ease of recollection (Serafinelli, 2018).

How have emerging economies responded or reacted to the social/cultural and technological shifts that have impacted on marketing and communication? There are suggestions for organizations to work closely with the communities and locals they serve in media planning and usage (Olaniran, 2018) for the purpose of promoting the brands. An example of sociotechnology-driven success can be found with Safaricom in Kenya. The success of mobile money in Africa has been driven by social innovation through the use of mobile telephony relying on available and user-friendly technologies (Tesar & Kuada, 2013). In Kenya, M-Pesa had nearly 80,000 agents (Olopade, 2014) substantially driven by the need to send money to rural relatives as well as easier method of payments generally including the majority who were previously not part of the banking system as an opportunity to digitally save money. It is worthy of note that most of these agents of M-Pesa are individuals/entrepreneurs who have seized on the benefits of new and mobile technology in order to meet the market needs of Kenyans. At the same time, word of mouth played a significant role in spreading the message on the effectiveness and reliability of Safaricom for sending money to rural relatives. Our tentative observation is that traditional and contemporary forms of marketing communication can co-exist. What is necessary is for the marketer to understand the emerging economy cultural context in order to select the relevant marketing communication tools—be they traditional or contemporary.

The role and the call for public relations resides in the identified context rests on its ability to enhance relationship development between the organization and its audience. In this regard, public relations as part of integrated marketing communication mix and viewed as a primary element of integrated communication has the advantage to help create long-lasting brand loyalty through credibility and trust, and in the process be a key contributing tool towards the long-term financial stability of the organization. A further advantage held by public relations should be viewed against the backdrop of the growth in digital marketing and social media. This accentuates the functioning of public relations in its interactive nature compared with the one-way traffic of traditional media. This interactivity gives a higher potential for spreading messages about products and services as a means of developing brands (Gesualdi, 2019) through the management of public perceptions (Naumovska & Blazeska, 2016). These developments suggest the need to exploit the free publicity embedded in the application of the public relations tool of communication. Consumers in this regard become the 'word of mouth' on digital platforms as they spread their experience and expectations of products and services.

The ability of social media to engender and support the speed of message delivery as well as reach out to the mass audience worldwide is notable. This may have dual effect of either creating positive outcomes with the audience where the message is positive and negative outcomes where the message is negative. This suggests that marketers in exploiting public relations should create content that will help create a positive perception about products and services to the public. Public relations as a tool has the embedded strength of communication to both internal and external stakeholders of the organization and in the process helps to build trust and brand awareness (Naumovska & Blazeska, 2016). The buzz that can be created via public relations drawing on both internal and external stakeholders can be channeled for the purpose of corporate social responsibility and in support of communities (Lyft, 2020).

Challenges in applying digital and social media including public relations in emerging economies such as inadequate business practices, lack of human and technological infrastructure, government regulations, internet access, cultural and religious beliefs can exist. In spite of that, the widespread use of mobile devices in emerging economies does mean that the mobile device avenue can be exploited to the fullest in application to engage communities (Schultz & Malthouse, 2017). In periods of economic decline and budget constraints on organizations, public relations can be deployed via digital platforms for the benefit and purpose of reaching out to the requisite audience at a minimal cost.

Another important lesson that can be drawn from this book is that corporate social investments have become an important communication strategy for firms in recent times (Chu et al., 2020). Communicating social investments has an impact on the overall performance of the firm, especially in EEs (Saeed & Zamir, 2021; Sarkar et al., 2021). For effective CSR message and strategic communications, organizations need to adopt strategies that will be in consonance with the intended objectives or outcomes. The corporate social responsibility (CSR) communication strategy adopted by firms determines how the other aspects of the CSR communication activities are conducted. The informational approach is appropriate for the purpose of providing information about the firm's CSR activities. The emphasis of the informational approach tends to be on the use of digital new media channels from the firm to the audiences—with audience more as mere recipients. A reactive CSR communication strategy demands that firms must understand through surveys and intelligence gathering, the interests and expectations of stakeholders and must come up with CSR communications that satisfy these expectations. Deliberative CSR communication strategy is interactive and seeks the involvement of recipients or stakeholders and perhaps to be seen as preferred option.

Under COVID-19, creativity in the design of the message is important and congruence between the organizational purpose and the CSR action or effort is necessary to achieve credibility among the audience. For greater effectiveness in CSR communications, multiple communication channels can be used to reach out to target audience with different needs. There is a greater likelihood for each channel chosen to add to the overall effect of the outcome. Organizations in emerging economies driven by a focus on achieving CSR strategic objectives, are more likely to resonate with the target audience to achieve a positive outcome via multiple channel choices involving the traditional and digital. In examining the development of brands through CSR for the purpose of realizing the enhancing effects on performance and influence customer preference, Lindgreen et al. (2016) observe that consistency between corporate branding and benefits and CSR effort by organizations should integrate the CSR policy as part of the strategic development or orientation of the brand such that the brand image aligns with the CSR activities. The strategic domain or policy must be clearly defined to the target market; resources need to be allocated such that the brand associations form a critical part of the overall choice of message, channel in reaching out to the intended audience in emerging economies.

In EEs, marketing communications that utilize both the traditional and contemporary approaches build strong brands through strong customer relationships. Brands are one of the most valuable assets possessed by firms. In the current intricate world, brands serve as distinguishing factor in helping individuals and organizations navigate the plethora of choices they are inundated with daily. It is said that developing and possessing strong brands simplify decision-making, reduce risk and set expectations for the consumer while such brands create a sustainable competitive advantage for the brand owner.

One of the key tools for managing brands in the current competitive and volatile business world is through a strong communication strategy development. The reason is that for the long-term success of a brand, there must be a consistent flow of information, persuasion and reminder to the consumer in terms of the benefits offered by the brand. A firm's ability to develop a strong marketing communications strategy enables it to give voice to the brand and establish a dialog channel between the brand and the consumer, which builds the needed relationship with the customer. Designing a well-integrated marketing communication agenda is an important firm-level capability that incentivizes the elicitation of customer response, which boosts brand equity.

12.3 A Mix of Traditional and Contemporary Marketing Communication Channels in EEs

Effective communication requires selecting an appropriate communication channel to send message to consumers. We understand, channel or medium is the vehicle of transmission for a message. In marketing communication, channel selection largely depends upon the consumers. A clear understanding of consumers is required to ensure the channel of communication for effectiveness.

Traditional forms of communication channel range from memos, face-to-face meetings, telephone calls, etc. to use of cultural art and form, rituals, customs, wall paintings, folk songs, street plays, to name a few. In contrast, with technological development in recent past years, digital media and platforms have paved the way to marketers for effective communication and mass reach. E-mails, text messages, video conferencing, blogs, websites, social media, search engines, etc. making it possible for marketers to reach their consumers and deliver millions of messages every minute of every day, and within affordable budget.

The use of digital platforms, in terms of who accesses and benefits from digital landscape, is significantly determined by age. However, age is not the sole determinant, other factors such as education, income, gender and generational status also contribute to digital inequity (Fang et al., 2019). In another study, Pieterson and Ebbers (2008) tested a number of hypotheses on consumers' channel use behavior and the determinants of this behavior. The study reveals digital divide issues still influence channel usage by consumers, so it is necessary to keep all the channels of communication open for consumers. A multi-channeling approach should be adopted especially in emerging markets. The geographical location in emerging countries also influences the choice of communication channel. The rural–urban divide still exists and makes it challenging for marketers to choose between various available channels. An increased use of non-conventional media along with other advanced channels of communication has also been observed in emerging countries like India. These non-conventional media are wall painting, folk theatres, magic shows, puppet shows, interactive games, haats/village melas, particularly for marketing products and services in rural areas. Many multinational companies, such as Philips, ITC, HLL, Colgate Palmolive, Toyota, Tata, LG, Samsung, Honda etc., have witnessed marketing success with increased use of the above non-conventional communication channels among Indian rural consumers. These channels also help to overcome constraints like illiteracy, multidialects, lack of education, gender inequality, lack of information, economic, cultural and social marginalization.

In current pandemic, COVID-19 situation, businesses have highly relied on these digital platforms to reach out to their potential consumers. Moreover, businesses are finding their way to integrate applicability of new age technologies such as artificial intelligence (AI), augmented reality (AR) and virtual reality (VR) into their business practices. Owing to social distance created by COVID-19, businesses are keenly moving toward adoption of such innovative technologies for their survival in declining economies worldwide. Consumers today have become augmented and more technically savvy with smartphones in their hands. EE have the fastest growth rate in terms of new digital technology adoption. Consumers are aware of and actually lead the conversation on these digital platforms. Recognizing the differences in EE consumer segments and choosing the right approach will determine the success or otherwise of both local and multinational corporations.

12.4 Public Sector Marketing and Marketing Communications

In general, marketing has been theorized as a concept for private sector and competitive engagement. From discussions on the evolution of marketing, the concept is described as a relevant component of the capitalist system (Applbaum, 2004). It is also evident in the conceptualization of the marketing mix as McCarthy (1960) put forward. Additionally, competition and the continuous quest to differentiate one's product or service from others on the market is what has elevated the discussions on communication and branding. Branding itself is thought to be germane to products, organizations and services (Wæraas, 2008). Although discussions on marketing and marketing communication did not initially articulate public sector concerns, there have always been some elements of the marketing concept in the public sector, although they may not have been seen in that light. What readily comes to mind is the promotion of local tourism sites for economic gains. As Walsh (1994) puts it, although some activities of marketing were carried out in the public sector, it was more of specific techniques rather than a full-blown out development of a marketing orientation. Further stating that, in recent times, attention attendant to marketing has given rise to a much broader look at the concept and that consideration of a fusion of marketing into core public services like health and education has become prevalent. Other scholars explain that the past few decades have witnessed the encouragement of librarians to implement marketing concerns in delivering services to their clients (Keane, 1990; Tuffield, 1992). Adding that, marketing is progressively being promoted for and implemented by public sector service organizations and departments in both public and private sectors of the economy. Concluding that, marketing can be thought of as one of the techniques of the new managerialism, which has to do with established private sector concepts being adopted and implemented in the public sector with the purpose of managing for positive outcomes.

The growth of marketing to encapsulate all activities with a resemblance of marketing including public sector activities has made the call for public sector adoption of marketing principles even more important. A more recent definition of marketing by the American Marketing Association captures it better as 'an organizational function and a set of processes for creating, communicating and delivering value to customers and for managing customer relationships in ways that benefit the organization and its stakeholders' (Keefe, 2004, p. 17). Although public sector marketing takes on resemblance of private or profit-oriented marketing it must not be implemented as a clone of private sector marketing or business-oriented marketing. Largely, the elements of the marketing mix, the 4 Ps (product, price, place, and promotion) will come into play but the dynamics of implementation may change.

The importance of all the 4 Ps in public sector marketing has been highlighted by many (e.g., Andrea, 2011). With communications, and like product, the central government basically determines how this can be done usually through its media agencies or some other legislative framework. For example, any newly inaugurated government sets its own agenda or budget for infrastructural development including accessible and quality healthcare and education. Usually, techniques adopted in the promotion of public service like education, healthcare and utility organizations include print advertising, internet advertising as well as outdoor advertising. General media platforms can also be used by the central government whereas other public entities such as universities can be promoted by its alumni and healthcare facilities by satisfied patients. But the most effective way to communicate to the public about a public sector organization that goes beyond the remit of promotion is the staff since their expertise, politeness and competence all speak to image of the organization (Andrea, 2011). Managing marketing communications with the public sector also requires the diligent work of understanding the needs and wants of your target audiences, the differences in these audiences, and their media consumption patterns.

As part of the promotional efforts within public sector marketing some engagement of communication tactics can be employed to elevate the image of the public service. One of the foremost ways to achieve that is through research to be able to understand clients' needs to create personalized citizen-centered communication. Another way is to rebuild trust and engender the feeling of undivided attention to the community. Also, the public sector institution can build a strong identity, create meanings and be open and transparent while relying on innovative techniques. As a result of some level of misconception and mistrust in the public sector, communication must employ simple and effective content and be able to tell a story, which means it must be coherent for citizens to follow without it sounding like government is forcing something on citizens. Today's world is data driven and public sector marketing efforts must also be seen to be building an effective data-driven marketing strategy. Knowing the citizenry and the issues that concern them the most is key with data. Finally, public sector marketing must build a strong and diverse team with a focus on both internal and external communication because employees can project the image of an institution better selling the organization's values and culture to the outside citizenry.

12.5 The Future of Marketing Communications Research

The discussions in this book have demonstrated that the landscape of integrated marketing communications has evolved largely due to social and technological changes. The onset of the fourth industrial revolution (powered by Artificial Intelligence) means that the field of marketing communication will increasingly become complex. The blurring of boundaries between digital, biological, and physical spheres has created opportunities for marketing communications to grow further. However, it has also introduced new challenges for practitioners of marketing and communication, especially those in emerging economies. There is a need to review current theoretical work on marketing communications. As the global environment continues to converge, consumer purchasing decisions will become more complex, product design and communication will be more personalized, mobile communication will become the center of marketing, while customer-brand relationships will be determined by the perceived level of transparency by organizations (Turpin, 2016).

Some scholars argue that the focus of marketing communications shifted from the traditional 4 Ps to what is now being described as the four 'es' (4 Es), namely: experience (emotions), engagement, everyplace, and exchange. The 4es not only focus on value and emotion but also on the why, when, how to sell, and who to sell to (Festa, 2016). This book has highlighted key issues in the marketing communications field including, but not limited to, how social media and other technological changes are contributing to marketing communications in contemporary times; the need for businesses to be interactive-based instead of the traditional one-way form of dialogue if they wish to succeed; challenges facing practitioners including inadequate business practices, infrastructural (communication) challenges, government regulations, etc.; the need to develop appropriate frameworks/strategies that will guide the practice; and organizational responsibility to communities in a pandemic era.

These issues have implications for the future of research in marketing communications in emerging economies. The extant literature shows that the focus of research and theory building has been mainly driven by the west (Mersham et al., 2011). This means that scholars in emerging economies are rarely heard or involved in the discussion toward the development of a body of knowledge. The present dispensation provides scholars in emerging economies the opportunity to scrutinize the current landscape of research and practice in the field of marketing communication from their perspectives.

Future research in marketing communications can be conducted in several areas taking cognizance of the current global and technological environments. One of the key areas to look at in the near future is mobile marketing and advertising and how that is shaping consumer behavior and brand reception or avoidance. Mobile marketing reflects the various marketing communications techniques accessed through mobile devices (e.g. video and text). Several research papers have advocated the need to look at this area. Grewal (2016, p. 4), for example, proposed a general framework for future research in mobile marketing to be linked to the environmental and technological variables, consumer-related variables, market factors, advertising, and metrics. There is a need to determine the effect of mobile marketing communication on generating and enhancing brand awareness, brand communication, customer satisfaction, customer retention, brand attitude, and word-of-mouth. Findings can be used to develop a framework for effective mobile marketing communication in emerging economies. There is also the need for research to focus on how the fourth industrial revolution is influencing public marketing communications practices in emerging economies.

Much has been said about the power of AI and analytics to positively influence consumer behavior, organizations, industries, and society (Cohen, 2018). Knowledge and understanding of how AI can fully be utilized by marketing communication practitioners to enhance organizational effectiveness is needed within the social, economic, cultural, and technological context of emerging economies. Marketing communication scholars have the fundamental responsibility to examine the application of AI (if any) in the practice, given the peculiar challenges that impact businesses in emerging economies.

Furthermore, future research should examine issues such as ethics in digital and social media marketing, electronic word-of-mouth communication (eWOM), and customized and personalized communication. Additionally, one of the fundamental research areas often talked about but hardly engaged in is measurement and evaluation. It is one of the most problematic areas in marketing communication research. Research illustrates that practitioners acknowledge the importance of measurement and evaluation but hardly do it giving varied reasons such as lack of time and budgetary constraints. Globalization has demonstrated the need for practitioners to show how they contribute to organizational effectiveness. If the body of knowledge on marketing communication in emerging economies is to improve, then the area of measurement and evaluation should be critically researched. This will allow for appropriate standards of measurement to be developed to serve the needs of practitioners.

Scholars in emerging economies must also focus on developing a standard framework for effective marketing communications that takes into consideration the characteristics of emerging economies. Several papers have identified that, in most cases, frameworks and models promulgated by western scholars are unworkable in the non-western environment. This presents opportunities for scholars in emerging economies to look at the possibility of developing a codified body of knowledge that reflect the context of emerging economies. In discussing Africa for instance, Rensburg (2007), noted:

> *The African continent is a greenfield for research, and scholars have finally realized that some, but not all, aspects of the Anglo-European-American concept and practice of communication management can be transplanted onto the field in Africa.*

The composition of the social fabric and the value system of Africa is still far too different from that of the developed world (p. 38). Although this statement was made more than a decade ago, it still applies today. There is, therefore, the need for a paradigm shift in scholarly works that reflect the needs of emerging economies. The current global environment requires theory building to be viewed from a holistic perspective. It is, therefore, important for scholars in emerging economies to demonstrate how they can contribute to the global discussion on marketing communication scholarship.

The issue of sustainability has also been discussed and embraced in several emerging economies. A classic example is soleRebels, which is an Ethiopian company that manufactures environmentally-friendly shoes. The company creates customer value in the form of handcrafted footwear. Accordingly, future research should explore the issue of sustainable marketing communication in the context of emerging economies.

Communication integration is slowly but surely becoming a norm in the business world. Nevertheless, literature on communication integration, in general, and integrated marketing communication, in particular, has been written beyond the borders of emerging economies. While this book makes a meaningful contribution in this regard, there is still a paucity of research evidence. Therefore, it is recommended that future research should continue to investigate communication integration in organizations in emerging economies.

Research into the Latin American context: We call for deeper understanding of marketing communications research in the Latin American context. The Latin American context is one of the thriving emerging market contexts, which requires attention in marketing and especially, marketing communication. Latin America presents a unique context to communication generally and marketing communication in particular. For instance, Cornaway and Wardrope (2004) indicate that specific emphasis and kind and level of engagement and deference of authority shape communication among Latin Americans. That the peculiar nature of the Latin Americans causes writers to 'write between the line' as such high-context cultures rely on implicit meaning to relay unpleasant news. This further emphasizes the uniqueness of this context and their people, and, therefore, demands special focus when discussing communications and marketing communications, in particular, within the context of EEs. A lot has not changed since the assertion that mass communication research in Latin America is complex and disjointed. The economic instability and political transformation as well as foreign influence (usually from the USA) keep shaping marketing communication in the emerging context of Latin America. Researchers should focus on the cultural context of Latin America and how culture shapes marketing communication. Diving into the rich oral traditions and exuberant humor of irreverence and the complicity of the complex, often seen as conflictual. Multiracial societies of Latin America and how that influences marketing communication in such EEs will bring insight to the marketing communication discipline.

***Research into the diaspora side of marketing communication*:** In marketing, one key aspect of the emerging market consumer market is the diaspora market. Kumar and Steenkamp (2013) emphasize that marketing to diasporas is becoming increasingly attractive. The immigrant population globally is increasing and this trend is expected to continue into the future based on logical trends. The diaspora market has become one of the key focuses in the emerging market literature. There is a suggestion that it is an important niche market that needs attention in the marketing literature. Kumar and Steenkamp (2013) highlight that understanding the marketing communication needs of various diaspora segments is critical in the emerging marketing discourse. In the USA, the Hispanic/Latino—people with Latin American origin—is about 18% of the population. This is a significant population with some specific marketing communication needs. Africans, Indians and other nationalities from emerging economies are growing in every developed country. Researchers call for a look into the possible creative marketing communication avenues for reaching diaspora markets such as the Latinos in the USA, Africans, Indians and Chinese in Europe and everywhere. A number of African countries are seeking to attract the diasporas across the globe to come back to their root. Investigations into how they can be attracted through creative value communication will enrich the literature.

12.6 Conclusion

We would like to conclude by stating that one of the important but usually neglected is the proper alignment of the firm's objectives and marketing communication objectives. Marketing communication should be seen as an integral part of the value management cycle and should be aligned with the other parts of the strategic pursuit. For instance, a firm's messaging strategy is the basis of its promotional campaigns. Successful promotional campaigns are those that the messaging strategies aligned with the corporate goals. Such an approach improves the firm's strategic positioning through a consistent revision of a firm's goals and continuous alignment of messaging strategy with the target audience's expectations. It also helps to enhance the firm's trustworthiness among the target audience by delivering messages consistent with the target audience's expectations.

Fully aligning messaging strategy to business goals is a prerequisite for value creation and communication. Some studies have discussed the importance of aligning communication messages and corporate objectives in the context of integrated communication. However, strategic alignment of message strategy with organizational goals has received limited attention by researchers in the integrated marketing communication literature. For example, how organizations can align message strategy to organizational goals is still an issue in many emerging economies. The strategic alignment of message strategy and organizational goals must start with the latter and systematically drive the message.

References

Andrea, M. B. (2011). Public sector marketing: Importance and characteristics. *Journal of Economics Practices and Theories, 1*(2), 12–25.

Applbaum, K. (2004). *The marketing era: From professional practice to global provisioning*. Routledge.

Chu, S. C., Chen, H. T., & Gan, C. (2020). Consumers' engagement with corporate social responsibility (CSR) communication in social media: Evidence from China and the United States. *Journal of Business Research, 110*, 260–271.

Cohen, M. (2018). Big data and service operations. *Production and Operations Management, 27*(9), 1709–1723.

Cornaway, R. N., & Wardrope, W. J. (2004). *Business Communication Quarterly, 67*(4), 465–474.

Fang, M. L., Canham, S. L., Battersby, L., Sixsmith, J., Wada, M., & Sixsmith, A. (2019). Exploring privilege in the digital divide: Implications for theory, policy, and practice. *The Gerontologist, 59*(1), e1–e15. https://doi.org/10.1093/geront/gny037.

Festa, G. C. (2016). The (r)evolution of wine marketing mix: From the 4Ps to the 4Es. *Journal of Business Research, 69*(5), 1550–1555.

Gesualdi, M. (2019) Revisiting the relationship between public relations and marketing: Encroachment and social media. *Public Relations Review, 45*(2), 372–382. doi.org./10.1016/j.pubrev.2018.12.0025.

Gil, A. G. (2020). The future of social media marketing. *Journal of the Academy of Marketing Science, 48*, 79–95.

Grewal, D. B. (2016). Mobile advertising: A framework and research agenda. *Journal of Interactive Marketing, 34*, 3–14.

Grönroos, C. (2004). The relationship marketing process: communication, interaction, dialogue, value. *Journal of Business & Industrial Marketing*.

Jabbar, A., Akhtar, P., & Dani, S. (2020). Real-time big data processing for instantaneous marketing decisions: A problematization approach. In *dustrial Marketing Management, 90*, 558–569.

Keane, M. (1990). Marketing and librarianship: Yin and Yang, or uneasy bedfellows? *The Australian Library Journal, 39*(2), 116.

Keefe, L. (2004, September 15). What is the meaning of 'marketing'? *Marketing News*, pp. 17–18. American Marketing Association.

Kuada. J. (2013). Danso fruit drinks Ghana limited. In Tesar, G. and Kuada, J. (eds), *Marketing management and strategy: An African casebook*. London: Routledge, pp. 164–175.

Kumar, N., & Jan-Benedict, EM Steenkamp. (2013). Brand breakout: How emerging market brands will go global. New York, NY: Palgrave MacMillan.

Lindgreen, A., Maon, F., & Vallaster, C. (2016). Building brands via corporate social responsibility. In F. D. Riley, J. Singh, & C. Blankson (Eds.), *The Routledge companion to contemporary brand management* (pp. 228–254). Routledge.

Lyft. (2020). Undercover Lyft [Video file]. https://www.youtube.com/playlist?list=PL-04sKrMar6Nnjw94V1zSjpgEDahng1X&app=desktop. Accessed 2 October 2020

McCarthy, E. J. (1960). Basic marketing: A managerial approach. Richard D. Irwin.

Mersham, G., Skinner, C., & Rensburg, R. (2011). Approaches to African communication management and public relations: A case for theory-building on the continent. *Journal of Public Affairs, 11*(4), 195–207.

Naumovska, L., & Blazeska, D. (2016). Public relation based model of integrated marketing communications. *UTMS Journal of Economics, 7*(2), 175–186.

Olaniran, B. A. (2018). Social media as communication channel in emerg ing economies: A closer look at cultural implications. *Journal of Advances in Management Research*.

Olopade, D. (2014). Africa's Tech Edge. Atlantic 10727825, 313, pp. 82–86.

Pieterson, W., & Ebbers, W. (2008). The use of service channels by citizens in the Netherlands: Implications for multi-channel management. *International Review of Administrative Sciences, 74*(1), 95–110. https://doi.org/10.1177/0020852307085736.

Rensburg, R. (2007). Communication management in the Africa context: Implications for theory, research, and practice. *International Journal of Strategic Communication, 1*(1), 37–51.

Saeed, A., & Zamir, F. (2021). How does CSR disclosure affect dividend payments in emerging markets? *Emerging Markets Review, 46*, 100747.

Sarkar, S., Chatterjee, M., & Bhattacharjee, T. (2021). Does CSR disclosure enhance corporate brand performance in emerging economy? Evidence from India. *Journal of Indian Business Research*. https://doi.org/10.1108/JIBR-06-2019-0201.

Serafinelli, E. (2018). Digital life on Instagram: New social communication of photography. Emerald Group Publishing.

Schultz, D. E., & Malthouse, E. C. (2017). Interactivity, marketing communication, and emerging markets: a way forward. *Journal of Current Issues & Research in Advertising, 38*(1), 17–30. https://doi.org/10.1080/10641734.2016.1233152.

Shimp, T. A., & Andrews, J. C. (2013). Advertising Promotion and Other Aspects of Integrated Marketing Communications 9th (ninth) by Cengage Learning.

Tuffield, J. (1992). Management and marketing: A client based framework. In *ALIA 92: Libraries: The heart of the matter: Proceedings of the Australian Library and Information Association 2nd Biennial Conference* (pp. 376–377). Deakin, ACT: Australian Library and Information Association.

Turpin, D. (2016). *Seven trends that will affect the future of marketing.* https://www.imd.org/research-knowledge/articles/seven-trends-that-will-affect-the-future-of-marketing.

Wæraas, A. (2008). Can public sector organizations be coherent corporate brands? *Marketing Theory, 8*(2), 205–221.

Walsh, K. (1994). Marketing and public sector management. *European Journal of Marketing, 28*(3), 63–71.

Index

A
Acceptance 103
Advertising Association of Ghana (AAG) 177, 178
Aesthetics response 223
Appraisal theory 129
Artificial intelligence (AI) 288
Attention 103
Attribution theory 179

B
Brand awareness 114
Brand purpose 199, 201–203
Broadcasting strategy 98, 99
Budgetary constraints 77
Business marketing 27

C
Cause promotions 105
Cause-related marketing 105
Channel strategy 150, 151
Coherence 230–232
Communicating Corporate Social Responsibility 5
Communication process 70, 71
Community volunteering 105, 106
Complexity 230–232
Comprehension 103
Consumerism 28
Consumer purchase 115
Contemporary marketing communications 4, 20
Corporate philanthropy 104
Corporate reputation 114, 115
Corporate social investment 282
Corporate social marketing 105

Corporate social responsibility (CSR) 93, 94, 282, 283
CSR appeals 94
CSR communication 94
CSR Skepticism 102
Customer communications 125
Customer Emotions 6
Customer evangelism 25, 26
Customer loyalty 116
Customer value 132, 133
Customer value proposition 132

D

Digital marketing communications 23
Digital media 39, 41

E

Egoistic-driven motive 106
Electronic word-of-mouth communication (eWOM) 290
Electronic word-of-mouth (e-WOM) 249
Emerging economies (EEs) 2, 277, 278
Engagement-focused strategy 258
Exposure 103

G

Global business environment 37

H

Hard selling 258
Hierarchical effect model 76, 77
Hispanic culture 50

Hispanic population growth 49
Human resource practices 183, 184

I

IMC planning 68
Integrated communications (IC) 40, 41, 279
Integrated marketing communications (IMC) 2, 39–41, 65, 66, 71
Interactive communication theory 18
International Advertising Association (IAA) 176, 177

L

Learning orientation (LO) 72
Legibility 230–232

M

Managerial processes 182
Marketing communication campaign 130, 131
Marketing communications (MCs) 1, 11, 13, 141, 142, 277, 278
Marketing communication strategies 148, 149
Marketing communication tools 147
Media channel consumption 37, 38
Message content 101
#MeToo movement 199
Modernism 12
M-Pesa 281
Multi-channeling approach 285
Mystery 230–232

N

New Product Adoption Model (NPAM) 76

O

Optimization strategy 258

P

Perceptual integration theory 18
Point-of-purchase advertising 8, 225
Product life cycle 73, 75
Product strategy 149, 150
Promotion and advertising strategy 148
Public relations 37, 38
Public Relations Society of America (PRSA) 40
Purchase intention 234, 235
Purpose-driven marketing 7

R

Reciprocity theory 18
Relationship marketing 26
Retention 103
Rural and Community Banks (RCBs) 142

S

Shared values 25
Small and medium-sized enterprises (SMEs) 5, 66, 67
Social construct 201
Social marketing 27, 28
Social media adoption 249
Social media brand communication 207, 208
Social media commercial-focused strategy 258
Social Media Communication 7
Social media consumption 7
Social media early extension strategy 258
Socio-technology 280
Soft selling 258
South African Tourism 130, 131
Stakeholder-driven motive 107
Stakeholder information strategy 97
Stakeholder involvement strategy 98
Stakeholder response strategy 97
Stimulus-organism-response theory 228
Strategy-driven motive 107

T

Technological advancement 180, 181
Theoretical framework 13
Traditional marketing 15
Traditional marketing communications 4
Traditional marketing mix 16
Transaction marketing 28

V

Value-driven motive 106
Visual aesthetics 224